MICROCREDIT AND POVERTY ALLEVIATION

Microcredit and Poverty Alleviation

TAZUL ISLAM
University of Tokyo, Japan

ASHGATE

© Tazul Islam 2007

Published by
Ashgate Publishing Limited
Gower House
Croft Road
Aldershot
Hampshire GU11 3HR
England

Ashgate Publishing Company
Suite 420
101 Cherry Street
Burlington, VT 05401-4405
USA

Ashgate website: http://www.ashgate.com

British Library Cataloguing in Publication Data
Islam, Tazul
   Microcredit and poverty alleviation
   1.Grameen Bank 2.Microfinance - Bangladesh 3.Poverty -
   Bangladesh
   I.Title
   332.7'42'095492

Library of Congress Cataloging-in-Publication Data
Islam, Tazul.
  Microcredit and poverty alleviation / by Tazul Islam.
       p. cm.
  Includes index.
  ISBN-13: 978-0-7546-4680-8
  ISBN-10: 0-7546-4680-7
  1. Microfinance. 2. Women--Bangladesh--Economic conditions. 3. Grameen Bank. 4.
Poverty. I. Title.

  HG178.3.I85 2006
  332.7--dc22

                                                                    2006021131

ISBN-13: 978 0 7546 4680 8
ISBN-10: 0 7546 4680 7

Printed and bound in Great Britain by Antony Rowe Ltd, Chippenham, Wiltshire.

Contents

因果关系的

List of Tables

List of Boxes

List of Appendices

Acknowledgements

Many people have contributed directly or indirectly to this book and deserve special mention and thanks.

It is no exaggeration to say that this book would not have been written if I had not the moral support from Professor Dr Yoichi Izumida, Department of Agricultural and Resource Economics, The University of Tokyo. He has stimulated my interest in writing the manuscript of the book and helped and guided me every step of the way. I am indebted to him for opening my eyes to contemporary theories and realities of microfinance movement that have become central for analyzing the gap between the intent and content of this movement. For all the things he has done for me, too numerous to mention, I sincerely thank him.

I owe very special thanks to Dr Kenneth E Jackson, Director of Development Studies, at the University of Auckland. The book could not haven taken this shape if I had not the moral support from Dr Jackson. His relentless support of my work, his comments, advice, and critique has enabled me to clarify my data, sharpen my ideas, and develop the organization of the book. I could not have had a better supervisor and I really cannot thank him enough for all that he has done for me.

I am deeply grateful to Helen Vicary, who despite her tight schedules, has commented on some of my early drafts. She has been a very good friend to me and she has helped me many times, in many ways. I do not know how to express my thanks to her. I appreciate all that she has done for me.

Tapan Kumar Nath and Lukytawati Anggraeni helped me immensely in computerizing my book. I would like to express my sincere thanks to them.

My specials thanks to Professor Koichi Fujita, Dr Yasuyuki Sawada, Dr Takao Yurugi, Dr. K.N. Ninan, Professor Du Zhixiong, Ryuji Yamoto, Tomoko Kaino, Supawan Nilkamhang, Masahiro Shoji, and Harunur Rashid for their interests in my book.

In Bangladesh, Dr Atiur Rahman of the Bangladesh Institute of Development Studies in Dhaka gave me requisite feedback on my field research and encouraged me to make a critical analysis of the success of the Grameen microcredit programmes for women. I express my sincere thanks to him.

During my fieldwork in Bangladesh, the Grameen Bank (GB) offered generous assistance and cooperation. My most sincere thanks go to Professor Muhammad Yunus, Dipal C. Barua, Harunur Rashid, Nafis Ahmed and all the staff of the GB I visited. I also thank the many bank workers in the field and GB members who spent time with me and answered my many questions. I must record my heartfelt thanks to the innumerable men and women GB members in villages who have taught me about their enterprises, their finances, and their lives. My knowledge of microfinance is largely derived from them. They are the ones who made the GB real to me.

My family has always been a source of strength and encouragement, often drawn from-to-face difficulties in life. Sufia, my wife, and Tanveer, my son, shared my life in various ways. Without their love and understanding, I could not have seen my work completed.

I would like to express my deepest appreciation and sincere thanks to the University of Auckland, New Zealand for the generous *The University of Auckland Research Grant* without which it would have been impossible to undertake the extensive yearlong field survey on the GB Bangladesh in 1998. It is also no exaggeration to say that this book, based on two more field surveys on the GB in 2004 and 2005, would not have been possible but for the generous *Research Grant* from the Japan Society for the Promotion of Science (JSPS). The author gratefully acknowledges the financial support extended by the JSPS and the Department of Agricultural and Resource Economics at the University of Tokyo for necessary logistic and support.

Last, but not the least, I thank all those at the Department of Agricultural and Resource Economics at the University of Tokyo for their support and interest in my work.

List of Abbreviations

ACCION	A Non-profit Microfinance Organization based in Somerville, USA
ADB	Asian Development Bank
ADBN	Agricultural Development Bank of Nepal
ADP	Annual Development Plan
AIMS	Assessing the Impact of Microenterprise Services
APDC	Association for Asia and Pacific Development Cooperation
ASA	Association for Social Advancement
BAMWSP	Bangladesh Arsenic Mitigation and Water Supply Project
BancoSol	Banco Solidario (Bolivia)
BARD	Bangladesh Academy for Rural Development
BB	Bangladesh Bank
BBS	Bangladesh Bureau of Statistics
BIDS	Bangladesh Institute of Development Studies
BKB	Bangladesh Krishi Bank
BKK	Badan Kredit Kecamatan, Indonesia
BNI	Basic Needs Index
BRAC	Bangladesh Rural Advancement Committee
BRDB	Bangladesh Rural Development Board
BRI	Bank Rakayat Indonesia
BURO	Bangladesh Unemployed Rehabilitation Organization, Tangail,
CDF	Credit and Development Forum, Bangladesh
CGAP	Consultative Group to Assist the Poorest
CIGP	Credit-based-Income-Generating Projects
CIRDAP	Centre on Integrated Rural Development for Asia and the Pacific
CNM	Comparable Non-members
CPI	Consumer Price Index
CPR	Contraceptive Prevalence Rate
CROP	Comparative Research Programme on Poverty
CV	Control Villages
DFI	Development Finance Institute
FAO	Food and Agricultural Organization
FFE	Food-for-Education
FFW	Food-for-Work
FINCA	Foundation for International Community Assistance, Washington
FS	Financial Systems Lending
GAD	Gender and Development
GB	Grameen Bank

GDP	Gross Domestic Product
GEMINI	Growth and Equity through Microenterprise Investments and Institutions
GKF	Grameen Krishi Foundation
GNP	Gross National Product
GPS	Grameen Pension Scheme
HDI	Human Development Index
HES	Household Expenditure Survey
HPI	Human Poverty Index
HYV	High Yielding Variety
IDA	International Development Assistance
IFAD	International Fund for Agricultural Development
IFM	Informal Financial Markets
IGP	Income-generating programme
IGVGD	Income Generation for Vulnerable Group Development
ILO	International Labour Organization
IMF	International Monetary Fund
IRDP	Integrated Rural Development Programme
MCI	Microcredit Institutions
MFI	Microfinance Institutions
MWR	Market Wage Rate
NCB	Nationalized Commercial Banks
NGO	Non-governmental Organization
NTG	Non-target Group
OECD	Organization for Economic Cooperation and Development
PARD	Pakistan Academy for Rural Development
PFA	Platform for Action, Beijing
PKSF	Palli Karma-Sahayak Foundation
PL	Poverty Lending
PV	Project Villages
RD	Rural Development
RFEP	Rural Finance Experimental Project
RFM	Rural Financial Market
RKUB	Rajshahi Krishi Unnayan Bank
RNA	Rural Non-farm Activities
ROSCA	Rotating Savings and Credit Association
RWI	Relative Welfare Index
SAARC	The South Asia Association for Regional Cooperation
SAP	Structural Adjustment Policies
SEWA	Self-employed Women's Association
SFDP	Small Farmers Development Programme
SDI	Subsidy Dependence Index
SDS	The Social Development Society,
SEEP	The Small Enterprise Education and Promotion, New York

SEWA	Self-employed Women's Association, India
SIDE	Studies, Innovation, Development, and Experimentation
TFYP	Third Five-Year Plan
TG	Target Group
UNCDF	United Nations Capital Development Fund
UNDP	United Nations Development Programme
USAID	The United States Agency for International Development
USI	User-led Innovation
WDI	World Development Index
WID	Women in Development
WHO	World Health Organization
VGD	Vulnerable Group Development

Glossary

Boro	Winter dry-season paddy, harvested May-June
Dhenki	Wooden mallet for husking paddy, mounted on a wooden beam and operated with the foot
Ghani	Stone mill for grinding mustard seed, turned with wooden arms loaded with stones and working on a pivot
Gram Sarker	Village Government
Grameen	Countryside or Rural
Krishi	Agricultural
Musti	A handful of rice kept aside as saving while cooking
Palli Karma-Sahayak Foundation	Rural Employment-generation Foundation Shomitis Groups
Taka	Unit of Bangladeshi currency (52 Taka in 1998 and 67 Taka = US$1 during 2006)
Thana	Sub-district
Unnayan	Development

Chapter 1

Microcredit and Poverty Alleviation: Pluses and Minuses

Background

Looking at the *good, bad,* and *room for improvement* in microfinance model of development, the book attempts to clarify the principles that could, and perhaps should be followed by the microfinance institutions (MFIs) when considering why and when microfinance works-and when and why it fails to achieve its promise. Critically analyzing the ugly facts of the *one-size-fits-all* microfinance fancy model, the book bridges the gap between the claims that microfinance is a panacea for poverty alleviation and the counter-claims that caution against such enthusiasm.

As the microcredit movement matures, we get a clearer idea of both its strengths and limitations. To move forward, we need to be more effective, and design flexible financial products and take any other measure needed to spread the poverty alleviation net wider, so that a significant decline in poverty takes place.

Taking the Grameen Bank (GB)[1] of Bangladesh as a case study, this book specifically explores the significance of changing the focus of the GB from a credit-centred organization into a client-led, flexible financial services organization. Transforming into a client-led organization requires refocusing on clients, listening to their demands and preferences, and learning about their financial strategies. Microfinance needs to be fundamentally re-examined, not simply fine-tuning the existing one-size-fits all approaches. In order to have a significant impact on poverty alleviation for poor clients[2], the entire industry must overcome its institutional inertia of simply replicating current models. The time has come to re-think the purpose and potential of microfinance, going far beyond microcredit for enterprise development to encompass the provision of demand-responsive flexible financial services to poor people, regardless of whether they own enterprises.

This study investigates the ways in which GB microfinance programme has ensured the access of the rural poor women to institutional sources of finance heretofore excluded from formal financial markets. In the process the study examines the extent to which the GB programme has alleviated poverty of the rural poor

---

1   Throughout the book Grameen Bank, Grameen, GB, and Bank have been used interchangeably.

2   For the sake of simplicity the terms clients, member borrowers, borrowers, beneficiaries, and participants have also been used interchangeably all through.

women, who are generally considered to be at the lowest rung of the poverty ladder in Bangladesh. The GB has pioneered a credit delivery system in rural Bangladesh, bringing banking services to poor villagers with a focus primarily on women.

Microcredit, or its wider term microfinance, the extension of small amounts of collateral-free institutional loans to jointly liable poor group members for their self-employment and income generation, is a GB innovation. The GB is the largest provider of microlending services in Bangladesh. Its 1,658 rural branches operate in 57,790 of the total 68,000 villages in Bangladesh. The cumulative investment of the GB in 2005 in rural Bangladesh is more than five billion dollars, disbursed among 5.3 million borrowers, 96 per cent of whom are women (Grameen Bank 2005). The GB operations have contributed between 1.1 to 1.5 per cent of gross domestic product (GDP) of Bangladesh (Grameen Bank 1999). By way of comparison, the small scale industries sector contributes less than 4 per cent and agriculture and fisheries around 3 per cent of GDP, suggesting that the GB's contribution is quite substantial (Wright 2000, 16). Through the GB, Muhammad Yunus, its founder, was able to institutionalize features that provide a model for some, if not all, microcredit providers today. MFIs including *Grameen replications* have since flourished in many countries around the world.

Few will disagree, though, that microfinance has already shaken up the world of international development. One of the most striking elements is that the pioneering models grew out of experiments in low income countries like Bangladesh and Bolivia, rather than adaptations of standard banking models in developed countries. Entrepreneurs, academics, and development practitioners from around the world have been drawn to the MFIs. Scores of doctoral dissertations, master's theses, and academic studies have now been written on microfinance (Aghion and Morduch 2005, 1-2).

The term *revolution* suggests a radical overturning of established order. By this definition, the microfinance movement qualifies as a revolution in that it radically overturned established ideas of the poor as clients of financial services. In the process, it has shattered stereotypes of the poor as not bankable, spawned a variety of lending methodologies demonstrating that it is possible to provide cost-effective financial services to the poor, mobilized millions of dollars of social investment for the very poor, given rise to thousands of MFIs dedicated to serving the very poor (Woller 2002, 305).

The GB is not the only microlender flourishing in rural Bangladesh. Bangladesh Rural Advancement Committee (BRAC), Association for Social Advancement (ASA), and Proshika as well as nearly 10, 000 other nongovernmental organizations (NGOs) are providing microfinancial services to the rural poor in Bangladesh. By the end of 2004, BRAC had 4.5 million, ASA 2.7 million, and Proshika 2.8 million members. Shares of different sources of microcredit in total domestic credit show that MF-NGOs are the principal contributors in micro-credit expansion followed by specialised institutions and banks (CDF 2004).

Microfinance programmes are credited with an amazing array of beneficial impacts, and at the same time are accused of promoting themselves as *panaceas*. The

GB microfinance programme is now into its second decade. Now it is time to stock-take and assess where the GB microfinance is and the extent to which it has achieved its promise of sustainable poverty alleviation of its rural poor women clients.

First, the pluses of microfinance. In the microfinance process, poor households are being given hope and the possibility to improve their lives through their own labour. Access to microfinance is credited with reaching the poorest, increasing their income to have a sustainable impact in alleviating rural poverty, and with providing a cost-effective, sustainable development model that is applicable not just in developing countries, but also among poorer communities in the developed world. The remarkable success that pioneer MFIs have had at extending and recovering millions of loans to the poor has attracted worldwide attention. Donors, governments, NGOs, and now some, though not all, large commercial banks have all enthusiastically redirected efforts and resources towards new microfinance and microenterprise development projects.

Many researchers and different organizations have now completed enough impact studies to allow a thorough and balanced assessment of the GB impact. Taken as a whole, the evidence demonstrates a positive impact on enterprise and household income and asset accumulation, household consumption, and positive influence on social welfare indicators (education, expenditure on health and nutrition).

Now the minuses, widespread accumulation of studies which indicate that the GB does not reach very far down the poverty spectrum, either in absolute terms or relative to other income categories (Matin 1998b). Instead clients in the GB tend to be clustered around the poverty line, being predominantly *moderately poor* or *vulnerable non-poor*. Exclusion of the very poor-whether by self-exclusion, or by GB-appears to be a widespread phenomenon. Of the very poor who do join the GB, a high percentage often dropout after only a few loan cycles, while many others eventually dropout in later loan cycles as loan amounts begin to exceed their repayment capacity.

The MFIs in Bangladesh have done many things right. But in recent years, there has been considerable self-examination by MFIs along with criticisms from analysts about product rigidity. The fact that MFIs have experienced high dropout rates and that many in the target population refuse to participate suggests that something may be amiss. Although no comprehensive studies have been done, case studies and fragmentary data on five different indicators can be interpreted as evidence of client dissatisfaction and unmet demands. The five indicators, as Professor Meyer (2002, 352-8) points out, are: exclusion and non-participation; dropouts; delinquencies; overlap; and use of informal finance.

For too long now, the GB and other MFIs have focused on the products and services they could produce rather than the products and services clients want them to produce; on institutional needs rather than on *client* needs. Beyond this, the GB remains locked into a paradigm that is proving increasingly out of step with the needs of the very poor. In exploring the room for improvement in the GB microfinance programme, this study argues that it is possible to offer a set of flexible financial services to the poor that meet clients' needs and preferences. To accomplish this, the

GB must place clients at the driving seat. This, if ensured, will also help bring the very poor under the GB microfinance net.

The microfinance movement stands poised on the brink of a second revolution: a revolution in which customers replace products as the primary industry focus. The first microfinance revolution was launched by innovations in methodologies that successfully overcame the many structural barriers to providing credit and savings to the poor (for example, information asymmetries, lack of collateral, high cost, high risk, and systematic market bias) effectively extending financial services to millions of the world's poor heretofore excluded from formal financial markets.

While such innovations, pioneered by the GB and some other successful MFIs, initially proved tremendously successful, they nonetheless suffer from a crucial defect. A defining characteristic of such innovations is that they are *inward-looking*, their primary purpose is to satisfy organizational and donor demand, not clients demand. Thus in the interests of delivering loans at low costs, many MFIs including the GB, have adopted a *one-size-fits-all* approach to microfinance. This approach implicitly assumes a largely homogenous market for financial services among the poor.

The widespread adoption of this approach together with underlying assumptions has had a profound impact on the development of microfinance industry. Today, the industry, as well as many MFIs, can generally be characterized as *product-centred*, defined as a tendency to place more emphasis on products and product design than their clients. In other words, product-centred MFIs find clients to match the demands of the product instead of developing products to match the demands of the clients.

There is mounting evidence, however, that the product-centred approach is becoming increasingly dysfunctional. The dysfunctionality of the product-centred approach is well demonstrated in the exclusion and non-participation of many rural poor into microfinance programmes, large number of dropouts, delinquencies, multiple memberships, and continuous use of informal finance among the MFIs' clients in Bangladesh (Meyer 2002, 352-7). To the extent MFIs can continue to expand and charge near-monopolistic interest rates, they can continue to compensate for high dropout rates and delinquencies and give off the appearance of vitality. But this process cannot proceed indefinitely. At some point, growth will slow, the competition will catch up, and the products and policies that worked well in the past will no longer work in the future.

It is now firmly established that neither the growth nor the reception of the microfinance movement has been without controversy. As with most other development efforts, particularly those that compete for scarce donor funds, there are disagreements over the appropriate role and vision of microfinance. Studies on the *downside* of microfinance (for example, Hulme 2000; Rahman 1999) reveal the way in which some microfinance programmes can damage the prospects of the poor. It is not a polemic that argues that microfinance has failed-there is much evidence that it can help many poor people. Rather, such studies are a reminder that MFIs need to monitor carefully not only their positive impacts but also their negative effects, look to the future, and not rest on their laurels. The MFI industry needs to practice more humility about what it has achieved and deepen its understanding of the clients' demand. With the growing interest among donors, governments, and practitioners in the merits of microfinance as a tool for reducing poverty and a cost-effective instrument for achieving sustainability of the lending institutions, it is time to pause and examine these claims and concerns, and to try to separate reality from the publicity surrounding the microfinance movement.

Statement of the Problem

Microfinance holds the promise of a series of exciting possibilities for reducing poverty and fostering social change. But it also presents a lot of puzzles, many of which have not yet been widely discussed. One aim of the book is to highlight the possibilities that have created the movement. Another aim is to clarify the debates, and assumptions that guide conversations but that are too often overlooked. Debates include whether the poorest are best served by loans or by better ways to save, whether providing credit without training or skill-enhancing efforts is enough.

The book, based on a critical analysis of the GB's credit-alone policy, argues that the rhetoric promising poverty alleviation has moved far ahead of the evidence, and that even the most fundamental claims of success remain largely unsubstantiated. It has therefore become increasingly apparent that there is a need to take stock of the services currently being provided by the GB and other MFIs to their poor clients. This stock-taking, depicting the *intent* and *content* of the GB, will help determine whether microfinance is a degraded palliative or really a panacea for reducing poverty of the poor.

There is little doubt that support for microenterprise has dramatically increased since the late 1980s. The book critically examines the credit-initiated microenterprise development of the GB as a strategy to promote poverty alleviation. Satisfactory though the performance of the GB is in ensuring access of the poor, particularly poor women, to institutional sources of credit, and alleviating poverty of some of them, the book argues that it could have been even more impressive if the GB provided not only credit but also voluntary savings and other client-responsive, quality financial services. It underlines the limitations of microcredit, which is fast becoming the main form of microenterprise support, in particular, and microenterprise development, in general.

Poverty alleviation is not just about the quantity of clients reached. It is also about discerning the quality and range of financial services that meets the needs and desires of the poor. Some of the poor can exit poverty through the returns from credit-initiated enterprises, but most of the poor exit poverty through the returns on assets purchased with their voluntary savings. Quality financial services help expand investment and generate income. They affect the management of asset portfolios and smoothes household consumption. More importantly, they reduce the dependence of the rural poor on the informal moneylenders.

While suggesting appropriate quality financial services matching the needs of the clients, this book also attempts to suggest policies to attract the extreme poor, especially poor women into the GB microfinance programmes. Despite the success of the GB in delivering loans to poor women and bringing socioeconomic changes to some of these borrowers, this study suggests that there are still many borrowers who cannot improve their poverty situation, but instead become more vulnerable and trapped in the rigid, supply-driven, credit-alone system. The study suggests that the "monotheistic microcredit formula" promoted as a panacea (Wright 2000; Wood and Sharif eds. 1997) is not only inadequate to meet the needs of the poorest, but is also monopolizing resources that could, and perhaps should be used for other more pressing or important interventions. There is, however, a trade-off between the quality of the services (necessary for significant outreach) and the cost of providing such services (necessary for sustainability). Getting the correct balance, which is difficult though, but not impossible, is the only way to succeed in achieving the goal of significant poverty alleviation of the clients.

Considering the demand side of microfinance services, the poor participate in microfinance programmes in the expectation that their participation will increase their income and sustain or create self-employment. The ultimate test of any institution is not whether it just exists or sustains itself, but more importantly, whether it manages to do something useful for its members. The GB's ultimate achievements must be measured in terms of the nature and extent of the benefits that its members enjoy.

The success of the GB, as such, depends on whether participation of the poor does in fact reduce poverty in terms of raising their income and ultimately improving the levels of their standard of living. The aim of the book is to assess the extent to which this objective has been achieved. The basic research question of the study is: has the GB's microcredit programme with its credit-alone approach resulted in a substantial reduction of poverty, however measured, amongst the clients? The answer of the research question will be empirically analyzed at chapter 5, the section that follows gives a brief historical overview of the GB.

The Grameen Bank

The Bengali word *grameen* stands for rural or countryside. Therefore, the GB means the rural or the countryside bank. It is, indeed, a unique financial institution in Bangladesh. There are some fundamental differences between the GB and other conventional financial institutions. First, the GB was founded exclusively for the poor people who have little or no assets of any kind. The GB provides credit to the rural poor, particularly women, who own less than half an acre of land or whose assets do not exceed the value of one acre of land. The distribution of owned cultivated land among the GB borrowers suggests that 95.8 per cent of the loans went to the target group borrowers (nil-0.49 acres), and only 4.2 per cent went to the members of non-target groups (Hossain 1988). Secondly, despite being a specialized financial institution, it incorporated many of the principles of dynamism of the informal sector, which has made it a bank for the poor most of whom are engaged in the informal sector for their livelihood.

Thus, offering credit to the rural poor women who, had historically been excluded from formal sources of credit, holds a promise and potential to play a pioneering role in bringing about a possible breakthrough in the otherwise stagnant society of rural Bangladesh. The dynamic aspect of this bank is that in recent years many other developing countries of the world have been replicating the Grameen Model[3], although always not successfully.

The GB is the product of a set of desperate socioeconomic conditions prevailing in Bangladesh during the early 1970s. The country had just been liberated from the Pakistani (the then West Pakistani) occupying forces after fighting a bloody war for a period of nine months. Bangladesh lost lives and property beyond measure in that war. The already poor economic infrastructure was devastated. Millions of refugees came back from India virtually empty-handed. The political system was fragile. Law and order was not fully restored. In the situation of chaos and confusion, the Bangladesh government faced a difficult task of reconstruction and rehabilitation.

Despite inflows of huge foreign aid the Bangladeshi planners and policymakers, based on their centralized planning from the top in the hope of trickling down benefits, could not make the best possible use of the foreign aid. They failed, on the one hand, to rebuild the socioeconomic infrastructure of the country, and on the other hand, to uplift the socioeconomic condition of the masses living below the poverty line.

It is frequently mentioned that Bangladesh is nothing but 68,000 villages put together. But the implication of this statement is rarely reflected in the national planning, policymaking and administrative arrangements. After three decades of development, the Government of Bangladesh has recognized that the strategies of economic growth (1960s), income re-distribution (1970s), and economic adjustment (1980s) have failed to reduce poverty, illiteracy, malnutrition, disease, slums, unemployment and inequality. Measured in terms of aggregate growth rates, development has often been a success. But measured in terms of employment, justice and alleviation of poverty, development policies of the past were mainly a failure.

The performance records of other anti-poverty policies and programmes like asset provision (for example, provision of cattle and equipment), income provision (credit for trading and small scale production), or direct consumption support (vulnerable group feeding, and various relief activities) to the poor have not been significant either.

Moreover, the unimpeded growth of population and continuous decline in food production during the early 1970s made the problems of unemployment and hunger worse. The increasing trend of landlessness continued throughout the early 1970s, before the advent of the GB. Being deprived of land, virtually the only means of

---

3   The GB model is a group-based credit delivery system to landless poor women and men to start microenterprises for self-employment to lift them out of poverty.

production in a predominantly agrarian society, the landless poor did not have any opportunity to improve their social and economic conditions.

The failure of conventional development strategies that emphasize large-scale interventions and the changing economic conditions, especially since the early 1980s, have further heightened the need to re-examine these strategies of development through centralized planning. Given this general context, micro-and small-scale enterprises are now being proposed as a new alternative for poverty alleviation, and in the process achieve sustainable development. Among the most typical aspects of these activities are self-employment, microenterprises, and women's initiatives in the informal sector. It is increasingly recognized that these activities through home-based self-employment can provide an opportunity to accelerate general levels of economic activity and at the same time reduce rural poverty by a significant degree.

In Bangladesh, with more than 70 per cent of the total population living in rural areas, rural finance must take centre stage in any meaningful socioeconomic development effort. With appropriate institutional and infrastructure support, rural financial institutions can be an effective means through which the vital impulses for economic progress can be transmitted to impoverished rural communities.

But the formal financial institutions do not branch out in the rural sectors due to the apprehension of negative impact on the economic viability of rural bank branches. Such institutions are overwhelmingly urban-oriented, in terms of both the distribution of bank branches over national territory and the concentration of their financial activities.

Due to the reluctance of the formal financial sector to deal with the rural poor, the informal sources of credit remain the only option for this group. Although the informal financial sector has dynamism of its own, it is true that the structure and functioning of the formal financial sector largely determine the nature and extent of the informal sector.

If development becomes a function of, *ceteris paribus*, the access to different credits, the informal sector, firmly rooted in traditional values and practices, performs a very important role in delivering flexible, speedy, collateral-free, and need-based credits to the rural poor, who for whatever reasons have found themselves excluded from the formal sector. Since adaptability and flexibility are its major strengths, informal finance is best suited to provide small loans of short duration.

However, informal financial markets (IFMs) in Bangladesh have been regarded as usurious in character, operating in segments, and wielding considerable monopoly power. As both the formal and informal sources of finance cannot meet the ever increasing demand for financial services of the rural poor, there is a desperate need for some type of specialized financial institution to help the poor with their financial needs to improve their poverty situation.

In such a situation when all the avenues of improving the lives of the rural poor were closed, the GB came into being with the ray of hope of helping the poor to help themselves to escape poverty.

The GB project started its microcredit programme in a single village nearly 25 years ago; it has continued to grow and extend loans in rural Bangladesh, particularly to poor women. Since its inception as a bank in 1983, the GB has grown remarkably in terms of its branches, centres, membership, and cumulative loan disbursements (see chapter 3 for an elaborate analysis on the establishment and the expansion of the GB). Since the mid-1980s, the bank has emphasized recruitment of women borrowers. The proportion of male borrowers among all borrowers declined dramatically from 34.9 per cent in 1985 to less than 6 per cent in 1994, but the number of female borrowers increased by about 700 per cent during the same period (Khandker et al. 1995).

The expansion of the bank, its incorporation of women as the principal borrowers, its investment portfolio of over five billion dollars, and its claim (a claim which is not free from criticism of using reporting definition that are lax by international standard) of maintaining a 98.7 per cent recovery rates (CDF 2004) on its investment have brought the bank international recognition. Before 1990, the apparent success of the GB, combined with Yunus's advocacy, attracted considerable international interest and encouraged some bilateral organizations to increase their funding for microcredit and microenterprise development initiatives in developing countries.

In the 1990s, the microcredit approach of the GB attracted even wider international interest and is being incorporated in mainstream development agendas. The popularity of the microcredit concept in the West and its incorporation in mainstream development seem to have a political context as well. The former US President, Bill Clinton, and the then First Lady, Hillary Rodham Clinton have publicly come out in support of Yunus and his concept. President Clinton was personally very impressed and interested in this model, so much so that he proposed Dr Yunus for a Nobel Prize. In recent years, primarily because of the support of political personalities in North America, both microcredit and Yunus have received extraordinary press attention in the West.

Given Bangladesh's extreme poverty, especially among rural women, successive governments have understood the need for massive investments in human resource development if poverty is to be overcome. However, progress has been very slow. Governments, finding themselves unable to mobilize enough resources at home, have been dependent on international donors. A second policy approach of accelerating the growth of industrialization through macroeconomic reform, deregulation and privatization, and to make the country attractive to foreign investors, has been hampered by political instability and an unresponsive bureaucracy. Therefore, the country arguably has had more success with a third approach to microcredit-initiated poverty alleviation programmes targeted at the poor by both government and the NGOs.

Currently, as many as 13 Ministries/Divisions of the Government of Bangladesh are implementing microcredit projects related to poverty issues. These projects have diverse sectoral orientation such as small scale industries, crop cultivation, livestock and so on, providing various inputs like credit, training, social mobilization, and education under different Ministries and Directorates. As microcredit is a multi-agency approach, the credit lines are also different depending on donors' tastes and preferences. Even within the same Ministry, there are different credit lines devoted to the cause of poverty alleviation. This has created duplication and overlapping among the programme participants. There could be an appropriate national model programme for poverty alleviation in which all agencies could participate within the framework of microcredit approach.

Moreover, the present attitude of publicly supported financial institutions of microcredit needs to be restructured. The credit product needs to be linked with training, skill development and other means of social as well as human capital so that the poor can make the best use of it. Above all, good governance is a primary means of eradicating poverty. Inefficient, corrupt and poor governance have adverse impacts on poor people who are least able to depend on themselves because they are lacking in resources and knowledge to assert their rights. The Government's microcredit programmes should empower the poor in demanding better governance.

Currently, almost all national and international development organizations incorporate microcredit as one of the main components of their programmes. There is scarcely a multilateral, bilateral donor, or private development organization, or voluntary organization not involved in the promotion of a microcredit programme. Most bilateral and multilateral development institutions have increased their funding for microlending programmes in order to reach the poor, particularly women. Through various development projects and financial institutions' microlending services now reach about eight million borrowers on six continents (Microcredit Summit 1998). In February 1997, the promoters of the microlending projects organized the Microcredit World Summit with a commitment to create a poverty-free world by the year 2025. They have launched a plan of action to provide microcredit for 100 million borrowers, particularly women, and to reach 500 million people (if family members are included) by the year 2025.

When Muhammad Yunus, an Economics Professor at Chittagong University in Bangladesh, started making small loans to local villagers in the 1970s, it was unclear where the idea would go. Around the world, scores of state-run banks had already tried to provide small loans to the poor, and they left a legacy of inefficiency, corruption, and millions of dollars of squandered subsidies. Traditional economic theory also provided ample cautions against lending to the poor that lack collateral to back up their loans. But Yunus argued very confidently that his poor clients would pay back the loans reliably.

Today, Muhammad Yunus is recognized as a visionary in a movement that has spread globally, claiming over 65 million customers at the end of 2002. They are served by MFIs that are providing small loans without collateral, collecting deposits, and selling insurance to the poor, who had been written off by commercial banks as being unprofitable. Advocates see the changes as a revolution in thinking about poverty reduction and social change, and not just a banking movement (Aghion and Morduch 2005).

The GB explicitly targets women, and to many, the GB is all about banking for rural poor women. The following section gives a brief overview (more on *women and poverty* to come at chapter two) of the rural poor women of Bangladesh.

Women and Microcredit: A Bangladesh Perspective

Development cannot be effective and efficient if women, who constitute nearly 50 per cent of the population, are excluded from the development process. Although women clients are often overlooked in the design of any development project including small and microenterprise projects, they are a potentially profitable population. Many Asian families depend increasingly on women as income producers, as household incomes decline. Women who are the primary income earners head many of the poorest families. Under such conditions, well-designed microenterprise projects can make an important contribution to poverty reduction efforts.

Targeting women to any development programme is justified in that the incomes earned by women tended to be spent in ways that were more beneficial to the household than that of their male counterparts. Women spend proportionately more of their extra income on things that help develop human capital that is, better nutrition for the family, better health care and education for children, and better sanitation. Moreover, *when women earn, children learn*. This gives rise to a new generation of efficient women to participate in economic activities, ultimately reducing the dependency ratio for the new generations to come. The payoffs from human capital development thus formed involve a gestation period much longer than is normally expected. However, despite their innate efficiency and strong desire to escape from poverty, the lack of proper technology and training for the poor women leads them to reach, at best, to a *low level of equilibrium trap* in productivity.

Despite the fact that women's labour makes a critical contribution to developing countries' economies, experience has shown that the poorest people, especially women, with little or no access to land, are most likely to be left out of any development programme. Women's access to financial services is often made even more difficult by gender discrimination, even though women have shown themselves to be very adept at saving, are highly creative entrepreneurs, and are consistent in ensuring that earnings go directly to meeting family needs (Microcredit Summit 1997).

In recent years, there have been increasing attempts to bring Bangladeshi women into the mainstream. Ever since the First World Conference on Women in Mexico, gender issues have increasingly become a predominant theme of worldwide development discourse. Bangladesh was one of the first developing countries to establish a *Ministry of Women's Affairs* in 1978, three years after the Mexico Conference. Concerted efforts by national and international development agencies, and the Government's own commitment to both national and international pledges, paved the way for the enhancement of women's position and status in society. The Government has already prepared a National Policy for Advancement of Women and made some noteworthy progress in implementing the National Action Plan, prepared in response to the Beijing Platform for Action (PFA).

In spite of these achievements, the status of Bangladeshi women is low. Early marriage, and a lack of social security, as well as low levels of human development and poor access to income, remains core issues. Given this situation, it is hardly surprising that many of Bangladesh's poor are women. Female poverty is further reinforced by cultural norms that favour men over women in numerous aspects of life such as inheritance and the prevalent (albeit declining) practice of marriage dowry. Such discrimination means that women's access to other resources such as education, health, and financial services are restricted, reinforcing their overall disadvantaged situation.

Bangladeshi women's activities are largely invisible because they do not operate directly in the market and are largely in the form of unpaid family labour and in informal sector work. Women's workloads are heavy and most Bangladeshi women work a *triple shift* split between their market and nonmarket work and household responsibilities.

The rural women's economic activities in the informal sector include post harvest activities, cow fattening and milking, goat farming, backyard poultry rearing, pisciculture, agriculture, horticulture, food processing, cane and bamboo works, silk reeling, handloom, garment making, fishnet making, coir production, and handicrafts. A good number of rural poor women are also involved in rural construction. Women workers are found in certain activities traditionally falling under the male domain (for example, earthwork, construction, and agricultural work in the field). This is particularly the case for landless women who largely belong to the *extreme poor* group. It indicates growing economic pressure and erosion of familial support and traditional beliefs and norms regarding women's outside work.

A dearth of money to hire household help, traditional time-consuming food habits and the absence of child-care facilities increase women's burden of household responsibility and impinge on the time women can use for productive activities. Moreover, the greatest obstacle women face is the lack of capital required for building the permanent structure of the enterprise, labour-saving tools to ease domestic burden, and raw materials and growth-enhancing machineries needed to increase productivity in their enterprises.

The extremely adverse conditions of Bangladeshi poor women call for far-reaching policies and large-scale, multi-faceted, and sustained programmes to provide them with the skills and the resources to enhance their contribution to the common challenge of development and to improve the situation.

Scattered evidence also revealed that an increasing number of poor women in Bangladesh being frustrated at the governments' inability to create avenues for employment were creating their own jobs in small scale agriculture, manufacturing, services, and petty trade. Inaccessibility to finance for many of those poor women who attempted to start up such small scale enterprises was recognized as a constraint for poor women to climb out of poverty.

To many, microfinance is all about banking for women. Not all microfinance institutions focus specifically on women, but a recent study found that women make up 80 per cent of the clients of the thirty-four largest microlenders (Mody 2000). Group-based institutional lending to women is a significant addition to development initiatives in rural Bangladesh, although saving and borrowing have a long tradition among rural women.

Bangladesh has nearly 10,000 NGOs and substantial efforts are made by many of these in rural areas to target women with the result that a large and growing share of NGO participants is women. Currently, the efforts of both the NGOs and the government have shifted toward credit extension and development with a special focus on poor women.

In terms of inclusion of women members into the microfinance programmes, the GB`s history is, as Aghion and Morduch (2005, 179) call, instructive. From the start, Muhammad Yunus recognized the importance of women when confronting poverty. But cultural norms, especially the Muslim practice of *purdah* (which guards a woman's modesty and limits her mobility and social interactions), made it difficult to approach potential female clients. At first, Yunus struggled to serve at least 50 per cent women; but now, 96 per cent of Grameen`s clients are women.

Besides the main impact on poverty alleviation, the positive impact of microcredit on healthcare practices, family planning and schooling behaviour is now well recorded. The impact seems to work mainly due to the increasing participation of women into the microcredit programmes. Bangladesh has made spectacular progress, particularly during the last decade or so, in such social development indicators as child mortality rates, birth control and school enrolment, especially for girls. This has also been a period of very rapid growth in the coverage of microcredit. Bangladesh belongs to a regional belt stretching across northern Africa, the Middle East, Pakistan and northern India which is particularly characterized by patriarchal family structures along with female seclusion and deprivation. That makes these achievements and the possible role of women therein, all the more noteworthy.

Studies on the Grameen Bank

The GB has been well-studied in terms of: its programme design and sources of its success as a rural financial intermediary and its impact on the poor and women by Ghai (1984); R.I. Rahman (1986); A. Rahman (1986); Hossain (1988); Osmani (1989); Stiglitz (1990); Varian (1990); Wahid (1993); Bhyian (1994); Fuglesang and Chandler (1994); Ameen (1996); Bornstein (1997); Jain (1996); Hulme and Mosley (1996); Steinert (1996); Beltran (1997); Krishna (1997); Khandker (1998); Rahman (1999); and Aghion and Morduch (2005); its subsidy dependency by Yaron (1992); its replicability outside Bangladesh by Hulme (1990); Gibbons (1992); Getubig (1993); Dahlquist (1994); Nabi (1995); and Renteria (1996); and its impact on women's empowerment by Holcombe (1995); Hashemi, Schuler, and Riley (1996); and Goetz and Sen Gupta (1996); and Todd (1996).

Besides these, scores of doctoral dissertations, master's theses, and academic studies have now been written on the GB.

Most of the above studies, though insightful, are not as rigorous as the ones by Khandker (1998) and Wright (2000). Khandker (1998) from the World Bank in his *Fighting Poverty with Microcredit* observed that the microcredit programmes of the GB, BRAC, and RD-12 have been successful in reaching the targeted poor, especially women, and that they have reduced poverty among borrowers. The effect on the economy as a whole has been small, however, because of the nature of the activities these microcredit programmes support. These programmes have developed a single-product credit delivery mechanism that may be effective in reaching a large number of small producers. Such programmes, however, cannot reduce poverty significantly. Poverty is caused by many factors, including lack of skills, entrepreneurship, and human capital. Providing only credit for generating self-employment cannot solve the multiple causes of poverty.

Wright (2000) in his *Microfinance Systems: Designing Quality Financial Services for the Poor* stressed the need for flexible financial services for significant poverty alleviation of the poor. His insightful book explored the provision of client-responsive, flexible, quality financial services and the principles that could and perhaps should be followed by the MFIs to design a microfinance system to achieve the goal of significant poverty alleviation.

This study, which justifiably stresses that microcredit alone does not and perhaps cannot alleviate poverty significantly, complements the studies of Khandker (1998) and Wright (2000). Elucidating the many causes of poverty other than credit, that is, lack of voluntary savings and other flexible financial services, lack of skills, entrepreneurship, human capital, and infrastructure, this study supports the views of Khandker (1998) and Wright (2000) and attempts to address the issue of client-led, flexible financial services including voluntary savings. This book would complement rather than compete with these two insightful studies. This study, however, does not address the issues of skill development, entrepreneurship, and infrastructure systematically. But this is a matter of focus, and definitely not meant as a suggestion that such issues are unimportant.

Most rigorous and insightful though Khandker (1998) study is which, concentrates on GB, BRAC, and RD-1 programmes, however, falls short of emphasizing the role of flexible financial services including voluntary savings, which is the need of the second generation microfinance. The over emphasis of the microcredit movement on loans is misplaced. Some people want loans and are creditworthy, but all people want savings, especially voluntary savings, and are depositworthy. Although some people can cross poverty line through the returns on credit-assisted enterprises, most people exit poverty through the return on assets purchased with their savings.

Wright's (2000) study, though insightful, does not elucidate the role of credit. The study is an attempt to explore the general overview of the potential of quality financial services in achieving significant alleviation of poverty. This book in fact extends the works of Khandker (1998) and Wright (2000) by concentrating on the GB, the pioneer and cradle of microcredit movement, as a case study.

The Significance of the Study

Most of the studies on the GB have focused on quantitative indicators of the GB programme, i.e., the numbers of clients reached, amounts of loans disbursed among these clients and recovered from them. The performance of the GB based on these indicators has established it as a successful financial institution lending to poor women.

Probably no in-depth research in terms of incorporating appropriate, quality financial services including voluntary savings has been conducted on the GB. While presenting a critical analysis of the microlending policies of the GB, this in-depth study focuses on the importance of client-responsive services in terms of attracting the extreme poor into the GB microfinance programme. The incorporation of such services will make the GB more poverty alleviating for which it was originally established. This study also shows that the MFIs of the first generation with credit-alone policies cannot solve the problems of the poor of the second generation with their diversified needs and preferences. It is also the understanding of this study that the promise of the GB microcredit has not taken into consideration the hard realities of rural poor women's situations. Rather it has been over-advertised and communicated to the public through success stories about women-owned, largely home-based, businesses.

In contrast to the general trend of focusing on the *empowerment* aspect, this study focuses on the productive role of women. In a situation of extreme poverty, where the survival of the rural poor women is at stake, productive role is of great importance to make development more effective. Although female productivity is on average below than that of male productivity, at the margin this ranking may be reversed if only because of low participation rate amongst females. By enabling poor women to enter the labour force, the GB is contributing to poverty alleviation through using microfinance mechanism, the underlying assumption of this study is that the poverty alleviation impact would be more impressive if the GB provides not only credit but also other flexible financial services including voluntary savings.

The expansion of the GB and its membership of more than five million, most of whom are women, do not necessarily reflect the significant poverty alleviating impact of the GB. The high and increasing levels of women's participation in the GB programme may in many cases be a desperate attempt by women with few alternatives, rather than a conscious choice. The majority of poor women, though not interested in the GB initiated microenterprise schemes, which could not alleviate their poverty, were forced to undertake such venture in their dire need for survival. Given their low productivity one should also consider what alternative avenues these poor women have had before joining the GB programmes.

The critical analysis of this work not only complements the existing research but also presents a different picture from other research findings on the GB. These insights on the GB address the international demand for new knowledge of microfinance and microenterprise development. This study is aimed at a diverse readership: economists; policymakers; donors; social scientists; microfinance practitioners; specialists in rural finance and rural development and members of the general public interested in development. Since the mid-1970s scholars and activists have shifted their attention from massive infrastructural development projects to small-scale participatory development. The critics of the modernisation paradigm argue that poor people need mechanisms to organise themselves and establish microenterprises that require small amounts of capital and in which they can use their local knowledge and skill.

The Roadmap of the Book

The book comprises five chapters including the present one. This chapter, *Chapter 1*, has set the background for considering microfinance. The chapter began by asking why microfinance is needed in the first place. Can microcredit alone significantly alleviate poverty? Or can the client-induced, flexible financial services including voluntary savings services deliver important added benefits to the clients? Taking the GB, the pioneer of microcredit movement, as the case study, the chapter takes into account the pluses and minuses of microfinance in alleviating poverty. It challenges long-held assumptions about what the poor can and cannot achieve, and more broadly shows the potential of effective, flexible financial services in significant alleviation of poverty. A preliminary analysis of the GB, women and microcredit, different studies on the GB and the significance of this study are also discussed here.

Chapter 2 presents the background to the Bangladesh economy. To understand the dimensions of rural poverty, and the situation of women's lives, and the institutions that have been evolved to help them cross the poverty line, one must understand as much as possible, the situation of Bangladesh. The chapter is mainly an attempt to locate the position of Bangladesh in worldwide and regional rankings in terms of its socioeconomic structure. It specifically examines: the rural economy and its importance to the national economy; poverty, its trend over time and women and poverty.

Chapter 3 presents the financial structure of Bangladesh-formal financial sector, informal financial sector, and the rise of microenterprises and microfinance organizations and NGOs. The low density of formal financial institutions in rural areas and their reluctance to deal with small loans force the rural poor to approach the informal moneylenders for their financial needs. Because of the scarcity of capital, and the monopoly power, the moneylenders in the informal sector charge exorbitant rates of interest. The poor cannot afford to pay such higher rates of interest. The failure of both the formal and informal sectors to meet the financial needs of the rural poor gives rise to MFIs, like the GB and other NGOs. The coverage of large MFIs in terms of clientele served, amounts of loans disbursed, and amounts of savings mobilized are also discussed. Finally, the contribution of the GB to the national economy of Bangladesh is also analyzed here.

Chapter 4 begins with the research methodology used in the empirical study on the GB. This is followed by a critical evaluation of the GB's impact in raising the economic situation of its members. The basic idea behind the setting up of the GB is that if credit is extended to the poor at reasonable terms and conditions, it can generate self-employment and thereby improve their economic conditions. The economic impacts in terms of income, employment, capital accumulation, productivity, and impact in rural credit market are highlighted here. The importance of the institutional innovations of the GB in terms of ensuring the access of the rural poor to the institutional sources of finance and the lessons for the rural financial markets is also analyzed here. Based on the extent of the economic benefits the GB members enjoy, the next chapter, chapter 5, finally explores the GB's impact on poverty alleviation.

The last chapter, *Chapter 5*, attempts to answer the basic research question, that is, has the GB microcredit programme resulted in a substantial alleviation of poverty among the clients? This being the ultimate test, the success of which will mainly, though not exclusively, determine the success of the GB.

Microcredit, or in its wider term microfinance, holds the promise of helping the poor in alleviating poverty, but it has also its limits. It is neither a panacea nor a magic bullet, and it cannot be expected to work for everybody, especially the poorest of the poor. The impact and the limitations of the GB microcredit in alleviating poverty are highlighted here. Different steps and the realistic policy options to enhance the poverty alleviation impact on the extreme poor are also discussed here. Contrary to general findings of many studies, the present findings are, however, not the first to paint such a gloomy picture of limited poverty alleviation impact of microcredit.

Microcredit alone does not and perhaps cannot alleviate poverty significantly. The significant poverty alleviation depends on, among other things, flexible financial services, including voluntary savings. The more flexible and better quality the financial services are on offer, the greater the take up and retention by the poor clients will be, ultimately leading to a *significant* alleviation in poverty.

The book closes with a discussion on Grameen Phase II. The discussion is brief and it just scratches the surface. The introduction of Grameen Phase II in 2002 embracing some client-responsive changes is a welcome one, because it recognizes the demand of the clients. The introduction of Grameen Phase II also distinctly demonstrates that the Grameen Classical System with its one-size-fits-all policy was not sustainable.

Chapter 2

The Bangladesh Economy and Poverty in Bangladesh

Introduction

To understand the dimensions of rural poverty in general, and the situation of women's lives, in particular, and the institutions in Bangladesh that have been evolved to help them cross the poverty line, one must understand as much as possible the situation of Bangladesh. This brief description cannot convey the complexity of its economic, social and political conditions, the variety of points of view through which these conditions have been interpreted, or the process of change that is affecting them. It is meant to indicate, rather than explain the situation of Bangladesh.

The main questions of the chapter are where Bangladesh fits in the world in terms of its socioeconomic structure? Being mainly a rural country to what extent has its rural development been emphasized? What is the extent of poverty, and has it declined? How significant are the poverty alleviation efforts undertaken in Bangladesh in terms of rural poor women?

It is never easy to establish where Bangladesh ranks in a league-table of statistics of per capita national incomes, translated into US dollars at official exchange rates. Per capita income in Bangladesh is unquestionably among the very lowest of the very low-low in the lowest deciles of world incomes per head. Classified as a low- level developing country, it ranks 138th globally with human development index (HDI) below 0.509. Bangladesh is included among the eight least developed economies in the Asia Pacific region. The World Bank estimated its per capita income at $400 in 2003 (World Bank 2005).

Bangladesh had faced many formidable economic difficulties. Initially, there were disruptions resulting from the war of liberation in 1971. Bangladesh lost lives and properties beyond measure. High rates of population growth in a relatively limited area, and a heavy dependence on agricultural production subject to the vagaries of nature, the two oil shocks and the worldwide recession resulted in deteriorating terms of trade of the country.

There is little of significance to examine in terms of development projects in the period from 1975 to 1988. With the substantial growth that was occurring in the East and Southeast Asian countries in the 1980s, the policymakers of this country no longer could ignore the need for restructuring the economy. The desire to emulate the growth path of the growing economies acted as an incentive when the political elite decided in the late 1980s to restructure the economy.

The policymakers of the country rightly realized the fact that Bangladesh faces the enormous challenge of achieving accelerated economic growth and alleviating the massive poverty that afflicts 40 to 50 per cent of its nearly 140 million people. Strategies for meeting this challenge have included a shift away from state bureaucratic controls and industrial autarky towards economic liberalization and integration with the global economy on the one hand, and undertaking pro-poor growth strategies, on the other.

Bangladesh embarked on market-oriented liberalizing policy reforms, known as structural adjustment, towards the mid 1980s. These reforms were undertaken against the backdrop of serious macroeconomic imbalance, which had been caused in part by a decline in foreign aid and in part by a preceding episode of severe deterioration in the country's terms of trade. The beginning of the 1990s saw the launching of a more comprehensive programme, which coincided with a transition to parliamentary democracy from semi-autocratic rule.

The large population of about 138 million living in a tiny land of 144 000 sq. km (about quarter the size of New Zealand but with more than thirty six times the people) is still growing at a high rate. Apart from very small countries such as Singapore and Bahrain, Bangladesh is the most densely populated country in the world. The nation, at 982 persons per square kilometer, has often been compared to Indonesia's Java (Wikipedia 2005). High population growth negates any social improvement for the people unless a higher economic growth in the 5-8 per cent range is sustained over a decade. In addition, a robust external sector is needed to help import resources through the trade sector for serious development to occur. Bangladesh is very poorly endowed with resources, and consequently has a savings rate of about 7 per cent. These are the facts of the economy, which have to be realized by the country's elite and development institutions in understanding how fragile the growth prospects are for this economy.

Aid dependence, like poverty, is one of the defining components of Bangladesh's image. Aid constitutes a lion share of all development budgets of the government. Such development assistance has been described as a double-edged sword. The assistance secures the survival of the country, but strengthens the power of a centralized, inefficient and elitist bureaucracy and allows the government to ignore the crucial structural problems of poverty (Hulme and Mosley 1996, 95-6). The value of debt in 2005 is $ 12.8 billion and aid per capita is $ 10.1 (World Bank 2005).

Economic and Financial Structures

Bangladesh is an agricultural country. The total cultivable land is around 24 million acres and there are a little more than 14.5 million cultivators. Major agricultural products are rice, jute, wheat, potato, pulses, sugarcane, tea, tobacco, and so on. Tea, leather, and frozen shrimp are also major foreign exchange earners.

The Bangladesh economy is dominated by agricultural activities with a highly protected pricing system justified during the 1970s to create order and encourage production in a period of civil disorder. Only 23 per cent of the population lives in the urban areas most of which only has a rudimentary infrastructure. Agricultural output, therefore, is the mainstay for almost 110 million people. In the 1970s GDP growth was under 6 per cent. It fell to an average of 3.9 per cent in the 1980s and, after limited reforms in the 1990s, expanded closer to 5 per cent until it reached 5.8 per cent in 1998. The most important sector, agriculture, grew at about 2 per cent, and this despite wrongly motivated incentives and price controls favouring this sector (Ariff and Khalid 2000, 285).

From the mid-1970s to date, the trend in the rate of growth of food-grains output has been fairly satisfactory, with marked short-term fluctuations, notably the instability of supply during the 1970s and mid-1980s. The rice sub-sector has now fully recovered from the unprecedented flood damage in 1987 and 1988. Food-grains production reached a record level of 20.3 million tons in 1996-97[1]. Bangladesh is at the moment not just self-sufficient in rice, it even has a small export surplus. The question is whether this is sustainable, and if so, what reorientation of agricultural and food policies might be necessary (Abdullah and Shahabuddin 1997, 30).

This does not, however, mean that access to food is equitable. According to the 1988-89 Household Expenditure Survey (HES), while the average consumption of rice was 0.44 kg per day, it was 0.31 kg per day for the bottom 20 per cent of the population, and for the top 10 per cent, 0.51 kg per day. Clearly, food security and foodgrain self-sufficiency are not identical. The supply of food-grains seems to have increased much faster than the effective demand, and the imbalance between food grain supply and demand was due primarily to very slow growth in rural employment.

The above situation has made one thing clear: whatever may be the food self-sufficiency, the technical potential for increasing rice production and thereby achieving growth cannot be sustainable unless the product finds a growing market at remunerative prices. While part of this growth in demand can be within agriculture (crop diversification), a large part will have to be outside of agriculture (mainly non-farm incomes).

Moreover, as the rural population of Bangladesh increases, landlessness among people once dependent on agriculture is a growing problem. MacIssac and Wahid (1993, 191) paint a very bleak picture of the extent of landlessness in Bangladesh. According to them, in 1951 the landless numbered eight million, years later, there were fifteen million; and in 1993 there were over fifty million. This mass of landless has been growing so rapidly that, even if agricultural growth were to meet the government's most optimistic targets, employment in this sector would still be insufficient to meet the employment needs of the rural poor landless.

The rice-led agricultural growth has brought new challenges and opportunities to make agriculture more efficient and flexible. It is in this context that the issue of cropping intensity and crop diversification needs to be addressed as part of the broader agricultural development strategy. Increasing the cropping intensity

---

1   *The Daily Star,* 23rd June 1997, Dhaka.

for the medium and large farmers (small farmers' cropping intensity is relatively satisfactory) may also be a possibility for increasing productivity. Multiple cropping promises to be more effective in creating rural employment and income than a rural works programme (Singh 1990, 128).

Irrigation systems are based around rice in Bangladesh but irrigation water is sold or transacted for growing nonrice crops as well. The diversification of crop production is recognized as an alternative strategy for improving the productivity and efficiency of the irrigation water market. In the context of poor farmers, an important policy implication is the potential scope for promoting the *intermediate* irrigation technologies as represented by hand-tube wells and treadle pumps. These labour-intensive irrigation techniques are particularly advantageous for small and marginal farmers and for growing crops like potato (a substitute for rice for the poor), vegetables and spices. A striking feature of the profitability estimates of these crops is that these are more profitable than those of high yielding variety (HYV) rice (Abdullah and Shahabuddin 1997, 61).

There is also considerable scope for increasing the yields of noncereal crops through better farm practices and varietal improvements even under nonirrigated and semi-irrigated conditions. Such yield improvements, rather than more intensive cultivation of land (which is already at its saturation point), perhaps offer better growth prospects for these crops. The technical and socioeconomic constraints to the diffusion of improved technologies in the case of noncereal crops are still little understood. Much will depend on how far adaptive research and extension activities can be strengthened to identify and overcome these constraints.

Despite a positive trend in agricultural growth, in general, and self-sufficiency in rice production, in particular, not enough progress has been made to turn Bangladesh's stagnant economy into a dynamic one. Regardless of this increase in agricultural production, it is unlikely that there will be a significant reduction in poverty in an environment of mass landlessness.

In order to have a significant impact on poverty, it is imperative that the potential for employment expansion that exists in various sectors such as crop production, non-crop agriculture and RNAs be assessed. A comprehensive rural employment policy commensurate with the rightly placed emphasis on both wage and self-employment expansion for the poor including the female poor needs to be formulated. With the ever increasing size of the labour force, it is quite unlikely that Bangladesh can raise the level of investment to a level that would create enough wage employment to absorb its millions of unemployed labour force.

With the favourable effects of reforms, industrial output increased to about 8 per cent in the 1990s, while manufacturing, now under a more liberalized regime, is growing at 13 per cent. Manufacturing, if managed properly, has the potential for increasing growth. It is a competitive sector with small and medium-sized enterprises working under such constraints as low productivity and constant power shortages. Fortunately, progress in generating a reliable power supply is being made with the entry of private sector in this area and power-sharing agreements with India (Ariff and Khalid 2000, 285).

However, considering the limited progress in industrial policy and public enterprise, it is imperative that the government introduces a comprehensive restructuring programme comprising the liquidation of nonviable enterprises, restructuring and good governance of public sector enterprises, and privatization of the restructured enterprises. The removal of subsidies and/ or price controls will reduce the losses of public enterprises, estimated at BDT 20 billion or about one-quarter of 1992-1993 ADP or one per cent of GDP (Rana 1997, 22)[2]. Entry of the private sector in all non-performing public enterprises will perhaps be a right step.

It is not easy for a poor country like Bangladesh to specialize in manufactured exports. While most low-income countries depend largely on the export of primary commodities, Bangladesh has made the transition from being primarily a jute-exporting country to a garment-exporting one. This transition has been dictated by the country's resource endowment, characterized by extreme land scarcity and a very high population density, making economic growth dependent on the export of labour-intensive manufactures.

Although Bangladesh still does not rank among the most globally integrated developing economies, the pace of integration has been quite rapid. Until hit by the global recession in 2001, there had been robust and sustained growth of export earnings, averaging about 15 per cent per year in the 1990s. In 2001-2, however, export earnings declined in US dollar terms for the first time in nearly 15 years. Although there was a recovery in the following year, the medium term outlook indicates that it will be difficult to regain the export momentum of the 1990s (Mahmud and Ahluwalia 2004, 14)

A greater integration with the global economy seems to fit well with the kind of pro-poor growth envisaged by Bangladesh's development efforts. The export-oriented garment industry presently employs around 1.8 million workers-mostly women from low-income, rural backgrounds. The second dominant export-dominated activity, shrimp farming, is also very labour-intensive, presently employing nearly half a million rural poor (Mahmud 2003). More generally, import liberalization is likely to have contributed to the creation of productive employment for the poor through the strengthening of many small-scale and informal sector activities that have benefited from improved access to imported inputs. The impact of trade liberalization, in particular, and economic deregulation in general, on economic growth and employment generation has been immense. These policies have also indirectly contributed to stimulating other parts of the economy.

Another issue of great importance to Bangladesh is that the free movement of temporary workers across borders be expanded, for workers' remittances play an important role in its fragile economy. A redeeming feature in the face of the export slow down in Bangladesh is the continued increase in the flow of migrant workers' remittances, which grew from about 2.5 per cent of GDP in the beginning of the 1990s

---

2   The accumulated losses of the state-owned enterprises in Bangladesh at the beginning of 2001 stood at BDT 31 billion, which is 1.3 per cent of the GDP of the country. See for reference *The Daily Star*, Dhaka, April 20, 2001.

to above 5 per cent (amounting to about $ 2.5 billion) in 2001-02 (ibid.,). Migrant workers are mostly unskilled or semi-skilled, and most of them come from poor rural families, making their remitted savings an important means for their families to escape poverty. There is, however, considerable uncertainty about the continuation of these remittance inflows, which depends on the economic fortunes of the host countries and their changing policies and attitudes towards guest workers. Most of Bangladesh's temporary migrant workers are in the Middle East, but increasingly they are going to more diverse destinations in East Asia and Europe, though often illegally.

In the wake of the 2001 global recession, Bangladesh's reliance on foreign countries as a market for exports and as a source of remittances has become obvious. If Bangladesh is to become less vulnerable to the economic fortunes of the other, it will need to strengthen its domestic economy, creating jobs and markets at home. A strong domestic sector and an improved overall investment environment will provide a more stable source of income-like what the garment industry has provided so far-and will rekindle and sustain Bangladesh's economic growth.

Given the limited growth of sectoral sources, an improvement in the Bangladesh's economic performance is likely to come from an increase in agricultural productivity as well as the spread of a dynamic rural non-farm sector. Rural non-farm income is becoming an increasingly important share of rural income, averaging 42 per cent in Africa, 40 per cent in Latin America and 32 per cent in Asia (FAO 2000, 4). The rural non-farm sector, which now accounts for nearly half of rural employment in Bangladesh, is poised for a much bigger contribution to the country's economy and to a more rural-urban balance in development. Bangladesh's achievement in rural areas during the last few decades has been quite impressive. Aided by the remarkable agricultural growth, the rural non-farm economy has now become a leading source of income and half of employment in rural areas. The potential of the rural non-farm sector is inherent in the structure of living conditions in rural Bangladesh. This sector has the potential to help the country meet many of the economic challenges it faces. Agricultural growth and urban employment cannot absorb the increased labour force. The rural non-farm sector will have to play a major role to generate employment for this increased labour force, slow down rural-urban migration, and contribute to a more balanced pattern of development. The most detailed recent source of information on RNA in Bangladesh is the Annual Economic Survey of non-farm activities conducted by the Bangladesh Bureau of Statistics (BBS) in 1988-90. It estimated that about 1.5 million households were engaged part or full-time in RNAs. In all, these households contributed four million workers-a tenth of the rural labour force. The RNAs accounted for 13 per cent of GDP[3].

The experiences of Southeast Asian countries that have built rural non-farm sector including rural industries from comparable resource endowments have prompted Yusuf and Kumar from the World Bank (1996, ix) to argue that the non-

---

3   Because of its limited coverage, this survey perhaps underestimates the scale of RNA but it remains the only comprehensive source of information.

Table 2.1   Key Economic Ratios and the Structure of Bangladesh Economy, 1999-2003

Economy	1999	2002	2003
GNI, Atlas method (current US$ in billion)	47.1	51.1	55.0
GNI per capita, Atlas method (current US$)	370.0	380.0	400.0
GDP (current $ in billion)	46.0	47.6	51.9
GDP growth (annual %)	4.9	4.4	5.3
GDP implicit price deflator (annual % growth)	4.7	3.2	4.5
Value added in agriculture (% of GDP)	26.2	22.7	21.8
Value added in industry (% of GDP)	25.2	26.4	26.3
Value added in services (% of GDP)	48.7	50.9	52.0
Exports of goods and services (% of GDP)	13.2	14.3	14.2
Imports of goods and services (% of GDP)	18.7	19.0	20.0
Gross capital formation (% of GDP)	22.2	23.1	23.4
Revenue, excluding grants (% of GDP)	..	10.2	10.1
Cash surplus/deficit (% of GDP)	..	-0.2	-0.1

Source: World Development Indicators database April 2005

farm sector in Bangladesh could greatly stimulate the rural economy, contributing one-third share of GDP and absorbing two-thirds of the populace, with substantial linkage effects to agricultural output, exports, employment, and the tempo of the urban economy.

Now, coming on to the question of where does Bangladesh fit in terms of growth experience it may be said that three characteristics of Bangladesh's growth experience stand out when compared with those of a sample of Asian and African economies. First, in terms of variance, Bangladesh is in the group of countries, which includes Sri Lanka, whose growth is exceedingly stable. Second, Bangladesh has relied far more on services whereas the Asian countries, especially the ones registering the fastest growth, have depended heavily on industry as the engine of growth. A third, conspicuous feature of Bangladesh's growth dynamics is that the incremental capital-output ratio is low, closer to that of African countries than that of Asian countries. The low value suggests that growth has been extensively concentrated on services, sparing the development of infrastructure, and industry.

To prevent poverty and unemployment from becoming socially insupportable and politically explosive, Bangladesh has only one meaningful choice: it must aim for a growth rate of GDP of not less than 7-8 per cent, holding all else constant. Growth of this order is roughly twice the average annual rate attained during the 1980s and 80 per cent higher than the average rate seen in the first half of the 1990s. It is a rate that very few countries have been able to sustain over a long period of time[4].

---

4   Only the East Asian Gang of Four and Botswana had been able to sustain growth rates at 6 per cent or higher during 1960-88. For details see Easterly et al., 1993.

The sectoral sources of growth in Bangladesh are limited. The share of industry in GDP is small, and the sector lacks dynamism. Although services account for 45 per cent of GDP, the likelihood of it providing much additional growth momentum is also quite limited. An improvement in Bangladesh's economic performance is likely to come from an increase in agricultural productivity and the spread and development of RNAs-with backward linkages to agriculture and forward to the urban sector. Table 2.1 illustrates the key economic ratios and the structure of Bangladesh economy in terms of contribution of each sector, to GDP.

Bangladesh has been struck by a widespread arsenic contamination of drinking water, the effects of which are long ranging. Dangerously high levels of naturally occurring arsenic, a colourless, tasteless poison, have been found in the water in underground wells, putting an estimated 35 million people-nearly one fourth of the population-at risk.

In 1998, the government launched the Bangladesh Arsenic Mitigation and Water Supply Project (BAMWSP) with support from the World Bank. Although some progress has been made, a viable long term solution of this problem is not yet in sight. National direction and coordination, along with local innovation and ownership, will certainly be essential. The Government has an important role to play in leading additional research on the sources of arsenic contamination and the likely impacts on health and food production, in verifying, promoting, and regulating safe water technologies, and in providing the resources necessary for the poor to have convenient access to clean, safe water (World Bank 2005a).

Although there has been a moderate success in population control since 1991, the population still increases every year. Investment in and development of human resources will help a nation enhance the quality and abilities of its workforce. In a country like Bangladesh with its still high population growth, the government with its scarce resources finds it almost impossible to either invest in human capital or to create enough opportunities for wage employment.

Despite the growth of the RNAs since independence, evidence suggests that the real per capita income has declined in most RNAs. This decline in income is higher for rural non-farm households than for those of farm households. One possible reason for this trend is underemployment-the RNAs did not grow proportionately with the labour supply (Khandker and Chowdhury 1996, 5). The population in Bangladesh has been growing rapidly (Table 2.2), and the farm sector is absorbing a falling proportion of new entrants into the labour market. Low growth and underemployment in rural areas remains a chronic structural problem. There are also workers, particularly rural poor women, who may work long hours, but do not earn enough to lift their families out of poverty. This is related to the concept of overemployment.

One factor underlying low growth in Bangladesh is a depressing domestic investment rate-only 10 per cent of GDP in 1991[5]. This is the lowest domestic investment rate in South Asia-indeed, one of lowest in the world. This had a

---

5   World Bank, 1993, quoted in D. Hulme and P. Mosley eds., *Finance against Poverty*, 1996, Vol. 2, p. 95

Table 2.2   Social Indicators of Bangladesh, 1999-2003

People	1999	2002	2003
Population, total in million	128.8	135.7	138.1
Population growth (annual %)	1.7	1.7	1.7
National poverty rate (% of population)	..	..	..
Life expectancy (years)	..	62.1	62.4
Fertility rate (births per woman)	..	3.0	2.9
Infant mortality rate (per 1,000 live births)	..	..	46.0
Under 5 mortality rate (per 1,000 children)	..	..	69.0
Births attended by skilled health staff (% of total)	..	..	14.0
Child malnutrition, weight for age (% of under 5)	61.3	..	..
Child immunization, measles (% of under 12 mos)	76.0	77.0	77.0
Literacy rate, adult male (% of males ages 15 and above)	48.9	50.3	..
Literacy rate, adult female (% of females ages 15 and above)	29.5	31.4	..
	78.0	73.0	..
Primary completion rate, total (% age group)	80.0	76.0	..
Primary completion rate, female (% age group)	88.8	85.1	..
Net primary enrollment (% relevant age group)	42.1	44.5	..
Net secondary enrollment (% relevant age group)			

Source: World Development Indicators database April 2005

direct bearing on the volume of investment, which at 12 per cent is far short of the investment rates in the successful East Asian economies. The situation is not appreciably alleviated by foreign direct investment, which is much lower than those of India, Sri Lanka, Malaysia, and Pakistan. The revenue base of the government is also less than for the other Asian and African comparators with revenue GDP ratios in the comparators range during the early 1990s. All these factors contribute to a rate of capital accumulation that has averaged less than 14 per cent of GDP in the first half of the 1990s (Yusuf and Kumar 1996, x).

Bangladesh faces a severe domestic savings constraint on its development efforts. This is because of a paucity of domestic savings caused by a weak institutional structure for mobilizing private household savings of the rural poor. The extent to which public savings can be increased is, however, constrained by the limited capacity, inefficiency and corruption of the government employees, the small tax base, and last but not least, the lack of innovative financial intermediaries to mobilize the rural savings of the poor. All this suggests that achieving and sustaining economic growth would require innovative reform strategies that extract the maximum developmental benefit from the existing endowment and lay the groundwork for augmenting that endowment.

Since independence, Bangladesh has been dubbed many things, from the *basket case* to the *test case*[6]. Despite these gloomy and pessimistic characterizations, it has made significant economic strides in a number of areas, even though the country remains one of the poorest in the world. During the 1990s, Bangladesh significantly improved both its economic performance and its human development indicators. Even with a significantly reduced and declining dependence on foreign aid, the economy appeared to begin a transition from stabilization to growth. The growth of GDP had been relatively slow in the 1980s by the standard of contemporary South Asia, at 3.7 per cent a year, but it accelerated to 4.4 per cent in the first half of the 1990s, and to 5.2 in the second half. The country is self-sufficient in food now, and there is also ample scope for food export if further improvements are made in food production. The country has achieved notable success in macroeconomic stability and, more importantly, it has achieved significant reduction in poverty, with the poverty incidence declining from over 70 per cent in the early 1980s to less than 50 per cent in the early 1990s. Progress in human development indicators was even more impressive, and Bangladesh ranked among the top performers in the 1990s in the extent of improvement in the UNDP Human Development Index (Mahmud and Ahluwalia 2004, 14).

Despite the above successes, the country faces a number of critical constraints, including poverty, in further economic development. Although agriculture experienced rapid growth in the post-independence period, analysis of changes in real income and wages shows that such growth had only marginal impact on alleviating rural poverty and income inequality. Though the incidence of poverty has decreased (a claim which has resulted in considerable controversy in the recent literature, see for example, Table 2.6) the number of absolute poor has increased. Poverty, malnutrition and hunger are endemic in Bangladesh. Poverty is also manifested in such factors as unemployment, underemployment, low literacy, inadequate schooling, and unequal female participation in economic activity.

If the economy is to move from a low-growth to a high-growth trajectory, reforms need to be sustained and credible. Unless the reforms are carried out on an urgent basis, not only will further progress be jeopardized but even the sustainability of the past achievements may be at stake. There is a growing concern regarding how far the economic growth momentum can withstand a *weakening* of the institutions of economic and political governance. The political instability that has existed in the past 25 years or so has not been particularly helpful in inspiring confidence in the credibility of the reforms. The prevailing confrontational politics is not only hindering democratic consolidation, it also carries the risk of causing serious economic disruption. Beside this issue of credibility of reforms, the other issues critical to the economic success of the country are largely political-economic in nature and relate to labour market flexibility and governance. The industrial labour force is

---

6   The *basket case* label is attributed to Henry Kissinger, former secretary of state of President Richard Nixon, and subsequently, President Gerald Ford. The *test case* label is attributed to J. Faaland and J. R. Parkinson 1976 (cited in Quibria ed. 1997).

highly politicized and the consequent strikes and lockouts have prevented industrial output from reaching its full potential. Similarly, the management of public sector enterprises remains inefficient. Regulation and enforcement of government policies remain mired in various levels of red tape and corruption. The capability of the government to maintain law and order and enforce contracts remains circumscribed and needs to be further strengthened. All these issues require broad-based societal support for their resolution in favour of the process of economic development.

The limited progress of the Bangladesh economy has to be viewed against this background of an increasing incidence of poverty and the pervasive inefficiencies and distortions in public sector policies.

Rural Development

Rural development is a process of development designed to improve the quality of life of village people. Rural development may be equated with rural prosperity, rural modernization and upliftment. Robert Chambers (1983: 147) sees rural development as a strategy to enable a specific group of people, poor rural women and men, to gain for themselves and their children more of what they want and need. It involves helping the poorest among those who seek a livelihood in the rural areas to demand and control more of the benefits of development.

Rural development refers to the economic, social, and political processes that go on inside rural society, the ways in which these processes influence and interact with each other and are influenced by processes in the society at large, and the outcome of these processes in terms of transformation of the rural society (Asaduzzaman and Westergaard 1993, 2). Identifying *rural* with *agricultural* is not correct as the rural economy consists of many other economic activities-small and cottage industries, trade, shop-keeping, services and the like. Rural development refers to development in each and all of these sectors.

The increasing emphasis on rural development is justified not only because of its quantitative importance, but also because this is where there is the greatest need for infusing the spirit of self-reliance. Self-reliance at a national level will enable the country to carry out developmental and non-developmental action programmes with little or no foreign assistance and aid. At the household level, individuals and households will be self-supporting in terms of their incomes. They will also be free from all forms of cultural, ethnic, factional and exploitative economic bondage. Rural development through economic emancipation of the poor reduces the differences between the rural elite and the poor.

Given that more than 70 per cent of the population of Bangladesh is rural, a national development plan should not limit itself to urban centres but should also encompass the population living in the rural areas. A satisfactory solution to the rural development problem must include the rural sector, and in particular it should indicate how to generate the means to combat rural poverty and unemployment.

While the government policies adopted from time to time was supposed to help the poorer sections of the population, they often ended up having the opposite result.

The rural sector in Bangladesh, if properly developed, will not only generate employment, income and foreign exchange from agriculture and RNAs, but also will provide markets, labour and raw material inputs to manufacturing and other urban industries. Policy bias against agriculture and rural development diminishes the marginal yield on rural activities. Successful expansion of the agricultural sector is the first prerequisite in the difficult process of achieving balanced growth at a rate higher than the population growth to alleviate poverty in the rural areas. The presence of buoyant rural markets will help reduce the rural-urban prosperity gap, and finally put a break on the rural-urban migration.

Diffusion of new agricultural technology, especially for the small farmers with the provision of access to uncollateralized credit, has been considered by many as the most important means for improving agriculture and thereby raising the welfare of the people dependent on agriculture. Large scale adoption of new technology among small farmers seems to run counter to the interest of the dominating groups in the rural areas as well as the import lobby within the ruling elite. The government policies in the past favouring the large and medium farmers resulted in low productivity in the agricultural sector.

Of the total crop production in the 1980s, the smallholders in Bangladesh produced 70 per cent of rice, 30 per cent of wheat and 80 per cent of other cash crops (Jazairy et al. 1992, 410). In terms of cropping intensity, the small farmers' performance is much better than the large and medium farmers. Whereas 53 per cent of the cultivated area in Bangladesh is multiple cropped, 58-82 per cent of the area of farms smaller than five acres is multiple cropped. Indeed, for farms of less than one acre the cropping intensity in Bangladesh is almost as high as that in Taiwan, which is often cited as the prime example of effective multiple cropping systems (Singh 1990, 117).

Moreover, a large number of case studies conducted in Asia found an inverse correlation between farm size and the value of output per acre. Singh (1990, 101) and Jazairy et al. (1992, 3) observe that small farms are at least as efficient as big ones-largely because they employ more labour per acre. They recommend that policies should favour and promote the fast growth of output on small farms. Such growth is usually needed for farm and non-farm employment and benefits both poor farmers and even poorer rural employees.

Although the share of agriculture in GDP and its share of employment in total employed persons have declined over the years, it still and will remain the largest contributing sector in the Bangladesh economy. Agricultural growth is also a significant determinant of industrial and overall economic growth.

Given the extent of massive landlessness as well as the limited absorptive capacity of the industrial sector to attract the increasing number of the rural unemployed labour force, agriculture and industry as a whole cannot alone be counted on to fully absorb the annual increases in population and labour force of the country. A high proportion of the landless rural population depends largely on RNAs for example, petty trade, poultry raising, and small manufacturing. Given that non-farm activities are an important source of employment in rural areas, they should also be an important source of rural income. Women's employment in rural industries is much higher than their labour force participation rate. The reason being that most of these activities are of the cottage industry type-run from the home premises, largely with family workers, and enabling the domestic work to be done as well as preserving the persisting social values. While crop and non-crop agricultural activities are dependent on availability of land and working capital to a significant degree, RNAs of small and cottage industries do not require that much land and capital.

Rural development in Bangladesh is a complicated task, particularly with its acute scarcity of resources, skewed distribution of land ownership and resources and widespread poverty. A large segment of rural population in Bangladesh has been by-passed by the mainstream of development. Despite the implementation of a comprehensive rural development programmes over the years, the number of landless has been increasing and rural poverty is growing.

The twentieth century has witnessed unprecedented successes in improving the living standards of people in most parts of the world. As the *Human Development Report 1997* succinctly observed that in the past fifty years poverty has fallen more than in the previous five hundred years (UNDP 1997). The same period has also witnessed historically unprecedented increases in the overall economic prosperity of nations, as reflected, for example, in the growth of per capita national income. There can be little doubt that these two phenomena are very closely related. By raising the level of personal incomes of the poor and by expanding the resource base of social provisioning, sustained economic growth must have laid the foundations on which the impressive record of poverty reduction of the past half century has been achieved.

In an attempt to answer the question if a strategy that maximizes the rate of growth also represents the best strategy for reducing poverty, Osmani (2001, 3) observes that the mere existence of a positive growth-poverty nexus does not imply that maximizing the rate of growth is always the right strategy for maximizing the rate of poverty reduction. The author shows that there are plausible scenarios in which the strategy of achieving the most rapid rate of growth may conflict with the objective of poverty reduction. The author, however, does not present this as an argument for abandoning growth *per se*, but as an argument against aiming at the maximal possible rate of growth regardless of circumstances.

The single-minded focus on growth has been dominated by a paradigm in which the growth of the overall economy is believed to lead automatically to wealth *trickling down* to the poor, making the rural economy a vibrant one. An early variant of this paradigm, popular in the 1950s and early 1960s, emphasized growth alone as defined by the rate of growth of GNP-not GNP per capita. The problem of development was conceived by some scholars to be a question of transforming traditional societies into modern ones by way of growth (Rostow 1960). Others defined the problem as how to achieve growth with an unlimited supply of labour (Lewis 1992).

The most damaging assumption made in those paradigms was that all developing countries were considered to be a homogenous group; each country was subject to a *vicious circle* of underdevelopment, which could be broken by a *big push* coming from foreign capital and know-how. The ability of the rural poor in different developing countries to keep their societies fed and functioning for a millennium or two apparently counted for little. The urbanized, industry-led economic growth of the 1980s was not accompanied by concomitant improvements in the living standard of the rural poor. Authentic development is perceived as being broadly concerned with the improvement of the conditions of the majority of the population and particularly of the poorest.

The failure of the trickle-down policies in alleviating the poverty of the rural poor has led to various institutional initiatives. The major institutional initiative in rural development for the first time in Bangladesh was forged in the early sixties under what has now become known as the *Comilla* approach. The rural works component of the project emphasized the mobilization of rural unemployed labour for infrastructural development, and, in the process, providing a major source of off-peak employment for the landless population. The project, entitled *Integrated Rural Development Programme* (IRDP), combined production and anti-poverty goals targeted at the landless population.

Over time it has become the single most important poverty alleviation programme in rural Bangladesh. Immediately after independence, another relief-oriented scheme called *Food for Works* (FWP) was added, and recent years have seen the addition of a huge number of similar projects, both in the public and private sectors. However, the impact of the works programmes on the original objective of infrastructural development and the concomitant contribution to sustained growth is very debatable. It has provided a crucial focus for local government activities by involving them in their implementation and thereby greatly strengthened local government presence within the overall structure of administration. However, it has also opened up major avenues of patronage and corruption for local elite. The Rural Works component of the Bangladesh Integrated Rural Development Programme, scored 50.5 out of 100 total marks, using the Project Sustainability Index of the World Bank (Bamberger and Cheema 1990, 102).

Hindsight reveals that the main shortcomings of the approach were the lack of participation of the poor both in design and implementation of the programme. Over the years, several development strategies and models based on growth and redistribution, on basic minimum needs, and on a decentralized development approach have been designed and applied in Bangladesh before and after its independence. The general conclusion of these efforts is that development cannot be achieved simply by throwing together the necessary physical and technical inputs. The success of the programmes is crucially dependent on the participation of its beneficiaries and should take into account their needs and preferences.

A durable institutional framework, built on existing structures and patterns that are acceptable and better understood by local communities, especially the rural poor, has yet to be established for the effective operation of rural development programmes.

The biggest institutional implication is that the ordinary people are in or closer to the driving seat of the activity (or project). This is what Chambers (1983) refers to as *putting the last first*. Achieving this while continuing to achieve other objectives is the major task ahead of all developing countries (Shepherd 1998, 15).

The critical constraints facing rural development in Bangladesh lie in targeting the poor, on the one hand, and the planning-administrative-delivery system, on the other. While some success has been achieved in grassroots cooperation and the delivery system, progress in planning and decentralizing administration remains as elusive as ever. The limitations of the partial, reformist framework in which rural development practice has been firmly set over the last few decades has resulted in the failure of rural development and thus the alleviation of poverty (Rahman 1990, 13-4).

Any attempt to view rural development as a sectoral, rather than a comprehensive development strategy, ignores the very philosophy of rural development. The full import of the term *rural development* can be realized only if it is viewed as a new planning philosophy and a new strategy for development. It stands in sharp contrast to the *same-path-for-all* development strategy, fondly advocated and enthusiastically pursued during the sixties. The new strategy, being a reversal of the old one, sees development emerging from the bottom of the pyramid aiming at immediately bringing the benefits of development to the rural poor.

The view that growth alone does not necessarily lead to development has been energetically espoused by many of the *new microfinance practitioners*, notably Muhammad Yunus, the founder of the GB in Bangladesh. Development should mean positive change in the economic status of the bottom 50 per cent of the population in any given society (Yunus 1992, 9). The conventional paradigm in rural development, which is planned from the top, is not capable of promoting sustainable development and has failed miserably to reduce poverty. The new paradigm would allow development practitioners to work in a participatory, gender-sensitive, holistic manner, evolving their strategy and organization to make the maximum possible contribution to positive and sustainable development process. The end-result of such an approach would be to put ordinary rural people firmly in the driving seat, with development agencies playing a supportive role (Shepherd 1998, 10).

With the realization that reaching the poor was not possible without effective and explicit targeting, a number of initiatives emerged over the seventies built around precisely such principles. An approach, which has become note-worthy in this regard, is that of the GB which combined targeting principles with an innovative credit scheme. The GB has emerged as an important antipoverty programme, targeting the rural poor, especially the poor women.

Decentralization of central government power and authority to the local level is just as significant in the fight against poverty as any number of schemes of resource-delivery to the rural areas. The Government of Bangladesh, on the one hand, advocates rural development as the key to overall development, but on the other hand, pursues centralized planning, favouring urban development. As regards rural development, it seems that the government has *one foot on the accelerator and one on the brake*, simultaneously encouraging and discouraging rural development.

Moreover, the government has in a sense moved a step away from the people because the functions, authority and jurisdictions of the organs closest to them i.e., the *Gram Sarker* (the village government) has been circumscribed. In spite of the shortcomings of the previous *Gram Sarker* approach, the present system is neither better nor a match for it. In the event of no structural change, the *Gram Sarker*, though not solving many of the problems associated with rural development, could have at least opened the Pandora's Box of contradictions prevailing in rural Bangladesh. The *Gram Sarker* was supposed to prepare a development plan for the village on the basis of priorities and objectives of the national government. It was responsible for mobilizing the internal physical and financial resources to implement the plan. Financial grants and loans were supposed to be made available to the villages by the national government.

To impose a rural development system by central fiat or to attempt its central control would be to preclude the very outcomes sought. In line with the principles of the *Gram Sarker*, group-based organizations, like the one in GB, may be formed. In the GB, six groups form a centre with proportional representation from each group. The centre is vested only with coordinating and clearing powers while the effective economic power lies with the coalescing group.

Finally, it can reasonably be said that in the existing sociopolitical environment of Bangladesh, the process of decentralization faces a host of problems. The broad outline of a policy package for rural development seems to lie in the following direction: an elastic supply of financial services to all including the poorest of the poor; a large increase in the supply of agricultural inputs and raw materials for rural industries; emphasis on small farmers-both on equity and efficiency grounds; extensive skills training and integrating the poor women into the development process. However, they all involve difficult political, economic, and institutional problems. Only a strong political will and participation in the development process at grassroots level can achieve the goal of rural development.

Poverty in Bangladesh

In order for someone to conceive of the possibility of escaping from a particular condition, it is necessary first to feel that one has fallen into that condition. For those who make up nearly 50 per cent of Bangladesh's population today, to think of development of any kind requires first the perception of themselves as poor: the dimension, nature and causes of their poverty.

Poverty is not a new phenomenon. It is an old concept with a new strategy. The content and extent of poverty has changed over the ages and so has society's concern over it. The face of poverty varies from country to country. During the last decade we have witnessed some kind of a historical peak in society's expressed and largely sincere concern over poverty. While all this expression is not sincere, a lot is. Poverty has increased dramatically in the 1980s, and half of the humanity could be living in absolute poverty between 2050-2075 (Third World Network 1989, 5).

The record of poverty alleviation in Asia seems better than that of other developing regions (Africa and Latin America). During the 1990s, Asia was the only developing region where the incidence of poverty (defined as the percentage of people living at less than $1 per day) registered a substantial decline. Despite this achievement, however, there is very little room for complacency. Asia still remains home to over two-thirds of the world's poor. And within Asia, there is a wide variation in the progress made in reducing poverty. While some countries in East Asia and Southeast Asia have achieved impressive reductions in poverty, the performance of the South Asian countries has been rather modest (Islam 2001, 2).

Comparing Bangladesh with South and East Asia

A comparison of Bangladesh with its neighbours will indicate the extent of poverty and other socioeconomic deficiencies of the country. Despite massive poverty, Bangladesh compares well in some areas with its South Asian neighbours, but lags in adult literacy, women empowerment, and life expectancy at birth.

Bangladesh has lower GDP per capita and human poverty index than all other South Asian countries except for Nepal (Table 2.3). Access to safe water in Bangladesh has been the highest in South Asia[7]. Despite Bangladesh lags behind in adult literacy, gross primary school enrolment is now approaching to 100 per cent[8].

According to the 2006 Index of Economic Freedom, published by The Wall Street Journal and the conservative Washington think-tank Heritage Foundation, Bangladesh ranks 141st among 161 countries ranging from the *free to the unfree*. Bangladesh's ranking was the worst among five of the seven-nation South Asian Association for Regional Cooperation (SAARC). Sri Lanka was in a better position and shared the 92nd position with Romania, followed by Pakistan with 110th position, India with 121st position, and Nepal with 125th position. Bhutan and the Maldives, two other member states of the SAARC, were not included in the list (The Daily Star: December 6, 2006).

Comparing Bangladesh with East Asian countries highlights the potential gains of growth and investment in human capital (Table 2.4). Growth in East Asia has been associated not only with poverty reduction but also with rapid improvement of other social indicators. For example, infant mortality in East Asia is nearly half the rate in Bangladesh and the illiteracy rate is nearly one-third. Vietnam is the only East Asian country closest to Bangladesh in terms of population below poverty line, life expectancy at birth, and population with access to improved sanitation.

---

7   This, however, is not taking into account the increasingly recognised problem of arsenic contamination of ground water in Bangladesh.

8   Investments in the *Food for Education* Programme's growth will have to be balanced with the need to improve the overall quality of primary education.

**Table 2.3   Bangladesh and South Asia: Comparisons of Selected
Development Indicators, 2002, or Most Recent Estimates**

Development Indicators	Bangladesh	India	Nepal	Pakistan	Sri Lanka
Population (millions)	143.8	1,049.5	24.1	149.9	18.9
GDP per capita (PPP US$)	1700	2670	1310	1910	3570
Human Development Index Rank	138	127	142	142	96
Human Poverty Index Rank	72	48	70	71	36
Gender-related Development Index	110	103	119	120	80
Gender-empowerment					
Measure Rank	76	na	na	64	74
Population below poverty line (%)	49.8	28.6	na	32.6	
Adult Literacy Rate (% age ≥15)	41.1	61.3	42.9	41.5	25
Life Expectancy at Birth (yrs)	61.1	63.7	59.1	60.8	92.1
					72.5
Infant Mortality Rate	51	67	66	83	
Children Underweight for age	48	47	48	38	na
Population with Access to					na
Improved Sanitation (%)	48	28	73	62	
					na
Population with Access to Safe					
Water Source (%)					
Source (%)	97	84	87	90	
					na

Source: UNDP, 2004. Human Development Report 2004

When compared with the least developed and developing countries of the world
in terms of growth, human development, and income-poverty, Bangladesh fares
well in terms of percentage change in total fertility, infant mortality, and under-five
mortality (Table 2.5). But in terms of per capita GNP growth, Bangladesh though
performs better than the least developed countries; it lags behind the developing
countries of the world. In terms of head-count index of income-poverty, Bangladesh
performs better than Nepal and maintains the South Asia standard and lags behind
the developing countries.

Around 70 per cent of the total population of almost 140 million in Bangladesh
lives in rural areas. In 1994, approximately 40 per cent of the rural population was
living below the poverty line (Rahman 1995, 2). The absolute number of poor has
steadily increased each year since independence in 1971. Two decades of sustained
aid flows and emphasis on the social sectors have still left Bangladesh's social
indicators among the lowest in the world (World Bank 1995, 3).

Table 2.4   Bangladesh and East Asia: Comparisons of Selected Development Indicators, 2002 or More Recent Estimates

Development Indicators	Bangladesh	China	Indonesia	Philippines	Vietnam	Thailand
Population (millions)	143.8	1,249.9	217.1	78.6	80.3	62.2
GDP per capita (PPP US$)	1700	4,580	3,230	4,170	2,300	7,010
Human Development Index Rank	138	94	111	83	112	76
Human Poverty Index Rank	72	24	35	28	41	22
Gender-related Development Index	110	71	90	66	87	61
Gender-empowerment Measure Rank	76	na	na	37	Na	57
Population below poverty line (%)	49.8	4.6	27.1	36.8	50.9	13.1
Adult Literacy Rate (%)	41.1	90.9	87.9	92.6	90.3	92.6
Life Expectancy at Birth (yrs)	61.1	70.9	66.6	69.8	69	69.1
Infant Mortality Rate	51	31	33	29	30	24
Children Underweight for age	48	39	45	38	39	28
Population with Access to Improved Sanitation (%)	48	40	55	83	47	96
Population with Access to Safe Water Source (%) Source (%)	97	75	78	86	77	84

Source: UNDP, 2004. Human Development Report 2004

The Household Expenditure Survey of Bangladesh 1991-92 indicates the incidence of rural poverty, measured in terms of the head-count index, was 52.6 per cent and that of urban poverty was 33.6 per cent. Nationally, this amounted to a poverty incidence of 49.7 per cent. There has been a sharp decline in the price of rice during 1992-93, and this is likely to have a substantially positive impact on poverty alleviation. Still, the high incidence of poverty at the start of the 1990s strengthens the proposition that the problem of poverty in Bangladesh remains daunting and monumental as ever.

**Table 2.5   Growth, Human Development, and Income-Poverty:
An International Comparison, 1970-1997**

	Bangladesh	India	Pakistan	Nepal	Sri Lanka	South Asia	LDC	Developing Countries
Per capita GNP Growth, 1975-95 (% per Year)	2.0	2.8	3.1	1.6	3.2	2.5	-0.2	2.3
Total fertility rate								
1975	6.8	5.1	7.0	6.3	3.9	5.4	6.6	5.0
1997	3.1	3.1	5.0	4.5	2.1	3.3	5.0	3.0
% change per year	-2.1	-1.5	-1.1	-1.1	-1.8	-1.5	-0.9	-1.6
Life expectancy at birth (year)								
1970	44.2	49.1	49.2	42.1	64.5	49.0	43.4	54.5
1997	58.1	62.6	64.0	57.3	73.1	62.7	51.7	64.4
% change per year	1.1	1.0	1.1	1.3	0.5	1.0	0.7	0.6
Infant mortality rate (per 1000 live births)								
1970	148	130	118	156	65	131	149	111
1997	81	71	95	75	17	72	104	64
% change per year	-1.6	-1.6	-0.7	-1.9	-2.7	-1.6	-1.1	-1.5
Under-Five mortality rate (per 1000 live births)	239	206	183	234	100	207	242	170
1970	109	108	136	104	19	106	162	94
1997	-2.0	-1.7	-0.9	-2.0	-3.0	-1.8	-1.2	-1.6
% change per year								
Head-count index of income-poverty								
Early 80s	52.3	46-50	29.1	42.5	27.3	45.4	na	33.9
Early 90s	47.0	37.36	26.3	45.0	22.4	43.1	na	31.9
% change per year	-0.84	-1.87	-1.37	0.53	-3.59	-0.84	na	-0.98

Note and Source:

1. Per-capita GNP growth data are from 1999 H DR.

2. Information on fertility, infant mortality, under-five mortality and human development index are from 1999 HDR; adult literacy rate is taken front World Development Indicators (CD-ROM version). For Bangladesh, adult literacy data for 1995 are taken from the Fifth Plan document.

3. Aggregate poverty estimates for South Asia and developing countries are from Ravallion and Chen (1996).

The determinants of rural poverty remain almost unchanged. Inequality in rural incomes and in land distribution remains high and this, with the traditional institutional set-up, has probably blocked the transmission of benefits to the rural poor. Benefits have also been blocked in those cases where there have been impressive gains in agricultural productivity. At the same time, high population pressure on limited cultivable land (without any significant expansion of RNAs) continues to mount and the off-take of rural population into the urban sector has remained relatively insignificant.

The main causes of poverty are a lack of productive resources, a lack of employment, low productivity of labour and low wage rates. Economists believe that even if a substantial acceleration of economic growth, say over 5 per cent per annum, can be attained, it will take a long time before the huge backlog of unemployment and underemployment can be cleared through the normal market mechanism. The total population in Bangladesh that has access to government and NGO services may be only ten per cent of the total poor.

The landless (35.5 per cent) and functionally landless (19.2 per cent) households together constitute 54.7 per cent of the households and possess only 1.2 per cent of the total arable land. The top 4.5 per cent of the households own 33.2 per cent of the total arable land. A strong correlation exists between the quantity of land owned and the amount of income, the co-efficient correlation being 0.76. The dependency ratio was 224.89 per 100 persons, meaning that every person employed full-time, seasonally employed or underemployed, supports on average, 2.25 persons with his/her income (Ahmed and Kabiruzzaman 1984, 43).

Characteristics of rural poverty include: landlessness; too little land; large families; higher dependency ratio; malnutrition; ill-health; illiteracy; high infant and female mortality; low life expectancy; irregular and subsistence income; weak bargaining power; isolation-owing to poor communications; preoccupation with survival and indebtedness. A descriptive analysis of rural poverty, however detailed it may be, does not give enough information to design effective strategies to raise the productivity of poor households to escape from poverty. It is, therefore, necessary to understand the processes that tend to perpetuate rural poverty.

National policies and institutions often have built-in biases, which exclude the rural poor from the benefits of development. They also accentuate the impact of other poverty processes and fail to recognize the productive potential of the poor, which could be unleashed with the right kind of support. Policy biases against the poor include: urban bias in investment; bias towards export crops; pricing policies favouring imported cereals at the expense of rural crops; subsidized capital to expand modern sub-sectors and failure to provide agricultural inputs to the rural areas.

The institutional processes which tend to perpetuate rural poverty include: lack of access to institutional sources of finance; marginalization of women; absence of grassroots institutions to encourage participation of the poor; inequitable share cropping and tenancy arrangements; underdeveloped markets; lack of access to land and water; population growth; internal political fragmentation and civil strife, and limited and ineffective extension services. It is needless to reiterate that poverty is negatively correlated with land ownership in rural society. Poverty-both absolute and extreme are heavily concentrated among the landless and functionally landless. The incidence of absolute poverty is sometimes twice among the illiterates and the figure is increased to nearly threefold in case of extreme poverty. There is very little poverty among school graduates or people with higher education. Poverty in Bangladesh is most concentrated among people with agriculture, forestry and fisheries mainly in rural areas.

Combining household and sub-regional data of causes and trends of poverty, Jazairy et al. (1992) have drawn a *Poverty Map* (Appendix 2A) showing the location of the poor and vulnerable groups. Generally speaking, poverty is more among the landless and small farm owners. The poor are also the land poor. Poverty is also more among the illiterate persons. It (poverty) reduces sharply with the increase in literacy level. This information, together with a detailed assessment of resources and an analysis of the poverty process, which prevail in any specific area, will determine the strategy and policy option for strengthening the role of the rural poor to growth and development process.

Regardless of the definitions and measures used, the ubiquity of rural poverty in Bangladesh has posed a serious challenge to the survival of its growing population. The level of consumption of most of the extreme poor is already far below the poverty line. It tends to cluster around the famine line- the level of consumption below which the probability of death is high. Over the last few decades deaths have occurred due to the inadequate intake of food grain and other basic foodstuff. The rural poor suffer not only from malnutrition, but also from under-nutrition. The food intake of most of the rural poor, especially the women, is not only qualitatively inadequate on the average, but also quantitatively below the starvation level. The rural poor are mostly illiterate, unemployed and underemployed, ill-clad, and nearly shelter-less. Bangladesh exemplifies a spectre of poverty, inequality and quasi-famine. One only has to recall the situation prevailing in 1974 when a famine struck Bangladesh and claimed an officially acknowledged 26,000 lives (Alamgir 1978, 2), although the actual death toll was much higher. Besides the famine of 1974, there were quasi-famine situations during the natural disasters of 1987-88 and 1990, which had claimed innumerable lives due to starvation.

As to the effectiveness of the government poverty alleviation programmes, it may be said that different governments, both past and present, and a host of NGOs undertook a number of antipoverty policies and programmes targeted directly towards the poor. However, the performance records of these programmes like asset provision (for example, provision of cattle and equipment), income provision (for example, credit for trading and small scale production), or direct consumption support (for example, vulnerable group feeding, relief activities) to the poor had not been noteworthy. They have been plagued by lapses such as wrong selection of the beneficiaries, outright leakage, failures of enterprises, low level of productivity, market saturation, greater indebtedness of the poor and perpetuation of the relief syndrome among the target group population.

The major weaknesses of these antipoverty programmes are perhaps their naïve assumption that there is a universal harmony of interests in the society. They have not managed to understand that there are classes in the society and each different class has its own interests (Griffin and Khan 1978, 302). Most of the poverty alleviation projects in Bangladesh have not considered the different perceptions and needs of the rural poor men and women, which has resulted in the failure of those projects.

The political representation of the poor through the existing electoral process remains limited in the political environment of the country. Poverty alleviation is one of the principal objectives of planning in the country, yet the poor; *the social constituency of the rejected*, do not have much participation in policymaking. The substantive apparent concern about poverty can be explained as follows: the pursuit of the poor as a symbolic and social constituency generates a profusion of populist rhetoric which cuts across the entire political spectrum; the state's concern for poverty provides a rationale for seeking higher levels of foreign aid; and if poverty is allowed to go beyond a certain limit-to a state of famine-so as to create a crisis of legitimacy, then the stability and continuance of the government could be at stake. Thus the political economy of poverty appears to dictate no descent into famine but no definitive escape from the poverty situation either (Hossain et al. 1994, 151-3).

Despite data limitations, it seems apparent that a modest decline in poverty has occurred in Bangladesh from the mid-1970s to the mid-1980s. According to the most recent analysis of poverty trends, the percentage of the population below the conventional income-nutritional poverty line has fallen from around 70 per cent to 40 per cent between 1973 and 1990 (Hulme and Mosley 1996, 95-6). The declining trend in poverty could be attributed to increasing informal sector activities, induced by the survival efforts of the rural poor, which remain virtually unrecorded in national income accounts. The remittances from the semi-and unskilled workers from the Gulf in the 1980s, have helped the moderately poor, but not the extreme poor, who are illiterate and unable to mobilize the initial finance needed for migration.

However, the findings that show the decline in poverty in the mid-1980s have resulted in considerable controversy in the recent literature. There are many estimates of poverty based on income and nutrition deficiency that can be made to support or contradict the statement of decline in poverty. All these studies used HESs data to estimate the head-count ratio of people below the poverty line. Rahman and Haque (1988) found that poverty rose between fiscal year 1973 and fiscal year 1981 but then declined until fiscal year 1985, while the BBS study showed that poverty declined throughout the period fiscal year 1973 to fiscal year 2000. Khan (1990) also showed that both extreme and moderate poverty declined in rural areas between 1973-74 and 1985-86 (Table 2.6). The differences in findings on poverty arose mainly because different studies used different techniques to calculate poverty and partly because the HES were not comparable from year to year. Different poverty estimates based on independent household surveys by the Bangladesh Institute of Development Studies (BIDS) show an increase in poverty in the late 1980s, followed by a decrease in the 1990s.

Table 2.6   Estimates of the Head-count Index of Moderate Rural Poverty (Percentage of the Rural Population below Poverty Line)

Fiscal Year	Rahman, & Haque (1988)	Khan (1990)	Ahmed & others (1991)	BBS* (1991)	Hossain & Sen (1992)	Ravallion & Sen (1994)
1973	65..3	56.0	n.a.	82.9	n.a.	n.a.
1981	79.1	70.0	71.8	73.8	65.3	n.a.
1983	48	39.0	n.a.	57	50	53.8
1985	47.1	35.0	51.6	51	41.3	45.9
1988	n.a.	n.a.	n.a.	n.a.	43.8	49.7
1991	n.a	n.a.	n.a.	n.a.	n.a.	52.9
1995	n.a.	n.a.	n.a.	47.5	n.a.	51.1[a]
2000	n.a.	n.a.	n.a.	44.3[b]	n.a.	n.a.

BBS. Bangladesh Bureau of Statistics, Note: n.a. Not Available
Source: Various studies, as presented in Khandker & Chowdhury 1996, Table 1, p-25
  a. Ravallion and Sen 1996.
  b. UNDP 2004

In addition to measures of poverty incidence, other independent evidence suggests that standards of living improved in the first half of the 1990s. Malnutrition in rural areas (as measured by the percentage of underweight children) since mid-1990 was at its lowest level in 1996. The percentage of underweight children had declined by approximately 13 per cent compared to 1990. Real wages also increased by about 7 per cent between 1991-92 and 1996, especially in the agriculture and manufacturing sectors. At a more aggregate level, the fact that GDP growth has consistently outpaced population growth over the last decade is consistent with a decrease in poverty over time (World Bank 1999, 5-6).

Over the period between mid-eighties and mid-nineties, the average annual rate of poverty reduction was less than one percentage point (indeed, national head-count declined by only 0.5 percentage point per year during 1983-95). Such a modest reduction rate could not prevent the rising absolute number of the poor. It may be a pertinent reminder that, in all the countries of South Asia, the annual poverty reduction rate hovered around one percentage point or less, compared with higher reduction rates (2-3 percentage points) observed in South East and East Asia. Binayak Sen (1998, 2) terms such poor rates as the *Sub-continental rate of poverty reduction*.

Despite the decline (albeit modest) in poverty in the 1990s, rural poverty is still higher than urban poverty and reducing the poverty of the very poor living in rural areas remains a massive challenge. The modest decline in poverty does not necessarily imply that there has been a reduction in the vulnerability of the rural poor. Despite some modest improvement in short-term directionalities as applied to some specific sub-periods in ratio and percentage terms, this should not detract our attention from the wider challenge of absolute numbers (persisting mass poverty).

It is this challenge that the current paradigm of poverty alleviation has failed to confront.

The aggregate allocation of resources, which have either a direct or indirect bearing on rural poverty, has gone up substantially in Bangladesh since the early eighties, from a level of 30 per cent to 50 per cent by 1994-95. In sheer budgetary terms, the situation with respect to supporting antipoverty projects and programmes is not as bad as may be observed in some other comparable countries faced with declining social sector allocations and de-emphasized rural focus (ibid. 6).

The pertinent question now is why the poverty situation changed as little as it did during the period since the early eighties through to the mid-nineties despite the *progressive* shifts in public spending. The broad conclusion one derives is that the allocation figures may be misleading. Public expenditure only effects poverty alleviation in so far as it is implemented effectively. In the final analysis, the quality of public investment rather than the increase in mere quantitative terms is going to determine the outcome in terms of the impact on poverty. It is well-known that an effective monitoring mechanism is lacking with the Bangladesh government.

Implementation of the projects, not to mention the quality of it, needs to be radically improved before one expects any favourable *impact* of their operations on poverty. Once the quality dimension is added to this, the governance problem in poverty alleviation projects and programmes becomes even more formidable.

The above analysis demonstrates the severe shortcomings of the existing programmes that pass under poverty alleviation. A number of welfare-enhancing programmes designed mainly for the extreme poor are now in place, ranging from Vulnerable Group Development (VGD) which provides food grain and training to disadvantaged women, and Food-for-Education (FFE) which initially provided wheat and now provides wheat and rice to poor children in return for regular primary school attendance, housing for the shelterless, grant for the female destitutes, and old-age pension. To assess the impact on poverty alleviation, one needs to look at the redistributive effects of some of these programmes.

Some of the above programmes are old-first-generation programmes (FFW and VGD would fall under this category); and the FFE and the Test Relief are second-generation programmes. Many of these programmes initially claimed to be highly successful, but their subsequent development proved much less encouraging, even showing signs of deterioration in their overall performance and rating.

The largest direct intervention targeted toward the rural poor, with little or no land, is the combination of food distribution, employment, and skill development under the FFW and the VGD, which was substantially, expanded (more than doubled) over the eighties. The FFW and the VGD together accounted for 43 per cent of total resources released through food-assisted programmes in 1994-95. Both these programmes are purported to reach the most needy, who may be left out of the traditional growth process (Sen 1997, 144).

Although the net effect of the FFW was a reduction in poverty, however, the employment in the programme involved a contradiction by lowering, instead of increasing, the nutritional status of the poor. The VGD during the mid-1980s had effectively targeted the poorest rural women and most vulnerable groups in rural Bangladesh. However, the development objectives of the programme were mainly not met and it is still a relief effort rather than a programme capable of self-sustaining development. In terms of reaching the poor areas to reduce overall poverty, the economically poor areas still do not get preferential access to these programmes. If alleviation of overall poverty is the declared objective, such safety net measures should first target the poor areas on a priority basis without compromising on the general principle of targeting poor households.

The case for public expenditures on education for the poor is strong, but quality and access must improve. The government has recognised the role of education in promoting growth and reducing poverty. School enrolment has increased dramatically, almost doubling in percentage terms in the 1980s. But, while 8 of 10 children aged 5 to 11 currently enrol in school, attendance rates are as low as 60 per cent. Dropout rates are high, since only 6 of 10 students complete primary education, repeats are frequent. It takes on average nearly 9 years for a student to complete the 5 years of primary school (World Bank 1999, 35).

The FFE Programme is not as well-targeted as the FFW and VGD, and improvements in targeting would further raise its social returns. Quality of education remains a major issue. Attending primary school does not ensure literacy. Acknowledging the low quality of education, the World Bank's 1996 Education Expenditure Review recommended shifting the focus from expanding enrolment to improving the quality and efficiency of schooling. Investments in the programme's growth will have to be balanced with the need to improve the overall quality of primary education (ibid.).

Despite already large and growing education budget allocations to FFE, public spending on education remains biased towards the well-off. Reallocating public education expenditures toward primary and secondary schooling would help to increase the benefits for the poor. The quality and efficiency of education must increase to ensure that primary school enrolments translate into literacy. Reducing repetition rates in primary, secondary, and higher education would reduce the cost of public education, thereby freeing up resources to encourage school enrolment and attendance among the poor. Although Bangladesh has achieved remarkable success in expanding primary education, especially for girls, despite continuing prevalence of widespread poverty and social repression of women and girls, the current challenge of improving the quality of education, however, may prove more difficult than the expansion of access to education.

Besides those food-based safety net programmes which have been relatively recent in Bangladesh, subsidized grain rations for the landless and near-landless households have been introduced to reduce food- intake poverty and to increase the purchasing power of the poor and hence, the demand for food. However, it has been argued that instead of subsidizing wage goods, it may be better to integrate targeted food distribution with an employment creation programme (Bardhan 1993, 319).

The above programmes targeted to the poorest yet to flourish into a holistic campaign for the eradication of extreme forms of deprivation from the face of the society. The evaluation of other development initiatives is also not favourable for the extreme poor, especially poor women. The effect of the green revolution on the alleviation of poverty, although mixed, clearly did not have any favourable effect on the extreme poor. The gender gaps in agricultural labour markets remain large in Bangladesh, the growth effect being counteracted by the major displacement of land-poor females from a traditional mainstay of agricultural wage-work, namely rice husking by landless women in the homesteads of the large farmers. The rapid increase in mechanised rice milling has displaced an estimated 3.5 million to 5 million days of female wage labour per year (Quibria ed. 1993, 338). Little attention has been given to compensating the job losses with job gains and to targeting additional employment sources.

There are, of course, some successful recent examples of groups of landless women acquiring and operating semi-automatic rice mills and conducting many micro businesses with the GB and other MFIs' financial support. The employment effects of export-oriented garments industry in Bangladesh has been a drastic turning point for women's engagement in the money economy. In 1978, Bangladesh had only four garment factories; by 1995, it had 2,400, employing 1.2 million workers. Ninety per cent of them are women who are mostly poor. The sector employed 70 per cent of the women in wage employment in the country (UN 1999, 33). It is, however, far from clear whether women from landless or near-landless households, especially from remote villages, where most of the extreme poor live, have gained much access to it.

The challenge of rural poverty is thus squarely one of scale and requires for its alleviation, multidimensional efforts on different fronts. To illustrate the orders of the magnitude of poverty, the World Bank (1995, 3) remarks that it would take 25 years for an average poor person in Bangladesh to cross the poverty line, if real per capita income continues to grow as it has in the past. Singh's (1990, xvi) concept of the *great ascent* from poverty, although perhaps evident in other South Asian countries, is still far from happening in Bangladesh. Khandker and Chowdhury (1996) from the World Bank, on the contrary, present a rather encouraging picture when they comment on the basis of the Grameen experience that it takes about five years for programme participants to cross the poverty line and eight years to achieve economic graduation, that is, stop taking loans from a targeted credit programme.

Despite the ongoing debate on the measurement of poverty, the main point of agreement in Bangladesh is that an unacceptably large number of its rural population remains poor even today. Given the mass influx of donor assistance since the liberation of the country, the persistence of poverty in Bangladesh originates less in the lack of resources for its alleviation than in the failures of governance (Sobhan 1998, 15). These failures consist of a lack of a developmental vision, absence of a commitment that goes beyond rhetoric and that could translate the vision into policies and programmes, and weak capacities at the administrative, technical, and political levels to implement such programmes. The programmes aiming at poverty reduction have suffered from rent seeking at various levels, which reduced efficiency and effectiveness, and deprived many poor of access to the services to which they were entitled.

Better results could have been achieved through the redirection of public expenditure to social services and improved governance, which would ensure better returns from such expenditures. This may be feasible if a political coalition can be built with those segments of the political and civil society genuinely committed to *putting the poor first*, that is, bypassing those elements of state power which have stood in the way of serving the poor. The roots of the governance problem in Bangladesh are the structural features of its polity. These features include the existing politics of confrontation, *mutual blame game* between the major political parties, weaknesses in the practice of parliamentary democracy, the malfunctioning of political parties, the role of money and muscle power in politics, and the rent-seeking collusion among the political parties, state machinery, and the vested commercial interests.

The Wall Street Journal and the Heritage Foundation (cited in The Daily Star: December 6, 2006) in their report on Bangladesh said,

> ...weak rule of law—manifesting itself in some of the world's worst official corruption, civil crime, and political violence—continues to burden Bangladesh's democracy. The chaos of a lawless society has added to other problems keeping economic growth to roughly 5 per cent annually, substantially below the 8 per cent needed for appreciable development. Until the government addresses Bangladesh's many structural weaknesses, there is little reason for optimism about the country's future.

Efforts for improving governance must be directed towards persuading the political parties of the advantages of reforms in the existing political institutions. The civic actions in creating widespread awareness of the benefits of better governance will also help achieve the goal of good governance.

At the societal level, this involves developing lateral coalitions among the poor, which could ensure their access to formal sources of finance and other public resources necessary for full realization of their potential to alleviate poverty. This would give way to good governance at the macro and micro level, which remains central to poverty reduction in Bangladesh.

While there are no magical strategies to reduce poverty, a set of measures, each measure with its own dosage and timing without distracting the greater emphasis on provision of microfinance services for the rural poor, may be undertaken. Such a set would include several of the following in one form or another, with greater or lesser intensity, and to be applied either immediately or in the future: provision of financial services to the poor; encouraging the participation of the poor in planning and implementation of poverty alleviation projects; elimination of the bias against females in the access to resources through policy inducement; removal of policy bias against rural development; and finally, instituting a set of fair and effective laws and regulations governing resource use.

Women and Poverty

Investment in women can broaden the returns of economic development. Because of the critical role women play in their family's health and nutrition and in the education of children, the benefits from investments in women's development tend to diffuse more widely through society and across generations (World Bank 1990, 2). Both equity and efficiency call for a female focus in antipoverty programmes because the female poor suffer from deeper poverty with respect to food intake, literacy and school education; moreover, women carry a larger load of low-return work

Women are poorer, and more deprived, than men. Women have to manage home and family with virtually nothing to manage with. If one of the family members has to starve, it is almost an unwritten law that it has to be the mother. Since the mid-1960s, the number of rural poor in general has increased, and the number of rural poor women has increased disproportionately as compared to the number of rural poor men. There are factors and processes which impoverish rural men that also affect rural women but, in some cases, with greater intensity. In addition, there are factors and processes, which affect women exclusively, aggravating their poverty. Rural poor women are affected more than rural poor men because of explicit gender bias in credit, land allocation, employment opportunities, and input and service delivery. Rural women also suffer more, particularly as heads of households.

The stagnant economic environment in certain respects affects the female poor more than the male poor. This is so because women and girls are overrepresented in certain activities that are made harder and costlier in time and energy expenditure by the lack of basic facilities and infrastructure; and because access to seasonal migration as a means of getting around the problem of lack of local opportunities is more constrained for the female.

The strains of poverty on rural poor women have had the impact of breaking up of extended families into nuclear family units. The familial support system is being eroded and female-headed landless households are expanding due to increasing numbers of divorces and desertions as men move away in search of employment. Cultural constraints have become irrelevant for women in situations of extreme poverty. To ensure their own survival and that of their families, women join the ranks of men in search of employment. An estimated 8 million women (40 per cent of whom are in rural areas) are seeking employment in a labour market where access has been restricted to date[9].

The situation of these poor women becomes even more precarious when droughts or cyclones strike and they can find no work; they fall even deeper into poverty. In general, because women are the poorest of the poor they are especially vulnerable to these variables which have had worsening effect on poverty. These variables have a triple effect on women's poverty: as *poor* people, they live under

---

9   The Labour Force Survey 1984-85 of Bangladesh (cited in the World Bank 1990, indicates that the familial support system is being eroded in an estimated 7.2 per cent of the rural households.

the same harsh conditions as men; as *women* they suffer cultural, social and policy biases; and as *heads of the poorest households* they are the hardest hit in times of economic crisis (Jazairy et al. 1992, 289). On the basis of twenty indicators related to health, marriage and children, education, employment and social equality, the status of women in Bangladesh has been ranked lowest worldwide by the 1988 Population Crisis Committee (World Bank 1990, 22).

Differences in the sexes, in terms of consumption, education and other policy biases, tend to perpetuate the poverty of the rural poor women. In terms of basic consumption, there is some evidence, though not conclusive, indicating that intrahousehold consumption disparity exists between sexes favouring the male members of the household. There are also similar inequities between sexes in relation to medical care. Disparity in literacy rates between poor men and women is also pronounced especially in the rural areas of Bangladesh. Parents in Bangladesh are less likely to send their daughters to school than their sons. The direct and indirect costs of education are higher for girls and the benefits for parents are remote and uncertain. To minimize the gender gap and enhance girls' enrolments, the World Bank-financed *Bangladesh General Education Project*, based on *package approach*, which provided, among other things, scholarships for poor girls, however, increased their attendance significantly.

Over the past two decades, life expectancy at birth has risen for men and women in almost all the countries of the world, where the average life expectancy for women is five to eight years longer than for men. But in Bangladesh, the female life expectancy is still lower than for men.

Although there is formal recognition of women's rights and a legal acceptance of women's equality with men, various surveys indicate that women continue to face discrimination and marginalization. There is still a significant gap between what should be, according to law and policy, and what is in practice. The constitution ensures equality of the sexes, but at the same time acknowledges unequal status by reserving the right of making special provisions for women, including the employment quotas. While women are granted equal rights with men, personal laws such as marriage, divorce, custody of children, and inheritance are discriminatory against women. However, in terms of political representation, women have gained ascendancy in key positions, both the Prime Minister and the Leader of the Opposition being women. But women are under-represented at the lower levels of the political hierarchy.

Describing the situation of the rural poor women, the World Bank (1990, 1) observes,

> Women's access remains limited to services that can equip them to acquire knowledge, obtain essential social services, and overcome gender-specific constraints to labour force participation. A woman's ability to be independent and take initiative, to acquire new ideas, skills, and contacts, and to obtain employment outside the home is restricted by her limited mobility. As a result, men have generally been the main beneficiaries of economic development while women have remained largely unskilled or semi-skilled.

Since the poor in many cases are working poor, many aspects of poverty are closely linked with the quality and quantity of work they do. The large load of low-yield work handled by poor women leaves little time and energy for family and personal maintenance and improvement (Bardhan 1993, 317). Women have limited access to employment opportunities and even if women are employed, there is often a considerable differentiation in the nature of jobs held by men and women. Women are generally engaged in inferior jobs, which provide fewer opportunities for advancement. Differences in human capital endowments (education, work experience) between men and women explain only a small proportion of the wage differential. Legal barriers and discriminatory hiring practices may explain much of the observed gender differences in wages and salaries. It is also argued that even if men and women have the same income/consumption, the same choice of leisure and employment, but women remain socially, politically, and psychologically more constrained with limited freedom of participation in the society and the polity, indicating their worse off position in terms of well being as compared to men. However, this is a much broader perception of well being and poverty, incorporating aspects which are neither quantified nor quantifiable (ADB 1993, 4).

The official female labour force participation rate (often patchy and underestimated though) in Bangladesh is one of the lowest in the world. Much of their subsistence and domestic work is not recorded in the official labour force participation rates. The 1989 and 1990 Labour Force Surveys had used an alternative wider definition of female participation, which included several household activities hitherto unrecognized as economic activities. This resulted in an unusually large figure of 62 and 58 per cent for the female labour force participation rate in 1989 and 1990 respectively. Women already contribute far more to the economy and to the family than is generally reflected in official labour force statistics.

The work of rural women is an integral part of the rural economy, which means, since Bangladesh is predominantly rural, an important part of the national economy. Women through their income-earning and expenditure-saving activities generate a large part of a household's income in Bangladesh. Rahman and Hossain eds. (1995) calculated the value of all expenditure saving activities as 20 per cent of the total household income of landless families. It is unlikely that the poor men would be able to maintain a household without women's participation in the productivity of foodstuffs and services, the loss of which would render most rural poor Bangladeshi households economically impotent. Rural women have to do the triple jobs of production, reproduction and family management. In spite of all their contributions, women were, and still are, largely seen as recipients of welfare and benefits and as *mothers* and *wives*.

Partly because women are under-represented in the formal sector, women comprise the majority of informal sector workers in most developing countries including Bangladesh. Informal activities generate little value-added, and incomes are so little that almost no savings materialize which are worth reinvesting to improve productivity or enlarge the scale of operation. They are a means of subsistence livelihood, rather than a form of entrepreneurial activity, and *need* rather than *profit* is the motivating factor. Women from poor households flock into these types of informal activities to generate whatever level of income they possibly can (UN 1999, 26). The poor women generally work for such a low income because they have to and not through choice. They are often concentrated in the lowest remunerated categories of self-employment and wage-labour. The female share of non-commercial subsistence work is, however, far larger than that of males. Despite the critical nature of their work for health, education and the basic needs of the family and their efficiency in commercial and subsistence work, a real shift of priorities is yet to be seen.

From the standpoint of poverty alleviation, it is important to increase employment and improve work options of the poor. However, the question that has increasingly been raised is how efficient is it to provide only employment options with almost nothing done to alleviate the technological problem. Efforts towards technological improvements in the areas of domestic work, and provision of microfinance and skills-enhancing services in microenterprises will help improve the poverty situation of the rural poor women.

The heterogeneity of the rural poor women calls for different poverty alleviation policies for the different groups of women. In the case of the landless or near landless, the suggested policies for poverty alleviation are: increasing counterseasonal wage-employment options through public works, preferably with partly in-kind wages as a buffer against the seasonal food price rise and the seasonal difficulty of fuel gathering; training for better jobs in garments and other labour-intensive export industries; distributing self-employment assets and promoting access to microfinance services and marketing channels, especially to those technologically displaced from traditionally female agricultural operations. In the case of women in smallholding households, the suggested policies include: provision of simple equipment and facilities to reduce the labour intensity of household work and subsistence gathering, and to help with increasing the productivity of kitchen gardening, animal husbandry and fuelwood production on the homestead. In both cases, promoting access to microfinance services and extending skills-enhancing efforts are of immense importance in increasing the productivity of the rural poor women.

It has become increasingly clear that targeting benefits to the poor in general, and hoping women will get their share, simply does not work. The relative isolation of poor women coupled with a lack of understanding on the part of many development administrators, has dramatically limited the entry of them into the development programmes. Many development programmes, because of a lack of proper targeting, have been of little direct benefit to women.

All this amounts to saying that to plan a strategy for rural development without acknowledging women, as a highly visible economic resource is to doom the plan to failure. Success depends upon a well reasoned and goal oriented national strategy incorporating both men and women. Regrettably, however, most of the Bangladeshi women share with women in many other countries the trait of *economic invisibility*.

A well-orchestrated female focus in poverty alleviation can be more effective in speeding up the pace of fertility decline in Bangladesh than the historically classic factor, the pace of industrial transition. A 1995 Household Survey of the programme areas of five NGOs in rural Bangladesh that offer microcredit programmes reveals that women who participate in them are more likely to use contraceptives, to want no additional children and to desire smaller families than women who do not participate or who live outside of programme areas. Non-members living in programme areas also desired smaller families, suggesting a diffusion of norms established by credit members to other women in the community (Amin et al. 1994, 555-6).

In addition to microfinance services, attempts through skills training, literacy and health education, and the creation of market channels could possibly have an impact on the situation of rural poor women in Bangladesh. The extremely adverse conditions of Bangladeshi poor women call for far-reaching policies and large-scale, multi-faceted, and sustained programmes to provide women with the outlook on life, the skills, and the resources to enhance their contribution to the common challenge of development, and to the uplifting of Bangladeshi men and women. To the extent that the female poor suffer from disadvantages of poverty and discrimination, efforts at alleviating female poverty need to address both the issues.

There are two main approaches for poverty alleviation: direct and indirect approaches. The direct approach for poverty alleviation encompasses various asset transfer programmes directed at women, redressing poverty through improving the asset-ownership position of women. It is sometimes debated, whether transfers should be targeted towards all poor or there should be special provisions exclusively for the female poor. The basic argument for a general provision for all the poor is that one should not discriminate among the poor, based on their gender, if poverty alleviation is the objective. Those who argue for a special provision targeted at the female poor contend that the female poor encounter additional social, cultural, and religious obstacles that deter them from taking advantage of these opportunities, and therefore, there should be special provision for poor women. The indirect approach encompasses various policies and programmes, including the provision of financial and skills-enhancing services to improve the economic environment to alleviate poverty.

To eliminate discrimination, changes in social attitudes and various affirmative action plans to ensure fair play are needed. Much of the deprivation of women can be traced to the differential endowment of assets (including education) on women, which often arises from disparity in intrahousehold allocation between the sexes. There is limited scope for public policy to influence intrahousehold resource allocation directly. To reduce sociocultural barriers against access to publicly provided services, including financial services, employment, education, training and extension services, one needs greater involvement of women in these services.

Poor women face gender-based obstacles in microfinance and microenterprise development (Table 2.7). Innovative policies alone can ensure their access in those services. Group-lending is one such innovation. Institutions that have experimented with such innovative strategies-such as the GB of Bangladesh-have much higher repayment rates than national commercial banking systems (World Bank 1994, 10-2).

**Table 2.7   Gender-based Obstacles in Microfinance
and Microenterprise Development**

Constraint	Individual	Household	Wider community/ national context
Financial	- lack access to banks/financial services in their own	- men's control over cash income - men's expenditure patterns	- perception of men as controllers of money/loans
Economic	- undertake activities which produce low returns - heavy domestic workload	- gender division of labour - unequal control of joint household produce and income stream	- women underpaid for equal work - lack access to markets for inputs and outputs due to lack of mobility
Social/ cultural	- women not literate or educated - girls education not prioritised	- limited role for women in household decision-making - violence towards women	- banks and financial organisations do not view women as potential market
Political/ legal	- lack confidence to claim political and legal rights	- women lack legal rights to jointly owned household assets	- women's legal rights to household assets not defined in law or useful for collateral - lack legal rights to land

Source: Johnson. 1998, p. 28.

Grameen's group-lending programmes have been more effective in generating self-employment in microenterprises for rural poor women without land collateral and in achieving an excellent recovery rate. However, the existing small scale of operations cannot meet the large and diverse needs of the poor women in Bangladesh. The financial market is a thorny area for women. Providing access to credit and other microfinance services remains the key to poverty alleviation among the rural poor women. Bangladesh's success in garment exports had a most beneficial impact in the form of employment for 500,000 women. This has perhaps done well to more women than any other single gender-oriented policies (ADB 1993: 24). The industrial strategy should emphasize efficient, export-oriented, and import substitution industries. Given relative prices and the resource endowments of Bangladesh, such industries are likely to be relatively labour intensive and are therefore likely to achieve positive impacts on employment and income, particularly for women. These policies will help reduce poverty but cannot effectively alleviate all forms of discrimination against women. They may, however, lay the groundwork for change in a male-dominated, institutionally biased, and relatively stagnant socioeconomic environment. The increasing discrimination against the poor women should at least be reduced, if not eliminated, to ensure that the average gains at the national level translate into gains for poor women as well as men.

To sum up, the evidence above shows that gender biases and inequalities in access to financial services and other public resources, and in labour market act as barriers to the effective and productive use of human resources in alleviating poverty. Similarly, there is also the recognition that as long as women are not provided with financial and other efficiency-enhancing services, mere participation of the rural poor women in the development process will not help them climb out of poverty. The broad conditions of poverty and gender discrimination have been the main stimulus for the provision of client-responsive financial and skills-enhancing non-financial services to generate productive employment, especially self-employment, in the non-farm sector for the growing rural poor women.

Summary and Conclusions

Bangladesh has achieved a remarkable success in attaining a near self-sufficiency in the production of rice, making the phenomenon of famine a matter of the past. The role of market-oriented policy reforms, particularly in respect of the liberalization and privatization of agricultural input markets has been immense in achieving such an impressive growth in rice sub-sector. Strengthening the role of the private sector in the input markets as well as larger allocations of public resources for agricultural research and water resource development will help sustain this increasing trend in rice production.

Although the rate of poverty remains still high, Bangladesh has been able to maintain a food security reasonably well even in the face of unanticipated natural disaster of the scale of 1998 flood. Major risks of entitlement failure could be averted largely because of an effective combination of public action, NGO efforts, and community awareness. NGOs played an important role during the relief phase of the post-flood months by helping the distribution of food and other forms of assistance to the affected areas.

Despite the relatively slow income growth and modest pace of income poverty reduction, Bangladesh's achievements in the broad area of human development were faster, and in some respects, were truly remarkable. The winds of change that swept the Bangladesh economy over the past two decades were truly remarkable on many counts.

Bangladesh's impressive record in social development, poverty reduction, and accelerated economic growth should not lead us to complacency. More recently the momentum of growth has slowed down and the course of social development is entering a more challenging phase. Major impediments to growth include frequent cyclones and floods, inefficient state-owned enterprises, a rapidly growing labour force that cannot be absorbed in agriculture, delays in exploiting energy resources (natural gas), and slow implementation of economic reforms. Economic reform is stalled in many cases by political infighting and corruption at levels of government. Progress also has been blocked by opposition from the bureaucracy, public sector unions, and other vested interest groups. The critical need of the time is institutional reform and better governance of Bangladesh if Bangladesh is to consolidate its development gains and make further progress in poverty reduction and social development.

Despite falling inflows of foreign aid, Bangladesh achieved macroeconomic stabilization and an acceleration of economic growth in the 1990s. For consolidating the transition from stabilization to growth, improvements are needed in many areas such as revenue mobilization and the efficiency of the financial system ensuring the access of the rural poor.

The contribution of RNAs to generation of employment and growth of rural incomes in the early stages of development is well recognized in the development literature. This sector has played a dynamic role, offering increasingly more scope for productive employment, though in many cases, self-employment and diversification of the rural economy. The unhindered growth of this sector, however, may worsen rural income distribution unless the poor have better access to quality financial, and skill-enhancing pro-poor training services. Critical to a better performance of this sector are sustained agricultural growth, right set of policies and institutions, good rural infrastructure, better security for rural entrepreneurs, and better mitigation of vulnerability to disasters.

It may reasonably be argued that with the ever increasing size of the labour force, it is quite unlikely that Bangladesh can raise the level of investment to a level that would create enough wage employment to absorb its millions of unemployed labour force. Employment in the non-agricultural sector has increased quite rapidly. A comprehensive rural employment policy commensurate with the rightly placed emphasis on both wage and self-employment expansion for the poor including the female poor needs to be formulated.

Despite the ongoing debate on the measurement of poverty, the main point of agreement in Bangladesh is that an unacceptably large number of its rural population remains poor even today. Given the mass influx of donor assistance since the liberation of the country, the persistence of poverty in Bangladesh originates less in the lack of resources for its alleviation than in the failures of governance. The programmes aiming at poverty reduction have suffered from rent seeking at various levels which reduced efficiency and effectiveness, and deprived many poor, particularly poor women, of access to the services to which they were entitled.

Women in rural Bangladesh suffer the double burden of poverty and discrimination. There is also the recognition that as long as women are not provided with financial and other efficiency-enhancing services, mere participation of the rural poor women in the development process will not help them climb out of poverty. The broad conditions of poverty and gender discrimination have been the main stimulus for the provision of client-responsive financial and skills-enhancing non-financial services to generate productive employment, especially self-employment, sector for the growing rural poor women.

In order to plan a strategy for rural development without ackn as a highly visible economic resource is to doom the plan to failur upon a well reasoned and goal oriented national strategy incorporating women.

Despite improvements in some development indicators, Bangladesh remains a poor, overpopulated, and ill-governed nation. Although half of GDP is generated through the service sector, nearly two-thirds of Bangladeshis are employed in the agriculture sector, with rice as the single-most important product. Major impediments to growth include frequent floods, cyclones, inefficient and corrupt state-owned enterprises, inadequate port facilities, a rapidly growing labour force, delays in exploiting energy resources (natural gas), insufficient power supplies, and slow implementation of economic reforms. Economic reform is stalled in many instances by political infighting and *mutual blame game* policies of the main political parties. Progress has also been blocked by opposition from the bureaucracy, public sector unions, and other vested interest groups. Even with the greatest imaginable efficiency and planning and administration, resource-poor and overpopulated Bangladesh cannot perhaps achieve significant economic improvements within a short period of time.

The limited progress of the Bangladesh economy has to be viewed against this background of a mainly traditional rural economy, an economy that has an increasing incidence of poverty and the pervasive inefficiencies and distortions in public sector policies. These policies do not encourage the mobilization of private and public savings nor do they provide formal sources of credit to the rural poor, majority of whom are women.

Appendix 2A   Poverty Mapping in Bangladesh

Who the poor are	Types of poverty	Location of the poor	Dominant processes
1. Small cultivators (owners and owner-cum-tenants) with holdings of 0.8-two hectares.	1. Overcrowding/ endemic		Domestic policy biases - Natural cycles and disaster - Exploitative intermediation
2. Subsistence cultivators (owner-cum-tenants) with operational buildings of 0.4-0.8 hectare.	2. Overcrowding/ endemic/ sporadic	Widely distributed • all over the country; • however, the people	- Population pressure - Gender biases
3. Marginal farmers with operational holdings of less than 0.4 hectare.	3. Overcrowding/ endemic/ sporadic	• in the north-east • and southern part of • the country • are relatively	
4. Sharecroppers.	4. Overcrowing/ endemic/ sporadic	more • vulnerable • to natural	
5. Pure tenants.	5. Endemic/ sporadic	calamities • (floods, droughts)	
6. Landless with or without homestead land.	6. Endemic/ sporadic	• and cyclones.	
7. Artisanal fishermen	7. Peripheral/ sporadic		
8. Rural women and households headed by women	8. Endemic/ sporadic		

Source: I. Jazairy et al. , "The State of World Rural Poverty...", 1992, pp. 96-7

Chapter 3

The Rural Financial Structure and the Grameen Bank

Introduction

This chapter analyses the financial structure of Bangladesh, which is characterized by the co-existence of a limited formal financial sector and a vast informal one. The main questions of this chapter are what the structure and potential of the financial sector is, and whether the GB and other MFIs have overcome the problems associated with formal and informal finance, and finally, where the microfinance programmes of the GB and other MFIs fit within a poverty reduction strategy.

In answering the first question, Sections 2 and 3 of the chapter analyse the financial structure of the country and demonstrate the failure of the formal and informal sectors in meeting the ever increasing financial needs of the rural poor, particularly poor women, which has led to the growth of innumerable MFIs. Sections 4 and 5 answer the second and third questions. The rise of microcredit has been illuminated in Section 4. Section 5 reviews the circumstances leading to the birth of the GB, its apparent successes and failures, and its relevance to the standard economic theories, and its similarities and differences with the informal sector.

The financial sector in Bangladesh, in terms of bank density and financial deepening, is one of the lowest not only in the world, but also amongst the very least developed countries. Bank density, is the ratio of the number of bank branches/ offices per 10,000 people, and financial deepening is the expansion of financial transactions of all kinds in rural areas to reach broader clienteles, provide wider choice of services and to offer additional contract terms and conditions.

The growing interest in rural financial deepening relates to the issue of poverty alleviation. The higher the financial deepening, in the context of the overall economy, the greater the share of lending by deposit banks rather than reserve banks, and the greater the share of credit to the private rather than public sector, the greater will be the rate of economic growth. These factors increase growth by raising both the amount and efficiency of investment. The relationships between poverty and finance are quite complex, however, and incorrect perceptions and expectations can have rather counterproductive effects.

The financial system of Bangladesh, as noted, is characterized by the co-existence and operation side by side of a formal financial sector and an informal one, a situation commonly denoted as financial dualism. Theoretically, the formal sector would refer to an organized, urban-oriented institutional system catering to the financial needs of the monetized modern sector, while the informal sector, itself unorganized and non-institutional, would deal only with the traditional, rural, and subsistence spheres of the economy. It is equally important to recognize the great diversity, which exists within each of these two sectors and the difficulty in accurately defining the precise dividing line between them.

The Formal Financial Sector

The formal financial sector in Bangladesh, a legacy of the British colonial role, includes: (a) Bangladesh Bank as the Central Bank; (b) four nationalized commercial banks; (c) five government-owned specialized banks; (d) thirty domestic private banks, 10 foreign private banks; and (e) twenty eight non-bank financial institutions. The financial system also embraces insurance companies, stock exchanges, and co-operative banks. Among these institutions, only the specialized financial institutions and commercial banks deal, though not exclusively, with rural sector finance.

Bangladesh Bank

The Bangladesh Bank (BB), as the central bank, has legal authority to supervise and regulate all the banks. It performs the traditional central banking roles of note issuance and of being banker to the government and banks. It formulates and implements monetary policy, manages foreign exchange reserves, and supervises bank and non-bank financial institutions. Its prudential regulations include: minimum capital requirements, limits on loan concentration and insider borrowing and guidelines for asset classification and income recognition. The BB has the authority to impose penalties for non-compliance and also to intervene in the management of a bank if serious problems arise. It also has the delegated authority of issuing policy directives regarding the foreign exchange regime.

In order to keep the main issue in focus, this study concentrates, though the discussion just scratches the surface, on commercial banking system and specialized financial institutions, which directly or indirectly affect the microfinance operations in Bangladesh. This is, however, a matter of focus, and not meant as a suggestion that those other formal financial institutions are unimportant.

The Commercial Banking System

As in other South Asian countries, commercial banks dominate the financial system of Bangladesh, and as such nationalized and private commercial banks are its backbone. The four nationalized banks dominate the banking sector. However, the private banks, domestic and foreign, are growing and increasing their market share. Because of the distressed nationalized banking sector, the growth of private banking is a healthy development. As the area of operation of private banks is still limited to a few nation-wide city areas, they have not yet created any effective competition with nationalized banks.

Inefficiency, mismanagement, corruption, and loan defaults are the main causes of distress of the nationalized banking sector. Loan defaults are often linked to the government's industrial policy and directed credit programmes to priority sectors. The problem started when the banks, industries, and foreign trade were nationalized in the early 1970s. A new loan classification procedure introduced by the BB in 1990 uncovered the fact that by mid-1991 around 25 per cent of the nationalized commercial banks' (NCBs) loan portfolios were non-performing (Khalily and Meyer 1993, 29)

Privatization of nationalized industries has often been considered one way of improving their performance and such a decision may improve the performance of the nationalized banks as well. The government has been facing opposition from vested interest groups, which include workers, trade unions, bureaucrats, and politicians (Humphrey 1990). The government, instead of dragging its feet for political reasons, must realize that privatization of nationalized industries is good for these industries as well as for nationalized banks. Until such a decision is made, the nationalized banks should at least have the autonomy in lending to nationalized industries according to commercial principles.

To develop a sound private banking system, the government must make strenuous efforts to recover the enormous defaulted loans of nationalized banks. Loan recovery by stringent measures would be a signal to future borrowers that once loans are taken, they have to be repaid. Without banking discipline and responsibility of all concerned, the banking sector cannot survive and thrive.

Private Commercial Banks

The long-term solution of problems in the commercial banking sector is the development of the private banking system in terms of geographical coverage, deposit-taking, and commercial lending. There are, however, concerns that some private banks might not follow the rules and regulations of the BB. Therefore, while the rapid growth of private banking should be considered a positive development, the BB needs to keep an eye on private banks' lending activities. The development of a healthy private banking system will take some time and require the prudential supervision and guidance of the BB.

Specialized Development Financial Institutions

The government-owned development financial institutions in Bangladesh, the Bangladesh Krishi (agricultural) Bank (BKB), the Rajshahi Krishi Unnayan (agricultural development) Bank (RKUB), the Bangladesh Silpa (industrial) Bank (BSB), and the Bangladesh Silpa Rin Sangstha (industrial credit organization) [BSRS] are in great difficulties. Many argue that their fate was decided when they were created on flawed economic principles. These government-owned institutions are not mobilizers of funds from the people. They are basically the dispensers of subsidized funds from government and foreign sources to priority projects. They rarely evaluate the quality of such projects on the basis of economic criteria. In the industrial sector, persistent political pressure leave industrial banks no choice but to provide large loans to well-connected borrowers of dubious business and industrial backgrounds for non-viable projects.

The formal financial sector is characterized by two different approaches: a closely regulated financial sector where government control over and intervention in the activities of financial institutions is extensive, often at the expense of the development of the financial markets; and a more liberalized financial sector where financial institutions have greater leeway in carrying out their intermediation activities. The financial system of Bangladesh could be described as mixed, with a tendency towards that of a regulated one. Until the early 1980s, the government owned, controlled, and directed Bangladesh's financial system with the objective of allocating funds for sectors, projects, and purposes of its choosing. The quality of financial intermediation judged by the percentage of total rural population served, the variety of services offered, women's participation, and above all, loan recovery rates was very poor.

Government intervention in policies of priority sector lending and subsidized credit has been common in Bangladesh. The nationalized commercial banks whose lending is frequently in response to government's directives, have accumulated substantial backlogs of non-performing loans, while the maintenance of interest rates at artificially low levels has acted to repress savings. These policies have led to extensive credit rationing by banks, which in turn has resulted in an inefficient and inequitable distribution of credit (APDC 1992, 17).

Huge funds are also pumped into the agricultural sector with a feverish political zeal and a patronizing attitude with the belief that such loans would help the poor increase agricultural production. Such loans are rarely repaid. The BKB lending mostly to farmers with land as collateral, has had overdue loans running at 30 per cent, and was severely affected in the run-up to 1991 election when rival parties vied to offer the highest rate of loan forgiveness for farmers[1]. During the1980s, a period of seriously deteriorating credit discipline, the government directed BKB and other NCBs to expand their rural branch network and increase lending to agriculture. During the period 1976-91, the amount of total loans made increased by about 87 times, while the rural banking network increased eight-fold (Khalily and Meyer 1993, 24). This expansion outstripped the institutions' ability to maintain the quality of its lending and recovery programmes. Poor debt recovery was exacerbated by the involvement of local government officials in borrower selection, mixed signals created by loan amnesty, interest remission programmes, and the use of credit for relief and patronage purposes.

Establishing smaller versions of the urban branches in rural areas has expanded the rural branch network, but this expansion was not coordinated. Consequently,

---

1   Rutherford, 1993, quoted in (Hulme and Mosley eds. 1996).

some rural areas are over-endowed with bank branches, while others do not have any at all. Banks have expanded their operation in rural areas by replicating the procedures and facilities they provide in urban areas, many of which are unsuitable for rural areas (Rana 1986, 40-41). The NCBs' efforts to improve their mobilization of deposits have largely consisted of increasing the number of branches, with little effort to improve or expand the services they offer. The activities of the NCBs have come to be viewed as quasi-government departments rather than as independent financial institutions. This is incompatible with the role NCBs should play.

While branches in rural areas have increased rapidly, there has been a concentration of banks in *thana* (sub-district) headquarters with many villages being left unbanked. Furthermore, the emphasis has been on providing agricultural credit, with only small amounts of institutional credit being provided for RNAs, which is an important sector, in terms of employment and income generation. Criticizing the uncoordinated expansion of rural branches, Choudhury and Phare (1993, 294) remark,

> ...the financial system in rural Bangladesh today stands fractured as a result of creating too many institutions covering similar areas of financial intermediation, and who often work independently of each other. This has bred numerous inefficiencies in the financial intermediation process, which in turn has impeded the expansion of rural credit.

What is true about agricultural loans is equally true for industrial loans. Industrial banks' huge lending to projects of dubious quality and very low rate of loan recovery has left them in a precarious state. Given the sorry state of development of financial institutions, one pertinent question to ask is whether such institutions are really necessary for economic development. Many believe that a country like Bangladesh may even be better off without them.

In such a situation, the private commercial banks (PCBs) would take care of the credit needs of genuine borrowers. To many borrowers, the quality of financial services is important for the success of their businesses. Given the dismal picture of the development financial institutions, many borrowers have turned to foreign banks for their credit needs. It was not subsidized interest rates but the quality of financial services of foreign banks that encouraged such borrowers.

Provision of subsidized loans to priority sectors should be removed. Specialized development banks have outlived their purpose. Sooner or later they are likely to be closed down. Until such a time comes, their main task may be devoted to loan recovery by stringent measures. The massive default of loans by large industrial borrowers has created shortages of loanable funds for small borrowers who are better repayers of loans and have entrepreneurial capability (Hossain et al. 1994). At the time of closure it is sensible for the BB to establish a special unit to look after the loan recovery of specialized banks.

In order to counteract the on-going criticisms labeled against formal financial institutions and to achieve a significant outreach to the mass of rural poor, the formal financial institutions need to offer microfinance services, which they have so long been reluctant to do. Formal financial institutions in Bangladesh, like in other developing countries, have not regarded microfinance as a genuine option, because they have believed it to be unprofitable. These institutions typically have three basic concerns: it is too risky; too expensive; and there are socioeconomic and cultural barriers.

However, the formal financial institutions are well positioned to offer financial services to ever-increasing numbers of microfinance clients and to earn a profit. These institutions have several advantages over non-bank, microlending NGOs. Many already have the required physical infrastructure, including a large network of branches; they have well-established internal controls and administrative and accounting systems to keep track of a large number of transactions; and finally, they have their own sources of funds, they do not have to depend on scarce and volatile donor resources as do NGOs.

Microfinance services from the formal financial institutions may differ from their typical collateralised commercial and consumer loans. These microloans, although they share similarities with NGO microcredit products, such as frequent repayments and quick and inexpensive disbursements, may be slightly larger in size and may be granted for longer maturities than typical NGO loans. These differences may prompt some formal financial institutions to offer microloans in separate locations from their traditional banking services, highlighting the differences between products. Higher interest rate charges and less rigorous collateral requirements may characterize microlending by most formal financial institutions.

While formal financial institutions are better suited to the needs of large and medium scale industry, organized trade and commerce, the rural rich, and well-to-do urban households, informal/microfinance institutions enjoy a comparative advantage in retailing credit to the poor, due to their lower transaction costs and non-reliance on collateral. The comparative advantage of the formal banks would lie not in retailing directly but in *wholesaling* to MFIs for on-lending to the poor. In the long run the linking of the formal banks with the semi-formal MFI sector as well as the informal financial sector in an integrated financial system increases the efficiency of the system as a whole, and is the optimal solution to the issue of outreach to the poor (Ghate 2000, 201-3).

The steps outlined above are necessary requirements for the development of a dynamic financial system. Diverse and complex financial services can only be provided by a financial system, which is innovative and responsive to market demand. Competition is the key to innovation and the quality of services. Thus the contribution of a financial system to economic growth depends on the quantity and quality of financial services and the efficiency with which it provides them to its clients.

The principal microfinance service providers are usually categorized into four major groups: MF-NGOs; specialized institutions; banks; and administrative ministries or divisions.

Table 3.1   Selected Microfinance Statistics at the National Level (Taka in million)

Items	Up to December 2004		Up to December 2003		Growth in Disbursement in 2004 Over 2003(%)
	Cumulative Loan Disbursement	Recovery Rate (%)	Cumulative Loan Disbursement	Recovery Rate (%)	
1. MF-NGOs (n= 721 for 2004, 720 for 2003)[a]	338,635.6 (44.4)	98.79	269,472.31 (42.8)	98.76	25.7
2. Specialized Institutions	237,098.4 (31.1)		207,251.2 (32.9)		14.4
i) Grameen Bank	217,313.9 (28.5)	99.05	191,440.4 (30.4)	98.7	13.5
ii) PKSF	19,784.5 (2.6)	97.5	15,810.8 (2.5)[b]	99	25.1
3. Banks	126,026.2 (16.5)[c]		99,352.3 (15.8)		26.8
3.1. State – owned / Controlled Banks	*119,212 (15.6)* [c]	*86.1*	*94,537.4 (15.0)*	*95.35*	*26.1*
i) NCBs	91,442.4 (12.0)	94.29	79,847.9 (12.7)	96.81	14.5
ii) Agricultural Banks (BKB & RKUB)	23,073 (3.0)	55.97	11,180.5 (1.8)	84.94	106.4
iii) Others (Ansar - VDP Bank & Basic Bank)	4,696.6 (0.6)	97.7	3,509.0 (0.5)	98	33.8
3.2 Private Commercial Banks	*6,814.2 (0.9)* [c]	*96.34*	*4,814.9 (0.8)*	*94.98*	*41.5*
4. Administrative Ministries / Divisions	60,670.8 (8.0) [c]	82.87	52,877.5 (8.4)	83.2	14.7
i) Rural Development & Cooperative Division (BRDB, BARD & RDA)	35,437.6 (4.6)	91.15	30,374.3 (4.8)	85.19	16.7
ii) Ministry of Social Welfare	6,020.4 (0.8)	90.95	5,503.5 (0.9)	90.89	9.4
iii) Ministry of Youth & Sports	5,699.3 (0.7)	84.49	5,331.7 (0.8)	81.87	6.9
iv) Others	13,513.5 (1.8)	64.89	11,668.0 (1.8)	75	15.8
Total	**762,431.0 (100)**		**628,953.1 (100)**		21.2

Note:-   a. Cumulative disbursement figures reported in the table must be higher because of the existence of many unreported MF-NGOs in the microfinance sector. b. Up to January 2004. c. Up to March 2005
Source: CDF Annual Report 2004

Comparison of the major players' market shares in 2004 with their respective shares in 2003 does not reveal any significant change (Table 3.1). MF-NGOs are holding the largest share of the market with more than 44 percent of the total microfinance disbursement in 2004. The GB, which is a specialized organization accounts for about 29 percent of total disbursement. Formal financial institutions are gradually scaling down to spread their operations in the industry. Combined share of the NCBs, PCBs and other specialized banks increased to 16.5 percent in 2004 from 15.8 percent in 2003. Administrative ministries/divisions, specialized institutions and the NCBs have lost marginal portions of their market share in 2004.

Despite the ability of the formal financial institutions to include the poor in their financial services, these institutions have deliberately excluded the access of the poor to institutional finance. Formal bankers perceive the poor to be bad credit risks; the poor often perceive banks as alien institutions, which exist to serve the needs of their social superiors. Such perceptions create powerful inhibitions limiting the use of formal banks by the poor.

Apart from some individual schemes, the national banking system has still been unable to replace a substantial informal financial market, and has largely failed to address the needs of the RNA-based microenterprise sector.

The Informal Financial Sector

The term informal sector does not refer to one single type of economic activity or market, but rather includes the multitude of transactions, which can be contracted informally on the commodities market, the labour market, and the financial market. The concept of the informal sector first appeared in economic development theory in the International Labour Organization's (ILO's) World Employment Programme early in the 1970s (Turnham, et al. 1990, 13).

The terms *informal, parallel, black, underground, fragmented, unorganized, segmented,* and *curb* markets have all been used interchangeably in the literature to describe various forms of economic activity lying outside the officially regulated or monitored realm. In this manner, all activity that lies beyond the bounds of official regulation or control is considered to be informal in nature (Scobie et al. 1993, 8). The traditional informal finance includes: moneylenders, pawnshops, loans from friends and relatives, consumer credit in informal markets, credit unions, ROSCAs (also known as Loteri Samities in Bangladesh), money-guards, hire purchase stores, check-cashing outlets, and NGOs.

Over time with the changes in definitional concepts, the relative importance of the informal sector has also shifted. In the 1970s, much energy was expended arguing over the terminology and the importance of the sector in the economy. In the 1980s, new terms emerged leading debates to focus more on understanding the phenomenon regardless of the label used. By 1992, terms such as informality were used interchangeably with informal activity, self-employment, microenterprise, the underground or black market economy, and casual work. Terms such as economic dualism, petty commodity production, marginality, and traditional sector had fallen from favour. Accordingly, the people who engage in informal activities are equally likely to be called *the poor, unprotected workers, informals, and entrepreneurs.* The popularity of the informal sector concept among policy advisers and governments arose from an interest in poverty issues (Rakowski 1994, 502).

A worldwide survey of the United Nations (1999, 57) observes that despite its subsistence nature, the informal sector has not withered away with economic growth. Throughout much of the developing world the informal sector has become the locus of employment growth since the 1980s. In an environment where austerity policies are dictated by structural adjustment programmes, by changing forms of production and by increased competition, the formal sector simply has failed to generate sufficient employment for the growing labour force. The informal sector works as a huge *labour sponge*, which mops up the labour force excess in the formal sector.

Informal finance, despite its ubiquity in Bangladesh, is largely invisible because of its relatively small size of loans to finance working capital, rather than fixed capital. The sheer diversity of informal credit arrangements and the heterogeneity of informal lenders is another factor making generalizations very difficult. Informal lenders do not operate out of offices and they maintain few records. Our understanding of informal finance is largely impressionistic in nature.

The operators in the informal finance sector are mostly individuals, and transactions are based on the confidence engendered by face-to-face relationships between creditor and debtor. There is usually no collateral involved; security of loans is contingent upon the borrowers' past credit record, personal good faith and social pressure to sustain payment. Interest rate flexibility allows the lender to cover the opportunity cost of funds and the risk of default. Borrowers cite the convenience of borrowing from informal sources repeatedly as their reason for dealing with them, despite occasional exorbitant interest rates and other explicit and implicit costs of borrowing. In the terminology of the theory of *financial intermediaries*, the risks of *asymmetric information* are likely to be less in the informal than in the formal sector. Table 3.2 below summarizes the different characteristics of informal financial institutions.

In emphasizing the role of informal finance in economic development, a number of recent writers have argued that informal finance performs a useful function, socially as well as economically (Rahman 1992). Informal finance is a source of financing for activities often not provided by the formal sector (for example, education, medical care and other emergency outlays), but of essential importance for the rural population. The contribution of informal finance in the economic field is that it creates value similar to formal finance. New venture capital to the poor will usually be available only from the informal sector. There is growing acceptance among academics and policymakers that under certain conditions (for example, structural adjustment, recession) many informal activities are valuable economic endeavours as opposed to their past classification as *marginal* (Rakowski 1994, 501).

The rural poor women have very dynamic financial lives. While they are generally believed to be unable to borrow in volumes that formal financial institutions might find attractive, even they are very active borrowers. Facing restricted access to formal institutions, self-employed women tend to rely heavily on informal sources of credit

Table 3.2   Characteristics of Informal Financial Institutions

Characteristics	Friends and Family	ROSCA*	Moneylender	Pawnbroker	Tied credit
Loan size	Small	Small	Small	Small	Small
Loan term	Varies	Short-term	Short-term	Short-term	Varies
Terms	Very flexible	Flexible	Flexible	Flexible	Flexible
Collateral	No	No; group peer pressure	Sometimes	Yes	Economic relation
Transaction costs	Low	Low	Medium	Low	Low
Deposits	No	Fixed amount	Usually not	Sometimes	Usually not
Interest rate	None or low	Medium	High	Less high	Low
Source of funds	Own	Members	Own, some borrowed	Own, some borrowed	Own, some borrowed

* Rotating savings and credit association
Source: United Nations. (1999a), p. 186.

and *social* assets, such as, family and friends, not only in the face of emergencies, but also for routine borrowing needs. Much of that borrowing comes through reciprocal lending and borrowing relationships with other poor people and is taken free of interest, but it is most certainly a form of household financial management through borrowing-as is taking household goods or food on credit from a shop, taking wages in advance from an employer, and retailing items on loan from a middleman.

The informal sector is sometimes justified on its *equity* and *efficiency* grounds. The ability to deliver small loans to the poor borrowers is responsible for its equity impact. Informal credit is better distributed, and small farmers, microentrepreneurs, and poor borrowers generally depend on it either exclusively, or to a great extent. Moreover, small borrowers often use credit more productively, which means informal finance meets the efficiency objective. This accompanied by risk premium for the lender (because such loans are often given without any collateral) may partly explain why the informal sector credit is usually more (100 per cent–300 per cent) expensive than the formal sector credit. It is nevertheless more popular and more accepted.

Moreover, empirical studies (for example, Chaudhuri and Gupta 1996, 433) indicate that the market for informal credit in Bangladesh is often created by the delay in disbursement of formal credit. The bank officials of the formal credit agency control the delay, and the bank officials frequently have to be bribed by the client in order to reduce the delay. Bank officials play a non-cooperative game in choosing the bribing rate. The informal sector interest rate and the effective formal sector interest rate (incorporating the bribe) are sometimes equal in equilibrium.

Rural poor women are unable and reluctant to bribe the bank officials. Even though women tend to be better credit risks then men, access of poor women to formal credit is more constrained and restricted than poor men. Rural private economic agents can be classified into three different categories according to their degree of access to the financial market: large farmers and wealthy households who have relatively easy access to the financial market; small farmers and some qualified professionals who also have limited access; and poor landless and unskilled labourers, both men and women, who have no access at all. For the last group, which constitutes over 80 per cent of the rural population, formal commercial channels within the financial sector of Bangladesh are virtually closed.

Informal finance can be a mixed blessing too. While informal finance is useful for some purposes, it is not dependable and often has high costs in cases of large consumer purchases and emergencies. Furthermore, the interlinkage of informal credit with other services, such as marketing or the supply of inputs, frequently channels the benefits of increased production to the moneylender, not the borrower. Participation in these institutions does not link women directly to the mainstream financial system; continued reliance on them is one cause of perpetuating the marginalization of women's economic activities.

Moneylenders are frequently criticized for charging usurious interest rates and taking advantage, especially in rural areas, of borrowers who may not realize the true rate of interest they are paying and either do not know of or do not have access to alternative sources of finance. This inflates the element of monopoly profit, which is one of the determinants of informal interest rates. Their interest rates can indeed be extremely high. An example is the so-called *five-six* arrangement under which market vendors acquire their trading capital needs; the borrower may receive $5 before dawn and repay $6 to the lender in the evening, with an effective interest rate of 20 per cent a day (APDC 1992, 15). Fuglesang and Chandler (1994) observe that the moneylenders charge a phenomenal rate of interest, which can be up to 330-400 per cent annually.

In response to the criticisms raised above, Ghate (1994, 14) from the ADB observes that high interest rates do not necessarily imply monopoly profits-they are often the consequence of the high transactions costs of making small and short duration loans and of the opportunity cost of funds (the informal lenders do not receive subsidized funds). However, Hoff and Stiglitz (1997, 432) on the other hand, observe that even subsidized funds do not improve the terms offered by moneylenders. They argue that the conventional economic analysis suggests that an increase in government-subsidized credits, which benefit the informal lenders must *trickle-down* to the clients they serve. The consensus of those who have studied these markets is that in most rural areas where large inflows of subsidized formal credit occurred; interest rates in the informal sector did not fall significantly, or at all, nor did the availability of informal credit increase. Being sceptical about the *trickle-down* effects of subsidies, they support the view that the formal sector, like the GB in Bangladesh, must lend directly to the poor households to increase their productivity. Rahman (1992) from the BIDS observes that the informal financial market in Bangladesh has contracted and expanded in relation to the volume of business undertaken by the formal banking institutions. This complementarity between the formal and informal sectors leads the author to conclude that Bangladesh's informal sector is largely *efficient* and *potentially developmental* rather than *monopolistic* and *exploitative.*

However, this does not deny the fact that the informal interest rates are high and difficult to afford for many amongst the poor. Although it is difficult to specify real interest rates, Rahman settles on a modal interest rate of 10 per cent per month (a rate which when compounded is equivalent to 214 per cent per year) for most loans, both large and small. In contrast the formal sector lending rates in the past decade have been between 12 per cent and 20 per cent per year, with only a few experimental schemes using higher rates, for example, 36 per cent under the USAID sponsored *Rural Finance Experimental Project* in 1978-80 (Montgomery et al. 1996, 97). Following the seminal works of Mckinnon (1973) and Shaw (1973) on financial repression and underdevelopment of the developing countries, many countries including Bangladesh have reformed their formal financial system. The market has been liberalized and with no restriction on interest rate and supply of credit. As a result of the policies pursued in both financial repression and liberalization regimes, banking network as well as credit have expanded enormously and financial deepening has been increased. Despite enormous annual injection of $700 million of microcredit through a network of 3000 branches of over 1000 MFIs, and equal amount through a network of 3000 branches of commercial and development banks during the past five years, the share of informal finance remains more or less the same, which is estimated at 52 per cent of the rural households (Khalily et al. 2002).

The share of rural informal credit, although declining in most countries, still accounts for one-third to two-thirds in Bangladesh (Ghate et al. 1994, 10). Sixty three per cent of credit in Bangladesh still comes from informal sources: informal moneylenders cover 77 per cent of farmers' credit needs; 50 per cent by friends and relatives; 13 per cent by rural *well to do* and 14 per cent by professional lenders (Germidis et al. 1991, 44). Roy (1994, 44-5) from the BIDS observes that about 38 per cent of the agricultural labour, 31 per cent of non-agricultural labour and more than one-third of cottage industry workers have received loans from professional moneylenders. If the poor borrowers are classified in terms of credit agencies, GB covers only 3.4 per cent of the total poor borrowers. By contrast, professional moneylenders and the category of friends and relatives cover 33 per cent and 42 per cent respectively.

The rural IFM in Bangladesh comprises a range of lenders-landlords, richer cultivators, traders and brokers, professional moneylenders and *dadon*[2] lenders.

---

2   Dadon has same link to sharecropping, where land is provided for share of harvest. In return for credit the borrower (farmer) contracts with a trader to sell his crop to him for a price

In the highly unequal social and economic environment of the countryside, most forms of credit, which are not directly cash-for-cash are explicitly or implicitly *tied* to additional conditions including clientelist ones. Reciprocity of patron-client relationship is also widespread in Bangladesh, as is evident from the comments of White (1992: 64) when she observes,

> Loans are not always given by richer patrons to poorer clients. While the norm is for employing households to give loans to their workers, loans may also be given by workers/share-croppers to employers/landowners. Usually this involves upper/vulnerable households, who can be under some strains to sustain the lifestyle appropriate to their status from their limited material resources. This is regarded as shameful, and kept secret, so it is difficult to assess its extent. Nonetheless there is sufficient evidence in my small sample to suggest that it is quite widespread.

The Islamic prohibition of interest seems to have had at least four identifiable influences on the informal market in Bangladesh: of *dadon* as a means of financing crop production, in which the price discount in the forward sale substitutes for interest; the relative frequency of profit sharing in lieu of interest; the extremely high share of interest-free credit; and the frequency of usufructuary land mortgages.

The large proportion of interest-free informal credit (between 35 per cent and 45 per cent) is normally attached to some conditions such as pledges of labour and political support, mortgage of lands and other assets, and so on (Montgomery et al. 1996, 98). Sen (1988) in his study of moneylenders in Bangladesh found that 80 per cent of the lending in his sample was against the security of land, about three-quarters of which took the form of usufructuary mortgages.

Overall, the informal sector is unable to satisfy the credit needs of all the poor. In the high-risk natural and economic environment, the informal markets are as keen to *screen* as are formal institutions. In such circumstances, many of the poor are not deemed creditworthy by informal lenders, and are thereby denied access to such financial assistance. Moreover, the high interest rates, which to some extent reflect high risks, are not affordable by most poor families without cashing in their existing assets. Debt at high interest rates, whether deemed as *efficient allocation* or *exploitation*, remains one of the downward pressures, which, along with other structural social and economic conditions, constitute the *deprivation trap* (Montgomery et al. 1996, 88).

Moreover, in order to be a proper financial intermediary the informal sector needs to mobilize savings from the clients and disburse it to the borrowers who need it to increase their productivity. In practice, limited financial intermediation does occur but the sector mainly relies on borrowing or contractual savings rather than on deposit mobilization. This characteristic plus the lack of suitable collateral severely limits the ability of informal financial agents and institutions to expand their

---

agreed upon in advance, its difference from the market value of the crop at the time of delivery after harvest represents the implicit rate of interest. For details see (Ghate et al. 1994)

operation to have a significant impact on outreach to the poor (Christensen 1993, 728). The market failures of informal credit have been summarized in Box 3.1.

Box 3.1   Failures of Informal Rural Credit

1. Market power: too few operators with too big a share of the market
2. Depositor protection: savers at risk from deposit takers who may run off with their savings
3. Imperfect information: borrowers don't know where to go for loans, lenders don't know much about potential borrowers to risk lending to them
4. Redistribution effects: existing patterns of transactions may worsen maldistribution of wealth and income in a society
5. Moral hazard: a borrower who gets a big loan may not make every effort to make his enterprise successful, since he knows his lender is sharing the risk
6. Adverse selection: lenders may favour certain borrowers but this may not serve the public good
7. Enforcement problems: informal contracts can't be pursued at law
8. Covariant risk: every borrower may default at the same time if they're all farmers and face a drought at the same time
9. Segmented market: only certain borrowers interact with only certain lenders, and funds get trapped inside localities instead if flowing to where they can be best used
10. Institutional underdevelopment: institutions (literacy, numeracy) too weak to support growth of good services
11. Scarce collateral

Source: S. Rutherford (1997)

Despite some of its advantages, informal finance cannot supplant formal finance. Formal finance is available at a relatively lower interest rate and is more readily able to accommodate large and long-term loans because of its greater reliance on the pooling of deposits and maturity transformation. It thus enjoys greater *economies of scale* and *scope*, although not necessarily of *specialization*. But it is less successful in serving the needs of the poor, microentrepreneurs, and small traders.

There is a growing consensus that a sustainable rural financial system with a reasonable degree of *outreach* including poor women cannot be achieved by focusing attention on the traditional formal sector institutions and markets alone. At the same time, the informal financial sector also cannot be left to its own devices.

The informal financial sector is neither a panacea nor the basis of an alternative development model.

Despite all what has been said about informal finance in Bangladesh, the microenterprise development approach (used synonymously with informal sector and poverty) has gained momentum amongst the development practitioners over the last two decades. This approach believes in the ability of the poor to support themselves and survive through increasing their incomes in their microenterprises. While these activities have no formal label, they are most easily identified by the use of the terms *poverty alleviation* and *microenterprise*. The term *microenterprise* is typically linked to credit, solidarity groups, and training in productivity-enhancing activities, and marketing skills. The NGOs and other welfare organizations of the late 1980s and early 1990s have been expanding their role. Despite the time and resources, which NGOs as a group have invested in the poor, a tremendous amount of need remains unmet (Rakowski 1994, 507-8).

While no new policy changes in the area of rural finance are apparent in the near future, the setting up of microenterprises with the assistance of NGOs and MFIs, adopting some of the features of informal finance, especially to reach the rural poor including women, will help alleviate rural poverty.

The Rise of Microcredit Programmes

The Evolution of Microcredit

Rural poor need credit to allow investment in their small and microenterprises. The lack of physical collateral restricts the poor to the formal sources of finance. The informal sector's loans are often available, but their usurious interest rates block the access of the poor microentrepreneurs into that market. Recognizing this, governments and international agencies created banks and other specialized institutions targeted at the rural poor. The track record of these institutions is, however, mixed, especially with regard to reaching the poor. Reforms and innovations have emerged in recent years to improve credit market opportunities for the rural poor, particularly poor women.

One such innovation is microcredit, or small loans targeting the poor, and this has transformed the way credit is viewed. Microcredit is intended to help the rural poor escape poverty by investing in their own enterprises. Microcredit schemes overcome some of the problems of delivering rural credit to the poor by offering collateral-free loans often at near-market interest rates through community-based programmes operated by financing institutions or NGOs (FAO 2000).

There are many antecedents to microcredit, which is a recently coined term that is applied to a diverse range of credit activities and types of institutions. Locally managed credit arrangements have existed for hundreds of years and continue to serve small borrowers despite the advent of the *microcredit movement*. Small loans to poor borrowers have also been part of the rural development strategies followed by many organizations and agencies since the early 1970s. Thus, microcredit is older than it first appears, but the efforts to promote it globally and the high-level endorsement of specific outreach goals have recently elevated the movement to far greater prominence.

Debates have, however, emerged over the fundamental philosophy and technical details of microcredit delivery. Adherents have produced a flurry of examples and studies to support their view that microcredit is a revolution that will pull people from the depths of poverty, while critics staunchly maintain that it is not a panacea for reaching the poor where other credit systems have failed.

It is widely perceived that growth in microcredit programmes has been phenomenal. In Bangladesh alone, a total of BDT 762,431.0 million microfinance loans were disbursed in 2004, the corresponding figure for 2003 was BDT 628,953.1 million. This indicates a 21.2 per cent increase in growth in disbursement in 2004 over 2003. The shares of microcredit in total domestic credit in Bangladesh were 9. 37 and 9.89 per cent in 2003 and 2004 respectively (CDF 2004, 2-3). A survey conducted by the Microcredit Summit Campaign shows that at the end of 2002, a total of 67.6 million microfinance clients were served worldwide by over 2,500 MFIs. Of these clients, 41.6 million were in the bottom half of those living below their nation's poverty line. Between 1997 and 2002, the numbers grew on average by about 40 per cent per year, and the movement's leaders expect to continue expanding as credit unions, commercial banks, and others enter the market (Aghion and Morduch 2005, 3). Despite this fast growth, many believe the microcredit industry is still in an incipient stage relative to the potential demand for its services.

What indeed are the impacts of microcredit and is it reaching its stated goals of poverty alleviation? What are the limitations of microcredit programmes in alleviating poverty especially of the extreme poor? Taking the GB, the flagship of microcredit movement, as a case study, the following chapter, chapter 4 illustrates the empirical evidence based on a year-long field survey on the impact and limitations of microcredit in alleviating poverty. The section that follows describes the arguments surrounding how microcredit works, how it overcomes the barriers to credit delivery, and what are the main aims of microcredit?

How Microcredit Works?

Many variants of microcredit have emerged as the geographical reach, clientele and aims of MFIs have expanded. Both in the conditions of lending and in the nature of the clients, microcredit is a hybrid of a development tool and a financial service. MFIs are more flexible in their operations than many formal institutions, but are more structured than informal lenders. Microcredit aspires to reach poor women borrowers with flexible financial and non-financial services to help them alleviate their poverty.

How Microcredit Overcomes Barriers to Credit Delivery to the Poor?

Largely informal moneylenders and other providers of informal finance-including rotating credit groups and savings associations address the financial needs of the rural poor women. Microcredit does not replace these local sources of credit and savings but combines characteristics of such mechanisms, such as the information advantages of village moneylenders and the rotational lending of Rotating Savings and Credit Associations (ROSCAs). These traditional mechanisms have fulfilled the primary role of credit delivery to the rural poor. Microcredit fills a credit niche for certain population groups, especially women.

The rural credit programmes of the 1970s reveal a history of credit market failures, including the capture of benefits by wealthy or politically advantaged elite groups. Those credit programmes experienced several types of institutional failure, including the lack of practical mechanisms for reaching the rural poor. The problems can be summarized under three main headings: information asymmetries; low-potential profitability; and lack of portfolio diversification. The novelty in rural credit introduced by microcredit is the way in which it tackles these well-known market and institutional failures.

Information asymmetries are created when the parties to a transaction do not have access to equal information, thereby creating an advantage to the party with a greater amount of information. Such situations can arise either before a transaction takes place, when a borrower may appear to be less risky than he/she really is, and after the transaction has occurred, when a borrower may have an incentive not to repay the lender as originally agreed. To deal with the problem, lenders usually require borrowers to have good credit histories and meet other requirements to ensure they are creditworthy, as well as requiring some collateral to be provided in exchange for granting credit. However, these usual remedies do not work with the group-lending aimed at by microcredit.

Microcredit resolves information asymmetries by creating peer group contacts in which liability is collectively accepted and regular payments are made at group meetings. In this way, peer pressure creates an incentive to remain current with loan payments, as well as to exclude those who might be considered poor credit risks.

Low-potential profitability is the second barrier to loans for the poor. It reflects a bank's perceptions of the high costs, high risk, and small market inherent in serving such a borrower population. At the individual level, such borrowers generally do not have steady or adequate incomes or any assets to seize, and they face great economic and cultural barriers to earning income. At the community level, they are relatively isolated, so it is expensive to provide financial services to them.

Microcredit resolves this problem through several practices. Many microcredit programmes provide training and technical advice to borrowers in an effort to increase their incomes. These integrated programmes try to increase the skills and capacity of their borrowers. The value of this is obvious, especially for poor women who lack experience and knowledge in running microenterprises.

High repayment rates are also important to microcredit's ability to lend to the poor. This is believed to be attributable to the emphasis on female borrowers, who are more responsible than men in making payments, and to the peer joint-liability system. Moreover, microcredit programmes generally charge market interest rates on loans to support their high costs. This is a contributing factor to the formation of a market niche for microcredit borrowing, and it helps overcome high costs.

Portfolio diversification is the third problem barring rural poor populations from access to credit. Microcredit institutions have only partially resolved this portfolio diversification problem. The peer group lending approach spreads the liability for repayment among the entire group of borrowers in a given village or peer group. This means that they accept responsibility for each other's debts. While this approach does not overcome the risk of calamitous losses when a poor harvest or natural disaster occurs, it does reduce the risk exposure when losses are not widespread among borrowers. Insurance products and emergency funds are also being adopted to address the lack of portfolio diversification. These sources provide compensation or additional credit during times of disaster, and they might include the suspension of loan repayment schedules until recovery is possible.

During the Bangladesh floods of late 1998, the GB and other MFIs allowed borrowers to suspend payments on their loans until they were on a sounder financial footing. The compulsory savings component of microcredit programmes is sometimes used to finance such concessions.

However, the success of targeted microcredit programmes to the poor lies in the alleviation of their poverty. Different studies (for example, Hossain 1988; Khandker 1998) indicate that the microcredit programmes have been successful in expanding the opportunities of self-employment in microenterprises. Self-employment thus provides a good prospect of alleviating poverty by creating more employment for women.

The poor in Bangladesh, especially those without adequate access to productive land or paid employment, support themselves with a myriad of self-employed activities in trade, services, crafts and petty manufacturing, as well as in agriculture. However, they lack access to credit, and other microfinancial services, including savings. These are crucial obstacles for them to climb out of poverty.

Distinction between Traditional Banking and Microcredit

MFIs dealing with microcredit deploy small amounts of short-term working capital and in some cases longer-term investment loans, and provide deposit facilities to the rural poor. MFIs differ from traditional financial institutions in terms of: client base; lending methodology; administrative costs, nature of the portfolio; and institutional structure and governance.

In addition to the above points of distinction, the MFIs and the traditional financial institutions also differ on many other issues. Appendix 3A reflects a summary of the main points of differences between the MFIs and traditional banks, commonly found in Bangladesh and also in other South Asian countries. Differences among formal commercial banks, semi-formal microcredit/NGOs, and informal lenders in terms of loan size, loan term, interest rate, collateral, and transaction costs can be seen in Table 3.3. The advantages of MFIs over informal lenders are also appended in Box 3.2.

Box 3.2   Advantages of Microfinance over Informal Lenders

There are three main advantages:

1. In contrast to informal commercial lenders, institutions providing Microfinance have an incentive to attain wide client outreach. Such institutions price their loan products on commercial principles. They also provide incentives and training to staff in order to expand the institution's Microfinance business and its profitability.
2. Banks and other formal-sector institutions providing commercial Microfinance can benefit from financial intermediation, and from economies of scale.
3. Financial institutions with well-trained and motivated staff can attain better information about large numbers of lower-income borrowers than can an individual moneylender. This is because:

    a) Voluntary savings services can provide good information about the economic activities and the character of large numbers of savers-who are also potential borrowers. This helps to keep loan repayment rates high and to lower the bank's costs for loan transactions.

    b) Staff of bank branches are generally local people who maintain social and political relationships and who, in aggregate, have access to multiple local information flows. For these reasons, institutions providing commercial Microfinance can offer loans to credit-worthy poor borrowers at much lower interest rates than the latter would normally pay to moneylenders.

Source: M.S. Robinson (1998)

Microenterprises offer an alternative to the conventional strategy for bringing development to poor nations-making large loans to governments for massive power or infrastructure projects. Such project-oriented development has justifiably come under growing criticism from grassroots activists, who say the projects often benefit large contractors and central governments more than they help local people. More investment in smaller, local industries, they argue, could bring economic and social benefits at far less cost. This view is reflected in an old Chinese saying, *Many little things done in many little places by many little people will change the face of the world* (cited in Grameen Dialogue #27, 1996).

Table 3.3   Characteristics of Different Financial Institutions

	Formal	Semi-formal	Informal
Examples	Commercial bank	Microcredit/ non-governmental organisation	ROSCA*
Characteristics	Regulated	Often not regulated	Not regulated
Loan Size	Large	Very small-medium	Very small
Loan term	All terms	Medium-and short-term	Short-term
Terms	Rigid	Less rigid	Flexible
Interest rate	Low	Medium	Medium-high
Collateral	Usually	No; group peer pressure, character lending	No; group peer pressure
Transaction costs:	High	Medium	Low**
For lender	High	Medium-high	Low**
For borrower			
Deposits	Yes	Sometimes; savings	Fixed amount
Main Clients	Corporations	Poor women, MSEs*** SMEs****	Poor, women, MSEs***
Use	Fixed investment, working capital	Consumption, working capital, fixed investment	Consumption, working capital and fixed investment
Financial intermediation	Large	Small, but growth potential	Small
Linkages°	Small	Small, but growth potential	Small, but growth potential

*   *Rotating savings and credit association*
**   *For ROSCA, lender and borrower are the same*
***   *Micro-and small enterprises*
****   *Small and medium-sized enterprises*
°   *Referring, for example, to linkages between bank on the one hand and non-governmental organisation or ROSCA on the other hand. Linkages between banks and moneylenders or traders who on lend are more common.*
Source: United Nations. (1999a), p. 187.

Microcredit has, however, not been portrayed as a substitute for agricultural credit, nor for traditional banking, as it is far smaller in scale and differently targeted than such lending. However, in its modest form, it fills gaps in credit delivery that are not addressed by other providers, and, in its ambitious form, it attempts to catalyse economic development that will reduce rural poverty (FAO 2000).

The rise of targeted microcredit programmes in Bangladesh over the last two decades, both state-and NGO-sponsored, derives from the inability and inefficiency of the financial sectors. Capital scarcity, the failure of the formal sector to reach the poor, and the limited ability of the informal sector to meet the needs of the majority of the poor people striving to survive in the non-farm sector have led to the rise of microcredit programmes (Getubig et al. 1997, 53).

Bangladesh has seen a remarkable emergence of national and international NGOs contributing to participatory, grassroots development. There are more than 10,000 NGO's (local and foreign) in Bangladesh engaged in various development activities including microlending (World Bank 1990).

Among the major players, which have dominated the microfinance scene along with the GB are BRAC, ASA, and Proshika. As of 2004, the four organizations jointly reached over 15.3 million rural poor (mostly poor women), accounting for 80 per cent of the total outreach achieved by all MFIs in Bangladesh. Table 3.4 summarizes the statistics on coverage, savings, and credit of the GB and three major MFIs in Bangladesh.

Table 3.4   Statistics on Coverage, Savings, and Credit of GB and Three Major MF-NGOs, 2004

	GB	BRAC	ASA	Proshika
Inception year of Credit Programme	1976	1974	1991	1976
Active Members	5313.871	4496.435	2672.476	2768.147
Total Net Savings (Taka)	28,830,130,000	6,904,671,948	2,853,893,432	1,450,500,000
Cumulative Disbursement (Taka)	249,471,800,000	133,211,720,000	96,034,636,950	28,937,050,000
Outstanding Loan Value (Taka)	26,504,840,000	14,491,540,000	11,980,071,220	4,857,180,000
Recovery Rate (%)	99.01	99.15	100.00	95.00

Source: The Grameen Monthly Report (October 2005) for figures on the GB and Credit Development Forum Report 2004 for figures on BRAC, ASA, and Proshika.
Current Exchange Rate: 1 US$= Taka 67.00

Though the lending methods of these four organizations have certain similarities reflecting the early influence of the GB, they nevertheless represent different approaches to poverty lending. The GB is considered to be the best example of the *minimalist* credit approach, attempting to minimize the number of subsidiary services accompanying credit.

The approach taken by the BRAC is often contrasted to this minimalist credit approach. It offers credit as a part of a broader package of services, typically including skills training, technical assistance, and marketing services. Proshika's credit operations work along the principles similar to BRAC.

ASA pursued the Grameen-style credit-based development approach rather more single-mindedly than BRAC and Proshika. In recent years, ASA has thrown off some of the lending methods formerly considered essential to the Grameen model. For example, it no longer requires all group members to come to the weekly meetings. It has also introduced a popular deposit pension scheme, a life insurance policy, and an open access savings scheme, apparently making a departure from the rigid replica of the classical Grameen model.

The microcredit programmes of the GB and other MFIs in Bangladesh predominantly support non-farm activities. About two-thirds of Bangladesh's population is engaged in agricultural activities which accounts for only about 45 per cent of total household income. Non-farm activities employ about a third of the population but account for 55 per cent of income. The rural non-farm sector accounts for 60 per cent of the loans advanced by MFIs, 48 per cent of the loans advanced by formal financial institutions, and 28 per cent of the loans advanced by informal lenders. The rural non-farm sector received the bulk of annual lending that is, nearly more than 90 per cent of the GB's loan portfolio in 1994 (Khandker 1998, 70).

The experiences and expertise of MFIs and other NGOs in various aspects of development could be used as an important resource for national development in general and poverty alleviation in particular. More specifically, NGOs could play an effective role in working with the poor at the grassroots level in areas involved in addressing the determinants of poverty, creation and testing of new ideas, strategies of poverty alleviation through various local experimentation, consciousness-raising, awareness-building, training among the poor, and their skill development.

One secret to Bangladesh's limited turnaround is microcredit, small loans given without collateral. Social workers have discovered that a start-up loan of as little as $20 can often be enough to rescue a family from starvation and a lifetime of indebtedness to village moneylenders. The World Bank and other donor organizations now acknowledge that loans to poor people can often do more good for impoverished countries than gargantuan investment projects that generate corruption and waste (The Times, London April 28, 1997)

NGOs' activities, even if sometimes local and financially modest, have strongly contributed to a radical change in the concept of development by means of small-scale projects aimed directly at the rural poor. The effective poverty alleviation efforts of NGOs usually comprise of income-generating activities, credit programmes for the target group, employment, asset formation, training, appropriate technology, and supply of inputs. It is often argued that NGOs and other MFIs are effective in reaching the poor, particularly the poor women.

All such activities of NGOs sound like *magic*, and although they do something very useful for the rural poor, they are subject to the following criticisms. In terms of *outreach* and *volume* of credit, the NGOs' performance is not sufficient to meet the growing credit needs of the poor microentrepreneurs in Bangladesh. Savings mobilization is still the forgotten half of many NGOs.

Moreover, most, if not all, NGOs' credit programmes have experienced the problem of very poor repayment records. Some now have improved recovery rates although this still remains a problem in many cases. NGOs had failed to make efforts to involve the banks in their lending programmes, not only because of indifference and resistance from the banks, but also because in some cases the NGOs were themselves reluctant to give up control of the programme. Many NGOs had the support of religious institutions and were less inclined to emphasize the business and profit-making character of the microenterprises. NGOs generally lack the staff needed to understand technology and business management and so are unable to advise microentrepreneurs.

Some researchers into NGO work conclude that the NGO's rhetoric of working with the *poorest of the poor* is overstated, that NGOs may be successful at reaching poor people but have yet to demonstrate that they substantially benefit the poorest. In the words of Sheldon Annis (1987), a prominent American analyst of NGO performance,

> ...in the face of pervasive poverty, *small scale* can merely mean *insignificant, politically independent* can mean *powerlessness* or *disconnected, low-cost* can mean *underfinanced* or *poor quality* and *innovative* can mean simply *temporary* or *unsustainable*. NGOs will describe at length the importance of *women and development*, however, there are studies to indicate that NGOs projects tend to enhance their (women's) domestic, not productive, role.

Despite some reservations against NGOs, it can safely be observed that they have several advantages over governmental organizations in terms of being more innovative in the provision of assistance to the rural poor who are given higher priority by NGOs and whose close contact with the poor is likely to suggest ways to adapt new ideas to succeed. Having autonomy, flexibility, and advantages in the area of management, NGOs can perform better compared to the government, because governmental efforts are hampered by factors such as centralization, lack of decision-making autonomy, and rigid hiring and firing rules.

The Bangladesh government, because of its command over the access to much greater resources and the broader institutional framework, has the potential for designing suitable programmes to reach much wider sections of the poor. On the other hand, in the extremely unusual cases where there is already a critical mass of good retail capacity and a large enough market for microfinance services, it makes sense to establish an apex to serve as a kind of Central Bank for microfinance. An indicative rather than regulatory coordination between the government and the NGOs through such an apex institution would be the most appropriate approach.

In line with the need to coordinate the NGOs' activities and to make the poverty alleviation programme more effective, the *Palli Karma-Sahayak* Foundation (PKSF), an apex organization, was founded in 1991 with the full financial backing of the Bangladesh government. PKSF is playing an important role in channeling donor funds to the credit-giving MFIs to nurture their financial and technical capacity. Although PKSF loans to the MFIs are subsidized, the fact that they are loans rather than grants is a major point of departure from the state-led subsidized credit operations in the past (Ito 1999, 19).

Despite the fact that few *apex* institutions produced impressive results; the PKSF in Bangladesh is playing a very useful role. What is different about Bangladesh is that there was already a critical mass of strong retail microfinance capacity when PKSF came on the scene, including *superstars* like Grameen and BRAC, who had the political clout to defend it against government interference. In the field of poverty alleviation, the experience of the foundation has been unique in the sense that it is for the first time that a private organization has been established in the country through government initiative.

Many MFIs and NGOs targeting the poor converted *en masse* in the late 1980s to Grameen-style credit operations. Over time, however, various innovations that have taken place among them making Bangladesh the *Mekkah* for a variety of different microfinance operations (Ito 1999). The GB, the cradle of microfinance movement, despite being a specialized financial institution resembles more a voluntary NGO in its activities. The following section analyses the circumstances leading to the birth of the GB.

The Grameen Bank

The word *grameen* in Bengali literally means *village* or *rural*. The story of the GB is almost a legend. The founder, Muhammad Yunus, is a former economics professor who returned from the United States in 1972 with his doctorate from Vanderbilt. He joined Chittagong University, which is located in a rural area among many villages. During his tenure at the university, Yunus was confronted by the poverty that overwhelms many people in rural Bangladesh, living in a world of debt alongside the rich people and being kept in an omnipresent poverty circle.

The political climate in Bangladesh preceding the birth of the GB was permeated by pessimism about the efficacy of markets[3], as in the rest of the world since the end of the Second World War. The belief that markets, left on their own, would not produce socially desirable outcomes extended strong support to the political arguments for state intervention and economic planning in many parts of the world. In the context of the Indian sub-continent, the most notable example of numerous

---

3   The neo- classical economists believe that the market mechanism is a neutral arbitrator ensuring optimal allocation of resources thereby promoting efficiency and prosperity for all.

government-sponsored rural development interventions was the Integrated Rural Development Programmes (IRDP) launched all over the sub-continent during the 1960s. In Bangladesh, the Pakistan Academy for Rural Development (PARD), later to be renamed as the Bangladesh Academy for Rural Development (BARD), became the hub of the GB programme.

The devastating Bangladesh famine of 1974 added to the extreme poverty in the country. Muhammad Yunus was convinced that it was not the shortage of food but the lack of *entitlements* that made people starve. He observed that the poor people, having virtually no assets, worked hard, and in the absence of any major shocks, could somehow survive. Thus, if the poor villagers were to succeed, Yunus discovered that credit was the key to integrate marginal actors into the formal economy as full-fledged members and to enable them to engage in income-generating activities through self-employment. Yunus found that most villagers were unable to obtain credit at reasonable rates, so he began by lending them money from his own pocket, allowing the villagers to buy materials for projects like weaving bamboo stools and making pots.

This was the economic policy climate at the time Yunus walked into Jobra village and realized how little economic theories of development had helped to change the lives of poor villagers there. To his own great embarrassment, he was the one who was lecturing on these formal economic theories at the university right in front of Jobra village. After that experience he spent many days discussing with the villagers what their problems were. He was fully convinced that the chronic capital shortage was the single biggest constraint to the poor's struggle against poverty.

In a political climate deeply suspicious of market-led neo-classical economic strategies, Yunus' attempt to promote self-employment through delivering loans to the poor was met with a great deal of scepticism by politicians, academics, and the development community at large. The more radical among them saw Yunus' attempt as counter-revolutionary, which served only to perpetuate the fundamentally flawed capitalist system. Yunus had no time to take heed of such criticism. Yunus' thought consisted essentially of devising an effective institution to implement what poor people themselves identified as solutions to their problems. In the process, Yunus gained the confidence of the poor whom the urban-based, leftist intellectuals had largely failed to mobilize (Ito 1999, 12).

In 1976, Yunus first experimented with the microcredit concept in the form of an action research project, the GB Project, in the village of Jobra. This project was financially supported by a national commercial bank and supervised by students of the Economics Department of the Chittagong University. From 1976-78, in collaboration with various commercial banks, the project was introduced in different villages of the same region. The experiment helped Yunus to fine-tune the supervisory and timely recovery measures of his microlending project. It was soon expanded to include the district of Tangail (closer to the capital, Dhaka), and then to three more districts: Dhaka itself, Rangpur (in the north), and Patuakhali (in the south).

While the project was being expanded, it was operated through rural branches of nationalized commercial banks and the agricultural bank. Over time, however, these bureaucratic banks began to show signs of reluctance to process the large number of small loans associated with the project. Eventually Yunus decided that the future of his project depended on its becoming an independent bank. In this way the GB, an independent financial institution, came into being in October 1983 and in 1986 it became a private specialized bank, with 94 per cent of its stock owned by its own borrowers.

The GB was founded to deliver credit to the poor so that they could increase income and assets through self-employment. Yunus conceptualized credit as a powerful tool for creating entitlements to resources. The poor, who included a vast number of non-cultivating rural residents, especially women, are capable of getting out of poverty if given access to credit. Yunus realized the implications of microcredit for the first time in 1976 through his interaction with a poor woman in the village of Jobra who made bamboo stools for a living. The woman could not afford to buy bamboo herself and borrowed money from a trader on the condition that she must sell her product to the trader at a price he decided. Because the woman could not sell her finished product to anybody else, the trader took advantage of the situation and paid a price that barely covered the cost of the raw material. The socioeconomic environment of this woman led Yunus to think that if the woman had a small amount of working capital then she could work for herself, retaining the surplus now appropriated by the trader. All she needed was the *small loans* necessary for working capital.

To provide the effective and sustainable institutional mechanism to make this happen, Yunus introduced the five-member solidarity group arrangements. In these arrangements members of the same group would be held jointly liable if one of them defaults. They would be denied access to further loans as well. Hence members of the same group are supposed to take the responsibilities of screening new members, monitoring their behaviour, and enforcing repayment if they delay in paying the GB's instalments. This would transfer the transaction costs otherwise borne by the GB to the borrowers, while ensuring that only the entrepreneurial poor would participate in GB's membership.

Starting in 1974 with the disbursal of $30 in loans to a group of 42 basket weavers, the GB has established itself as an integrated community development organization that has disbursed over $5 billion in credit to more than 5.3 million clients in more than 57,790 of Bangladesh's 68,000 villages (Grameen Bank 2005). Drawing on lessons from informal financial institutions to lend exclusively to groups of poor households, the GB disburses non-collateralized credit to small groups of microentrepreneurs, mostly women, who are jointly responsible for repayment of the total group loan. Even with an interest rates of about 20 per cent, the loan recovery rate has consistently been above 98 per cent. Elsewhere, loan performance was something of a comedy. Despite their security requirements, the wall of collateral that poor people encountered-commercial banks in rural areas had repayment rates as low as 30 per cent, wherein for industrial development banks the figure was as low as 10 per cent (Bornstein 1997, 176-7).

Microfinance statistics are often calculated in idiosyncratic ways and are vulnerable to misinterpretation. The GB has, however, been relatively open with its data, and it provides a full set of accounts in its annual reports. The GB's rapid increase in scale between 1985 and 1996 has been phenomenal with the size of the average annual loan portfolio increasing from $10 million in 1985 to $271 million by 1996. Membership has expanded 12 times over the same period, reaching 2.06 million by 1996 (Morduch 1999, 1589). The membership has expanded more rapidly from 2.36 million in mid 2002 to 4 million in December 2004 (Rutherford 2005).

The Grameen has become a success story. It has grown from a one-man enterprise to an institution with branches almost all over Bangladesh. The Grameen is doing what it can to alleviate rural poverty. Its enormous popularity is tribute to its success in reaching the women of Bangladesh (Beltran 1997, 14-5). Comparing the GB approach with that of the Gandhian approach to development, Mascarenhas (1993, 475) observes,

> The initial success of the Grameen Bank has encouraged Yunus to advocate an indigenous model of development in which resources are invested in the rural economy, and from which basis the economy can then grow outwards. He believes that such a strategy will encourage development suited to local resources and capabilities and will reduce dependence on foreign capital and technology, which only produce luxury goods. In many ways his model of development resembles the Gandhian approach to development.

Moreover, much of the corruption that can be rampant in the underground economy of the informal sector is curbed by the microlending structure. In the GB, all transactions occur in the presence of group representatives and other colleagues. This transparency, coupled with an annual rotation of leadership positions at the centre, reduces the opportunities for abuse of power (Grameen Bank 1996, 2) Describing the GB as the most commercial bank in Bangladesh, Jackelen and Rhyne (1991, 9) note,

> While Grameen is a subsidised effort and therefore not *commercial*, it needs to be understood within the context of Bangladesh where institutional credit (granted on a secured basis) only achieves a 30 per cent recovery rate in rural areas and less than 10 per cent in urban areas. Grameen, lending smaller amounts on an unsecured basis, has consistently maintained recovery rates of 97 per cent. Thus, Grameen may be considered the least subsidised, as there is no subsidy greater than the failure to collect loans, and therefore the most commercial bank within the distorted banking environment of Bangladesh.

The success of the Grameen as a financial institution lies in its creation of a market niche. Its success as a poverty alleviation organization, on the other hand, is its outreach to women among the rural poor who constitute over 95 per cent of its membership. What has been difficult for many development finance institutions (DFIs) to accomplish for several decades with the support of government and various bilateral and multilateral agencies, has been accomplished by the GB in a decade (Grameen Bank 1994, 10-13). While demonstrating that tiny sums of money can help to alleviate rural poverty of landless people, the GB has contributed to 1 to 1.5 per cent of the total GDP of Bangladesh (Table 3.5).

**Table 3.5   Contribution of GB to GDP of Bangladesh
1994-1996 (Taka in million)**

Item	1994	1995	1996
Value added in Grameen Bank	1,890.7	2,181.9	2,750.8
Value added in linked sectors due to supply of inputs to Grameen Bank	75.9	88.9	97.2
Value added in linked sectors attributed to Grameen Bank loans	7,341.8	7,222.1	6,257.1
Capital supplying sectors	1,348.9	1,362.7	1,152.8
Input supplying sectors	5,992.9	5859.4	5,104.3
Wage payment from loans	547.8	553.9	468.9
Return on loan-financed activities at 40%	5,556.8	5,464.0	4,751.2
Total contribution of Grameen Bank to GDP	15,413.0	15,510.8	14,325.2
Total GDP	1,030,365	1,170,261	1,301,600
Percentage contribution of Grameen Bank to GDP	1.50%	1.33%	1.10%

Source: Grameen Bank. (1999)

This apparently remarkable success has led many to term the evolution of the GB as the *paradigm shift* in the theory of development. Proponents of the GB are of the view that the Grameen should be increasingly considered the rule rather than the exception as is evidenced by a number of other experiences in the developing world. It is a remarkable rural development experiment in a poverty-stricken country like Bangladesh (Jackelen and Rhyne 1991, 11). Grameen's success and its no-frills, no-charity, poor-people-are-entitled-to-a-fair-deal approach (Bornstein 1997, 177) has drawn worldwide attention and the Grameen model has been replicated both inside and outside Bangladesh. Because of Grameen's innovative programme design, outreach to women, and poverty reduction potential, development practitioners are increasingly interested in learning more about its potential, constraints and replicability.

A successful rural financial institution must overcome, as Hulme and Mosley (1996, 8) suggest, three particular problems with regard to credit to the poor: first, how to ensure that large numbers of poor borrowers can *access* loans; second, how to provide a mechanism for *screening out* bad borrowers in the absence of written records and business plans; third, how to give borrowers who cannot offer collateral an *incentive to repay* or, failing this, compel them to repay on time. Any organization seeking to provide financial services to significant numbers of poor people needs to adopt approaches that make it attractive for the poor to make savings and that make effective lending feasible (from both borrower and lender perspectives).

The GB, through its innovative credit delivery model has been highly successful in overcoming the aforementioned problems. It has solved the *access* problem directly by excluding borrowers, who are *too rich* to be eligible, the *screening* problem by abandoning direct interest rate subsidies and by providing loans for *fail-safe* projects and the problem of *collateral* by peer monitoring and peer pressure. If all else fails, the compulsory savings scheme developed by the GB will partially insure the lender against default.

It is inconceivable that anyone writing on microcredit will not discuss the role of the GB of Bangladesh. Morduch (1999) among others, has given a pivotal place to the GB. Though the GB remains sceptical of the role of general economics taught in universities in terms of alleviating poverty, its model is based on standard economic theory. As shown by the Baker-Hopkin model of credit, which describes the relationship between equity capital and credit, as long as the return on assets was larger than the interest paid on loans, credit would increase the income of the household that received the loans. The larger the ratio of loan to capital, the higher would be the growth of household income. Under normal circumstances, because of large marginal propensity to consume and excessive pressure of poverty, it was extremely difficult for the poor to accumulate savings. However, if the credit programme could be designed in such a way that the loan and interest were recovered in small instalments, over a longer period of time, the loan might force compulsory regular savings of small amounts. Despite being more inclusive, the GB is more or less based on the Baker-Hopkin economic model of credit.

Moreover, the GB concept also is in agreement with a sound banking principle, a basic economic premise, theory of prices, theory of risk, theory of innovation, and theory of poverty.

Banking Principle

Banks make profits by lending at higher rates of interest than the borrowing and deposit rates. In free markets, the demand for and supply of funds will determine rates of interest. When a government imposes price restrictions on banks, such as requiring them to advance credit at below-market rates of interest, the banks' capacity and incentive to operate as a sustainable business is compromised. The GB started and has remained as a private bank and has fortunately not been subjected to the country's populist policies. As a private bank, it was able to follow the pricing rule by charging real rates of interest higher than the open-market real rate of interest. Had the GB been required to advance credit at below-market rates of interest, the GB probably would not have become a pioneer of microcredit, as it is today.

Basic Economic Premise

Intuitively, the GB believed that the poor are basically honest in repaying their loans irrespective of collateral. At the same time the GB must have also assumed at least implicitly that the poor, too, would work hard to maximize their incomes to repay their loans as well as improving their poverty situation. The fact that over 98 per cent of them could repay their loans is evidence confirming that behaviour.

Theory of Prices

A basic economic principle of a rational entrepreneur is to raise the value of his/her product above the cost of production. In a situation where the value of production is lower than the cost of production, producer subsidies are a way of accepting such lower values. It is therefore not surprising that the South Asian countries, which have used subsidies extensively to alleviate poverty, are still among the poorest in the world. The GB, while still dependent on donor subsidies, is increasingly less so as evidenced by its declining SDI. It has been charging real rate of interest higher than the open-market real rate of interest, though its rate is only a fraction of the moneylender's rate. Its clients must produce a value that covers the cost of credit, in addition to making their labour more productive to alleviate poverty. Thus, the GB has incorporated the pricing principle of economic growth.

Theory of Poverty

Contrary to the general impression, subsidies in the form of lower prices, or income transfers rarely reduce poverty. Rather they sustain poverty and may perpetuate it. They introduce dependency. Instead of augmenting their income-generating capacities, subsidies put the recipients on crutches. The South Asian advocates of subsidies to the poor have confused egalitarianism with poverty reduction.

Despite the inflow of billions of dollars of foreign aid the poverty situation of Bangladesh has not improved significantly. The GB thinks that an effective long-term remedy against poverty is to ensure the access of the poor to financial resources. The GB's policy in ensuring access of the poor to financial services probably relates to the Chinese proverb which states; *To a hungry man don't give your fish-give a fishing rod*. The ideas behind the birth of the GB, at least on the basis of its experiences, if not for sheer logic, provide some scope for a well-founded holistic approach to emerge[4].

The GB, though a bank *par excellence*, has incorporated most of the user-friendly principles of the informal finance, and its activities resemble, as noted, more the voluntary NGOs than the public sector enterprises.

The Grameen Bank, Moneylenders, and NGOs

From the user's point of view what the GB does is similar to the moneylender. Like the moneylender, the GB offers a lump sum, which is recovered in a series of fifty

---

4   Those supporting the view of Yunus treat Muhammad Yunus as an institution and his contribution as a paradigm shift in the flawed neo-classical theories of economics. Terming the ideas of Yunus, as *yunusonomics*, they observe that there are at least six areas, which form the basis of Yunusonomics. These are: recognition of the potential of self-employment; the human claim to entrepreneurship; credit as a human right; the role of women in business; social-consciousness driven enterprise; and institutional innovation. For a critical analysis on *Yunusonomics* see (*The Daily Star*, August 27, 1998).

weekly payments over one year. Like the moneylender, the GB takes interest, but instead of deducting it at the time the loan is given, the GB takes it in small easy-to-find instalments along with the repayments. As with the moneylender, most clients immediately embark on a fresh cycle as soon as one cycle is complete.

The GB, to use the term of Rutherford (1999, 52), *a better kind of moneylender*, differs from the traditional moneylenders in several respects. Unlike the moneylender the GB does accept savings deposits in small regular fixed weekly instalments from its members.

The main differences lie in the use of group-guarantees, the GB insists that the group members cross-guarantee each other's loans. Moneylenders rarely use guarantees of any sort, let alone peer group guarantees, preferring to rely for good repayment on their personal knowledge of the client, on the mechanism of small-but-frequent instalments, and the client's dependence on them for future loans. The GB's rate of interest charges on advances is much less than charged by the average moneylenders. There has always been public concern at the antics of the crueller moneylenders (one may think of Shylock in Shakespeare's play, *The Merchant of Venice*). Britain's colonial administrators regularly fretted about moneylenders and in many colonies introduced legislation against *usury* (exploitative moneylending).

The main problem poor people face with moneylenders is often the price and availability of loans-the poor find it hard to persuade someone to give them an advance. This is where the GB really scores, because once a client is a *member* of a group, he/she is guaranteed access to a series of advances, as long as he/she repays on time and his/her fellow-members do the same. Moreover, the GB, unlike most moneylenders, tends to raise the value of the loan after each cycle. To secure this rare right, the GB clients, however, have to struggle, sometimes at considerable cost, to maintain their repayments and retain their right to borrow.

Finally, the GB differs from the traditional moneylender in being a formal organization with a massive outreach-around five million clients in 2005. There is no mystery about why the GB has been able to scale-up so much faster. Since the GB controls all the management of the financial service process, it can reap the benefits of scale if it makes its management efficient. It does not have to wait around while a group of illiterate village women slowly learn the basic skills of enterprise management. This view of the GB as a benevolent alternative to the moneylender has been helped by the political context in which the GB's reputation grew.

As criticisms of the state's role in the rural financial markets (RFMs) gained momentum in the 1980s, the Bangladesh government started reducing its interventions in these markets by easing interest rate regulation and withdrawing subsidies. Simultaneously, it started to delegate the job of poverty reduction to the non-state sector comprised mainly of NGOs.

The NGOs' efforts were at first concentrated on the *conscientization* of the rural poor so that they could organize themselves to fight against the exploitation of big landlords. However, they were soon confronted with the problem that their programme components were not attractive enough to sustain the interest of the rural poor. The attention of the poor was instead increasingly captured by the credit services offered by the GB which was by then operating widely across the country. Most of the NGOs in Bangladesh eventually came to the point where, whether they liked it or not, they could no longer ignore the pressing demand for credit among the rural poor. As a result, these NGOs started trying to integrate their rural development programmes with the GB-style credit services. This in turn enhanced the image of the GB as a model for NGOs trying to combine an effective lending mechanism with the social objective of poverty alleviation. On top of this, the GB's emphasis on lending to women to help make development more effective and efficient coincided with the international development discourse that increasingly saw productivity of women as one of its top priorities.

This is the context in which the GB ushered in the new era of donor agencies' enthusiastic support for microcredit schemes for poor women all around the developing world. And this is the context, too, in which an effective group-based lending mechanism and a commitment to poverty alleviation have come to be seen to work together in harmony within the GB and similar microcredit programmes.

Compared to other MFIs worldwide, the GB's financial performance was deemed good in spite of its dependence on subsidies[5]. The GB's outreach to the poor is satisfactory, given the smallness of the loan size compared internationally. Despite this, the exclusion of the poorest from programme membership is a rising concern among the practitioners and researchers alike (Ito 1999, 56). Opinions about the GB's impact on poverty reduction are also mixed both at the household level and at the macroeconomic level.

The GB's credit-alone approach even in the best of circumstances helps fund self-employment activities that most often supplement income for borrowers rather than drive fundamental shifts in employment patterns. It rarely generates new jobs for others. The best evidence to date suggests that making a real dent in poverty rates will require increasing overall levels of economic growth and employment generation. Microfinance may be able to help some households take advantage of those processes by establishing a partnership with local government and other public authorities, but the performance of the GB on this front is not encouraging either.

Moreover, the Grameen has stopped growing, and many of its existing branches are suffering lower repayment rates than they have been used to, as clients find that loan sizes that grow year-by-year finally turn out to be more expensive than they can handle out of weekly income (Getibug et al. 1997, 63). Donors are also having second thoughts with regard to the potential of *credit-alone* approach in terms of alleviating poverty. Microcredit represents an instructive case of a first-generation poverty alleviation programme that is increasingly being confronted with second-generation problems (Sen 1998, 15).

---

5   The SDI summarises the subsidy data by yielding an estimate of the percentage increase in the interest rate required in order for an MFI to operate without subsidies of any kind (Yaron 1992). The result for 1985-96 indicates that in the early 1990s GB would have had to increase nominal interest rates on its general loan product from 20 per cent to above 50 per cent (Morduch 1999, 1591).

The GB, a claimant of a model of poverty alleviation through its group-based credit delivery model, has perhaps been successful in achieving an excellent recovery rate of its uncollateralised loans. Be that is it may, even if the GB becomes a model, its existing policies will help at best to reduce poverty marginally, but definitely not remove poverty. Nevertheless, the performance of the GB, although not highly impressive, it is a step forward in reaching the poor (if not the poorest) rural women in Bangladesh, who have historically been excluded from all formal banking institutions. Even if the GB cannot effectively alleviate all forms of discrimination against women, it may lay the groundwork for a change in an institutionally biased, relatively stagnant, poor socioeconomic environment.

Moreover, even if the GB fails to alleviate poverty significantly, it can be argued that the poverty situation of those borrowers who could not improve their situation could have worsened had it not been for their participation. The limitations of Grameen credit in alleviating rural poverty does not imply that microcredit should not be seen as a major antipoverty tool. The idea is to point out that microcredit of the type we have seen in the past cannot significantly solve the problem of poverty today unless there are other interventions.

Despite the limitations, targeted credit programmes of the GB show how one good idea in the right place in the right time can spark off a whole new industry. A massive expansion of microcredit took place over the past decade, encompassing about half of the target group households in rural areas of Bangladesh. Indeed, the presence of NGOs in rural Bangladesh has become a common phenomenon so much so that it is now difficult to find villages without a NGO presence. Some of the large NGOs are in the nature of corporate entities, employing under its auspices a quite large number of staff, often exceeding 12,000 people.

Even if the current enthusiasm about the success of GB microfinance ebbs, it has demonstrated the importance of thinking creatively about mechanism design, and it is forcing economists to rethink much perceived wisdom about the nature of poverty, gender, markets, and institutional innovation. In the end, this may prove to be the most important legacy of the microfinance movement.

The enabling Bangladeshi environment has helped the uninterrupted growth of microfinance movement. Despite political instability, Bangladesh has not proved a hostile environment for MFIs. At the macroeconomic level there has been no hyper inflation and the government has also never legislated against NGO microfinance.

The invisibility of the NGO-MFI sector to the formal regulators has, so far, largely worked to their advantage. It has allowed them to charge high rates of interest on loans, a factor that has been crucial to the growth of the bigger MFIs, and has allowed them to set their own rules.

Although politicians could not resist promising loan forgiveness in the run-up to elections, the major MFIs have been able to present their programmes to the public as a special sector to which such loan forgiveness does not apply. There have of course been enemies within; for example, some fundamentalist groups have targeted MFI groups and placed anti-MFI stories in the local press, but the leaders of big MFIs are not without their own power and influence, and little lasting damage has been done.

In a country where formal employment opportunities are scarce, organizations with thousands of jobs at their disposal are important.

However, the decade of the nineties is fast accumulating a large body of *anecdotal evidence* on the widening gaps between the intent and content of many NGO programmes, which cannot be ignored any more (Sen 1998, 14). There have already been several instances of simply incompetent MFIs going out of business at the expense of poor rural savers. The microfinance regulation in the country is now underway, which will provide a legal basis and streamline the current and future MFI activities (Rahman 2001).

The development of a healthy financial sector appears to be far more difficult than it was thought to be two decades ago (Jong and Kleiterp 1991, 28). The task is even more complex in a country like Bangladesh where more than 80 per cent of the rural population is *unbanked*. Financial liberalization will help little, if any, to develop the rural financial sector in a country where the financial density is the lowest in the world, and where there is the presence of a largely heterogeneous informal financial sector with an anti-poor colonial institutional set-up. While some policy reforms have begun to occur, it may take decades perhaps before a vibrant and rational financial sector emerges in Bangladesh capable of reaching the poorest of the poor.

At the end of the day it may be said that the Bangladesh economy seems to be at a crossroads. If the limited financial sector reforms already initiated can be sustained; if provision for deliberate, flexible, client-responsive, and quality financial services are further reinforced; if the efficiency of the rural poor, especially women can be enhanced; if the economic, political, and social institutions can be reformed to integrate the tiny efforts of MFIs; and if the broad consensus that exists in favour of the potential of microfinance in alleviating poverty, then the economy has a fairly bright future. However, if the present consensus in favour of reforms, including financial sector reforms, flounders; if the vast majority of the poor remain excluded from quality financial services; if the productivity of the poor is not enhanced as it is today, then alleviation of poverty will not only be difficult but may suffer an irreversible setback. In this particular sense, the present microfinance movement in Bangladesh may lead either to a virtuous circle of growth in incomes of the poor or to a vicious cycle of poverty.

Whatever happens, the world will not forget that it was in Bangladesh where it was first proved that an institution lending exclusively to the poor could become a large, successful and near-self-sufficient financial organization.

Summary and Conclusions

The financial structure of Bangladesh is characterized by the co-existence of a limited formal sector and a vast informal one. In Bangladesh, nationalized and private commercial banks dominate the financial system. The activities of the nationalized commercial banks have come to be viewed as quasi-government department rather than independent financial institutions. This nationalized banking system is characterized by inefficiency, mismanagement, corruption, and loan defaults.

There is agreement that the traditional formal sector institutions and markets alone cannot achieve a sustainable rural financial system. However, it is also recognized that the informal financial sector, despite its popularity among the rural poor, cannot be left to its own devices.

Neither the commercial formal finance, which targets the rich and does not reach the poor, nor the informal finance with its usurious interest rates and limited jurisdiction, is suitable for sustainable poverty alleviation. Incorporating the advantages of both formal and informal finance through a microfinance institution has the potential of being effective and efficient for poverty alleviation on a sustainable basis. Informal finance has a lot to teach microfinance. Knowledge of the virtues of informal finance, however, does not imply knowledge of how to acquire those virtues. Policy advice must not only instruct microfinance organizations to imitate informal finance, but it must also say how to do so. Moreover, there is increasing recognition that microfinance programmes with a *credit-plus* or *integrated* approach including voluntary savings and other client-responsive and flexible financial services are more effective than programmes with a *credit alone* or *minimalist* approach.

The success of the GB as a financial institution lies in its creation of a market niche. Its success as a poverty alleviation organization is its outreach to poor rural women who make up over 95 per cent of its membership. What has been difficult for many DFIs to accomplish for several decades with government support and various bilateral and multilateral agencies, has been accomplished by the GB in a decade.

However, there are increasing concerns about the GB's performance. The deliberate exclusion of the poorest from programme membership is a rising concern among the practitioners and the researchers alike. Opinions about the GB's impact on poverty reduction are also mixed both at the household and the macroeconomic level. Moreover, the GB's credit alone approach, without any partnership with local government and other public authorities, supplements income for self-employed borrowers but does not assist in making fundamental shifts in employment patterns. It rarely generates new jobs for others.

Appendix 3A   Distinction between Microfinance and Traditional Banking

- While the Microfinance institutions don't require any start-up (paid-up) capital, the traditional banks require.
- Microfinance institutions, in most cases, are owned by the clients, the traditional banks are owned by the governments and other investors.
- Microfinance primarily deals with the RNA, traditional banks prefer farm and industrial sectors.
- Microfinance is based on the Asian approach of trust and confidence, the Western-style traditional finance is based on legal contracts.
- Microfinance deals with rural, poor and illiterate clients, traditional finance

prefers urban, rich and literate borrowers.

- Microfinance deals with credit and savings services, traditional finance, dealing with credit, does not prefer savings services.
- Microfinance insists that the bank should go to the people, while the traditional finance insists that the people should come to the bank.
- Microfinance, dealing with both financial and non-financial services, attempts to achieve the twin goals of poverty alleviation and commercial viability, the traditional finance, on the other hand, does not prefer non-financial services to undertake, deals only with commercial viability.
- Microfinance sees social development inextricably linked to economic development and as part of its own interest as a bank. Improved nutritional and health status for example, is a sound banking investment. It correlates with increased productivity and creativity which, in turn, must influence loan turnover and stability. Formal banks find it unacceptable.
- Microfinance emphasises motivating clients directly under its supervision to perform better: bank workers to clients; branch managers to bank workers etc. Traditional bank does not think it necessary to undertake such activities.
- Microfinance experience indicates that economists should concentrate more on microeconomics than on macroeconomics, usually emphasised by traditional banks.
- Microfinance believes that their business is with its clients, not with paper. Formal bank, under traditional finance, assumes that every client is a crook. It ties the crook client with all kinds of papers.
- Microfinance believes in decentralisation and participation in management. Formal banks follow the centralised top-down management process.
- Formal banks tend to view their functions as one of *inspection and control*, while the Microfinance views them as *supportive and co-operative*.
- Formal banks ask clients to pay back at the end of a long period i.e., 6 months or even longer, while the Microfinance clients pay back their loans in weekly instalments.
- More importantly, the traditional banks prefer large manufacturing and agricultural sectors to finance, whereas, Microfinance predominantly support small manufacturing and nonfarm sectors.

Source: Heavily drawn from Rock and Otero eds. (1997), p. 20

Chapter 4

Economic Impact of Grameen Microcredit

Introduction

In chapter three we examined the dual financial structure (coexistence of formal and informal sectors) in Bangladesh, wherein we observed that a sustainable rural financial system cannot be achieved either by the traditional formal financial sector alone, or by the informal financial sector, despite its ubiquity and popularity amongst the rural poor. The failures of both the formal and informal sectors to meet the growing financial needs of the rural poor, majority of whom, are women, led to the creation of the GB and many other MFIs.

The ultimate test of any institution is not whether it merely exists or sustains itself, but whether it manages to do something useful for its members. The GB's ultimate achievements must be measured in terms of the nature and extent of the benefits, especially economic benefits that its members enjoy.

The success of the GB, as such, depends on whether participation of the poor does in fact reduce poverty in terms of raising the income of its members and ultimately improving the levels of their standard of living.

This chapter begins with the approach and methodology used in the empirical study conducted on the GB. This is followed by a critical evaluation of the GB's impact in raising the economic situation of its members. This analysis looks into the economic impact of the GB's microcredit upon the members in terms of income, employment, capital accumulation, productivity, and impact in the rural credit market. The importance of institutional innovations of the GB in terms of ensuring the access of the rural poor to the formal sources of finance and the lessons for the rural financial theory are also highlighted here. Based on the extent of the economic benefits the GB members enjoy, the next chapter, chapter 5, finally attempts to assess the GB impact on poverty alleviation.

Approach and Methodology

Reasons for Impact Study

The microfinance movement was born of the ideal to create new banks with the mission of poverty alleviation. Completing impact evaluations is an important way to determine if the mission of poverty alleviation is being achieved. There is no study yet that has achieved wide consensus as to its reliability; and this reflects the inherent difficulty in evaluating programmes in which participation is voluntary and different clients use the services with varying degrees of intensity. While some observers have despaired at the impossibility of generating reliable evaluations, their despair is, as Aghion and Morduch (2005, 223) think, misplaced and too pessimistic. It is true that rigorous statistical evaluations are seldom easy. Still, a set of solid impact evaluations are within reach.

The measurement of impact is particularly relevant for poverty alleviation programmes. It is important to identify the range of factors which contribute to the creation of poverty, and which must therefore be addressed to achieve sustainable solutions to poverty. In the poverty alleviation policy framework, especially when the issue is one of allocating scarce public resources among different poverty alleviation strategies, policymakers, NGOs, and donors ask how credit programmes affect broader social goals. Goals such as income generation, attainment of food security, nutritional adequacy and enhancement of skills and sometimes even broader goals, such as the empowerment of women or the quality of the environment.

In recent years, donors are becoming more concerned about the quality of their interventions, and with the experience they have gained on the limits and possible negative effects of microfinance, the need for impact assessment has arisen. Reliable impact assessments can provide both donors and practitioners with evidence that interventions have a positive effect and that financial support is justified. At the same time, practitioners can assess to what degree, under what conditions, and through which mechanisms they can reach the poor. Impact assessment can also help to improve programme performance through a better understanding of clients' specific needs.

Although it is pointless to argue that financial constraints do not matter in poverty alleviation, it would be equally wrong to ascribe to the theories that "only credit matters, or credit is seen as a panacea, or credit is a magic skyhook to pluck poverty from the earth". The realistic assumption is that credit needs to be delivered along with other services to alleviate poverty within a reasonable time frame. The relevant question in the poverty alleviation debate is not so much whether financial constraints matter or not, but the relative importance to be given to credit programmes vis-à-vis alternative poverty alleviation programmes. These could include programmes relating to investments in infrastructure, health, education, and various kinds of services related to a social safety net.

The monetary value of marginal benefits must be at least as high as the price paid for the service. In this sense, the general health, profitability, and dynamism of a microfinance organization are important indicators of its significant impact because they attest to the success of client's projects: the returns accruing to the household from whatever is financed by loans are high enough to pay for services received in full.

Issues in Impact Studies

In making an impact assessment or evaluation, a number of methodological issues need clarification. A narrow view of impact assessment is to assess the impact with reference to the stated objectives of a project intervention. However, a project may have unintended impacts-either positive or negative-not foreseen by a project intervention. A broader view, therefore, is also to take note of those unintended impacts or changes in an impact evaluation. This study used the broader approach to assess the GB impact on poverty alleviation. This broader approach encompasses not only the impact on GB clients, but also unintended impacts and changes brought about among the non-GB members.

Microfinance may affect household outcomes through a variety of channels. It may make households wealthier, yielding an *income effect* that should push up total consumption levels, and holding all other constant, increase the demand for children, health, children's education, and leisure. But running microenterprises may also take time, yielding *substitution effect* that may counterbalance the effects of increased income. With increased female employment, for example, time spent raising children may become costlier in terms of forgone income, pushing fertility rates down. Only evaluating impacts on business profits may thus miss out other important changes within the household (Aghion and Morduch 2005, 201-2)

Another issue in impact study is to attempt to prove *causality versus plausibility.* The scientific method of impact assessment attempts to ensure that effect can be attributed to causes through experimentation. A particular stimulus to a particular object in a rigorously controlled environment is judged to be the cause of the observed effect. This relatively complex approach focuses on ensuring high levels of reliability with regard to the attribution of causality and has an exclusively "proving" orientation. A much wider set of income and asset variables will be measured and the focus will be on high precision through interval measurements. A set of related studies on institutional performance would be conducted, but the heart of the study would be the econometric and statistical analysis of survey findings.

The mis-specification of underlying causal relationships arises most commonly because of the assumption that causality is a one-way process. This may be a reasonable assumption in physical sciences. This experimental approach is virtually infeasible in the social sciences, because of its enormous demands for data on other causal factors and its assumptions. For human activity it is commonly invalid, as causation may also run from impact back to intervention. Mosley (199, 76) illustrates this with the example of a programme whose field staff put pressure on a borrower to repay her loan; this may succeed in the short-term but may induce the borrower to sell assets (machinery, land) which reduce the probability of repayment in the longer-term. Such reverse causation need not necessarily be negative, and from the perspective of more process- oriented analytical frameworks, is essential if programmes are to continually learn from their experience and improve (rather than prove) their impact.

Such problems can be overcome by the adoption of models that conceptualize causation as a two-way process, the use of two-stage least squares technique and multiple regression analysis. Such an approach is enormously demanding in terms of data requirements, technical expertise and costs. It will only be feasible on very rare occasions (for example, see Khandker 1996). For most researchers adopting this scientific method, reverse causality is a problem to be coped with rather than overcome. The main means of dealing with it are (i) tracing dropouts from both the treated and control groups; (ii) conducting impact studies on relatively mature programmes; (iii) interim impact monitoring activities to gather qualitative information about the complexity of causality; and (iv) retrospective in-depth interviews with clients (ibid, 6).

A second approach is the control group method which has been widely used. This requires a before and after comparison of a population that received a specific treatment, and an identical population (or as near as possible) that did not receive the treatment. While this idea is elegantly simple a number of biases like sample selection bias may befall its user. In practice, no two households are identical.

Selection bias may occur because of: (i) *programme placement bias*: difficulties in finding a location at which the control group's economic, physical and social environment matches that of the treatment groups. If programmes tend to be placed in locations that have a better infrastructure, not accounting for this fact will lead to overestimation of benefits and the opposite will occur if they are placed in communities with a worse infrastructure. Sharma and Zeller (1999) examined the way in which three NGOs in Bangladesh place their services. The results indicated that, although the placement of branches of NGO institutions is tied to poverty, NGO services are geared more toward poor pockets of relatively well-developed areas rather than toward servicing the poor in remoter, less developed areas. (ii) *selection bias*: factors such as entrepreneurship, social skills, management abilities, and other abilities make some households more productive than others but cannot be fully observed or adequately measured. These same factors also affect the household's decision to participate in credit programmes. At a household level, members of the household self-select the person to participate in the credit programme. The impact will be different depending on whether a male or a female member participates in the credit programme. In many case, benefits attributed to credit programmes will be overestimated if the non-observable attributes are not accounted for. As reported in Morduch (1998), selection bias can lead to overestimation of benefits by as much as 100 per cent. It could also lead to underestimation of benefits in cases where programmes take special care to select clients who have some inherent but unmeasurable weaknesses; (iii) receiving any form of intervention may result in a short-term positive response from the treatment group (the Hawthorne effect); (iv) the control group becoming contaminated by contact with the treatment group; and (v) the fungibility of the treatment (for example, when a loan is transferred from a borrower to someone else).

Problems (i) and (iv) can be tackled by more careful selection of the control groups and ensuring that the control group is located far away from the treatment group. Problems (ii) and (iii) are more intractable, but in many cases they can be tackled by using programme-accepted *clients-to-be*, who have not yet received microfinance services, as the control group (Hulme and Mosley 1996, chapter 4).

Another issue related to impact assessment is the *dilemma of attribution*. In other words, how can the observed changes or impacts be attributed to the given project intervention. The changes or impacts after a project intervention may have been influenced by other factors, or some other projects, unrelated to the particular project being evaluated. In this situation attributing an observed change or impact to the project being evaluated becomes difficult.

This problem of attribution is compounded further in the case of Grameen project, which is now nearly three decades old, since initial beneficiaries may be difficult to trace, impacts may have dissipated, a lot of changes may have taken place in the lives of the beneficiaries and the villages which had benefited from the GB project. Establishing a cause-effect relationship in these circumstances is a Herculean task. There is indeed no specific formula to solve this problem, and one needs to exercise one's value judgment to attribute to the observed changes or impacts to a given project intervention.

Still another issue is the problem of *fungibility*. The poor have very dynamic financial lives. An overwhelming majority of the poor engage in some type of financial transactions. The fungibility of loans implies that loan demand and use are driven by the overall budgetary needs of the households. It is difficult and sometimes even misleading to undertake impact studies on the basis of the expressed demand of the microfinance clients. It is difficult to estimate the income of a female member separately from the household in which she belongs particularly when she is self-employed. Due to fungibility of money, the resources of the household may be jointly pooled for the activity pursued by a female member and she may also help male members in other income earning activities of the household.

Fungibility can be seen as an intractable problem, as no study has successfully controlled for the fungibility of resources between the household and the assisted enterprise (Gaile and Foster 1994, 24). Using case study materials to cross-check actual loan use against intended loan use and thus estimating *leakage* is one possible approach to controlling for fungibility (Mosley 1997). However, for all studies except those that focus exclusively on *the enterprise*, then a concern about fungibility may be irrelevant. For studies looking at the household, the community or the household economic portfolio fungibility is not a problem for the assessor.

But Aghion and Morduch (2005, 223), however, consider fungibility as a minor limitation to trace the impact of a particular loan to a particular change in enterprise profits. Even if a given loan cannot be attached to a given change in profit, it is still possible to evaluate how profits change with capital (for example, to measure the marginal return to capital) and how borrowing affects household-level variables such as income, consumption, health, and schooling.

Besides the problem of *fungibility* of money, which does not ensure control of loan use, it is really difficult to isolate the effect of credit from other variables, such as group membership or training. Methods for measuring changes in household income rely on respondent's recall, which may be weak in reporting on an activity stretched over a year or two. This is especially the case where numerical skills are low and records are not maintained. Translated into quantitative data it takes on a potentially misleading degree of precision and authority. It is important to get details right, and that, for analytical purposes, having one very reliable evaluation is more valuable than having one hundred flawed evaluations.

Measuring asset accumulation at the household level is an approach that is also increasingly recommended as a focus of impact study, especially as a way to get around the inherent difficulties in measuring income changes accurately. The income level of the household can be assessed by attaching a current monetary value to assets and liabilities. The biggest quantitative problem, however, in such an approach involves depreciating and valuing physical assets.

Poverty line based on household expenditure is a widely accepted measure of poverty-as far as economic dimension is concerned. Expenditure is a good proxy of income. The standard practice is to record food expenditures using a recall period of one week, and to collect information on various nonfood expenditures using a combination of monthly or yearly recall periods.

Several studies on rural poverty in Bangladesh used a consumption bundle providing an intake of 2,112 calories and 58 grams of protein as the norm, which by and large conforms to the minimum diet recommended by the Food and Agriculture Organisation of the United Nations (ILO 1986, 59). This is the standard practice in the Bangladesh development literature (Khandker and Chowdhury 1996, 12), which has also been accepted by the Planning Commission of the Government of Bangladesh. We use this norm to identifying the extent of poverty across different groups of population in the sample areas. Given average village-level prices, the level of consumption that qualified as *moderate poverty* was fixed at Taka 6, 250 per person per year, while the level of consumption that determined *extreme poverty* was Taka 5, 312 per person per year[1], which would satisfy 85 per cent of the required calorie and protein needs. The figures include a 30 per cent provision of the cost of non-food items.

Although this approach has been criticized as it is *undesirably simplified, reductionist, universal, standardized, quantified, and bias to the measurable*, it has considerable strengths in terms of permitting quantitative comparisons and the analysis of changes in the access of different people to their most pressing material needs (Hulme and Mosley 1996, 105).

The social welfare indicators that became popular in the early 1980s, (education, access to health services, nutritional levels) have recently been extended into the impact assessment tool to assess whether microfinance can promote such indicators.

---

1   This almost conforms to the figures of Taka 5,270 and Taka 3,330 per person per year for moderate and extreme poor respectively. These figures were used by Khandker and Chowdhury (1996) while evaluating the impact of targeted credit programmes in Bangladesh. If the figures are adjusted in terms of inflation, it might cluster around the figures used in the present study. See Khandker and Chowdhury, (1996), p. 12.

Besides assessing the impact on poverty, the study also undertook consideration of some social welfare indicators, in which the GB women clients fared well vis-à-vis their counterparts in project and control villages.

The study, undertaken from August 1998 through February 1999, is based on a sample survey of 300 households, located in three different regions of Bangladesh. As far as the field investigation is concerned, the selection of study area is very important. A schedule was worked out with the GB to choose 6 different project areas in three different zones, taking into consideration three different stages in the GB's development. The zones selected were: Tangail; Comilla; and Bogra. Tangail is the oldest zone and it has the highest number of profitable branches. Comilla is comparatively a new zone experiencing growth and with new branches opening. Bogra zone has been operational for some years and has branches moving toward the stage of profitable branches. Logistically, the three zones make sense.

Besides using individual interview as the main method of collecting data, the survey took into consideration the participatory group discussion and key informants' interviews as well. Data were collected through a detailed structured questionnaire. The open-ended method was preferred over other methods (for example, discrete choice method) because of its inherent advantages such as this method would give a crystal picture of the day to day harsh realities of poor people's lives. Even though poor households in developing countries consume a small number of goods, accuracy in reporting is a valid concern given the long recall periods. Even if consumption items can be accurately recalled, ways have to found to value home-produced foods when market prices are lacking; irregular weights and measures cause problems in the computation of quantities; and information on a number of high-value items is likely to be seriously deficient. To minimize the scale of these problems the recall period of the study was kept minimum i.e., 1997-98, and extensive training was imparted to the research assistants. Moreover, multiple household visits, and cataloging of informal weights and measures were undertaken to minimize such problems.

Questionnaire: The survey was carried out by three experienced research assistants, one each in three different zones. All of them had prior experience in interviewing and the objective of the study had been explained to them. After the first 50 interviews were completed, all the questionnaires were examined and the research assistants informed of any mistakes that had occurred. The questionnaires were protested twice, changed and simplified. Care was taken to ensure that there was proper responses form the households selected for the interview. When the final questionnaire were handed in, less than 1 per cent of questions showed indications of having been improperly filled in. Data collected were analysed in terms of the objectives set for the study.

The social welfare indicators that became popular in the early 1980s (education, access to health services, nutritional levels), have recently been extended into the impact assessment tool to assess whether microfinance can promote such indicators. Besides assessing the impact on poverty, the study also considered some social welfare indicators, in which the GB women clients fared well vis-à-vis their counterparts in project and control villages.

In the absence of comparable benchmark data, the impact of the GB's operation on income and poverty had to be estimated using a *before* and *after* approach. This conventional approach relies on quantitative data and structured interviews and is favoured by economists and project analysts. The alternative approach usually favoured by sociologists and anthropologists is to adopt a *Participatory-based approach* or *Participatory Rapid Appraisal* (PRA) techniques to evaluate a project. Both these approaches have their advantages and disadvantages. While the former may be time consuming and requires more resources in terms of time and budget, it relies on solid quantitative data, whereas the latter though less time consuming and resources relies largely on qualitative data and impressionistic accounts. The present study relied more on the former approach in assessing the GB impact on rural poverty.

The survey collected information from households in six project villages covered by the GB and six control villages outside the GB's area of operation. The sample households were classified into four groups: (1) GB-members in project villages; (2) non-participating households within the target groups of the GB project villages; (3) target-group households in the control villages; and (4) nontarget- group households (those who own 0.5 acre or more) in both project and control villages. A total of 300 GB borrowers, 50 each from 6 project villages and 30 non-members, 5 each from the same project villages, were randomly selected for interviews. Another 30 non-members, 5 each from 6 different control villages (where the GB has no credit operation) were interviewed to measure the extent of poverty in the absence of the GB. The selection of the control villages was more or less purposive, keeping in mind similarities of land distribution and occupational structure between the project and control villages. Despite all these, this methodology is still not completely free from criticisms[2].

To assess the impact of the GB's credit on the economic condition of the borrowers' households, a census on land ownership and occupation was undertaken in the project areas earmarked for the field survey. The households were then randomly stratified into four land-ownership groups (large, medium, small, and marginal/ landless) and two occupation groups (farm and non-farm) within each land-ownership group. A proportional random sample was then drawn from each of the eight strata to get 50 sample households from each village. They were interviewed for an indepth survey to collect information on employment, assets, income, expenditure, investment, and sources of credit to finance their working capital.

---

2   The drawback of the control-group approach is that, unlike regression analysis, it cannot tell us the quantitative impact of project-in relation to non-project influences; on the other hand, it is free of biases associated with regression analysis in those cases where the standard assumptions of the normal linear regression model (normally distributed disturbances, constant variance of the error term and so on) do not hold.

Methods and Tools

1. Structured interviews with the GB members in GB project villages and comparable non-members in villages without GB branches,
2. Indepth interviews with the group and centre leaders,
3. Focused group discussions, d) Key informant interviews (village leader, teacher, village doctor),
4. Indepth interviews with the GB officials,
5. Documentary study (GB project documents, GB Annual Reports, Research Reports),
6. Analysis of project data and secondary data, and
7. Compilation and analysis of materials and secondary data.

Study Objectives

The main objectives of the study are:

1. To assess the changes in incomes of the GB members and
2. In the process explore the potential and limitations of the GB microcredit programme in significantly alleviating poverty of its clients.

The GB's Impact on the Level of Income of its Members

The primary process by which financial services are envisaged as reducing poverty is through the provision of income- generating loans. According to Muhammad Yunus, founder and Managing Director of the GB, credit provision can create a virtuous circle: *Low income, credit, investment, more income, more credit, more investment, more income.* As analysed below, this notion of continued growth in income, production, credit and investment captures part, not all, of the experience of poor households. The heterogeneity of poverty and as such the differing abilities of borrowers, their social positions and initial economic endowments ensure that no simple model can explain its straightforward solution. This is evidenced in the field survey conducted to evaluate the GB's microcredit programmes in terms of alleviation of rural poverty in Bangladesh.

Table 4.1 shows that the yearly household income of the GB members is higher than those of comparable non-member households both in the project and control villages. Household incomes mean the monetary and non-monetary value of all goods and services of the household members. Household incomes include cash in hand, and incomes from agricultural and non-agricultural products. Gross incomes of the GB households mainly from agriculture and non-agriculture products were estimated to assess their incomes. The incomes from agriculture included: crop cultivation; homestead garden; livestock and fisheries; and agricultural wage labour. Incomes from non-agriculture included: processing and manufacturing; trade;

Table 4.1   Level and Structure of Household Income of GB Members and Comparable Non-participant Groups 1997-98

Income Component	Grameen Bank Members (Group 1)	Target-Group Nonparticipants		Difference	
		Project Villages (Group 2)	Control Villages (Group 3)	Group 1 Over Group 2	Group 1 Over Group 3
	(Taka/household)			(percent)	
Agriculture	11,230	10,506	13,469	6.9	-16.6
Crop cultivation	5,392	4,125	5,013	30.7	7.6
Homestead garden	1,143	756	999	51.2	14.4
Livestock & fisheries	2,083	1,683	1,700	23.8	18.4
Agricultural wage labour	2,612	3,942	5,757	-33.8	-54.6
Nonagriculture	26,888	20,262	14,315	32.7	87.8
Processing & Manufacturing	9,453	5,936	2,988	59.2	216.4
Trade	7,977	5,736	3,134	39.1	154.5
Transport Operations	2,795	1,335	1,300	109.4	115.0
Nonagricultural wage labour	1,461	1,683	1,528	-13.2	-4.4
Other nonagricultural (earthwork & self services)	5,202	5,572	5,365	-6.6	-3.0
Household income	38,118	30,768	27,784	23.9	37.2
Per capita income	6,930	6,032	5,292	14.9	30.9

Source: Household Survey in GB Project and Control Villages 1998

transport operations; non-agricultural wage labour; and other non-agricultural work, for example, earth work and self-services.

Most of the GB members surveyed were poor and they fulfilled the GB's land ceiling criterion of less than 0.5 acre of land. Their household average annual incomes were Taka 18, 224 at the time of becoming GB members. This was verified from the membership applications of the borrowers with the GB.

On average, a borrower household is found to have nearly 24 per cent higher income than the target group non-member households of the project villages and more than 37 per cent higher than the comparable households in the control villages. The statistical test, one way analysis of variance, was used to find out the significant differences among the means of some variables. The mean differences in incomes among three groups: GB members, comparable non-members in project villages; and comparable non-members in control villages were statistically significant (P<0.000). The incomes of the GB members were significantly higher than those of other two groups.

However, the income impacts recorded above are only, to borrow the term of Hulme and Mosley (1996), *a snapshot* of a constantly changing situation and evidently different income-generating projects are achieving different results among the sub-groups of different poor households.

The increase in the incomes of borrowers is higher, though not as much as has often been claimed, and this was, perhaps, due more to an increase in the profitability of the assisted enterprise, rather than to incomes deriving from outside that enterprise. The information furnished in Table 4.1 clearly indicates that the higher incomes of the GB members compared to non-members in project and control villages (villages with identical socioeconomic condition but without GB programme) stems overwhelmingly from industrial activities, trading, construction, and transport services. These are precisely the major non-farm activities usually financed by microcredit programme of the GB.

On the other hand, non-members of the same economic status (owing less than 0.5 acres of land) are traditionally dependent on wage income. This is reflected in Table 4.1 showing higher wage and income from other sources for the non-members. The figures reveal the fact that the growth in the level of income of GB members is not at the expense of other poor of the project villages. The non-members of the project villages have household incomes, which are nearly 11 per cent higher than those of comparable households in the control villages. This implies that some proportion of the benefits from the GB members have also *trickled out* to local non-member households. As GB members (some of them formerly wage labourers) withdrew from the labour market (Table 4.3) and became self-employed, the employment area opened up throughout the year for the remaining wage labourers. This proposition, though highly speculative, that the wage rate also increased with the reduction in supply of labour (Table 4.4). This again led to the multiplier effect, causing an increase in demand for goods and services, including food.

The receipt of credit did, however, directly increase the incomes of assisted enterprises both for borrowers in the *middle* and *upper* poor and to a lesser extent, for *hard core* poor. This conforms with the findings of Hulme and Mosley (1996)[3], which is analysed at the end of the analysis on poverty alleviation.

The size of loans taken from the GB is a major, if not all, determinant of household income of the members. There is a positive relationship between the size of the loan and the average household income. On a priori ground, there are reasons to believe that the income-earning capacity of the member households depends directly on the number of times a member has taken loans from the GB. This is evidenced from the following Table, which shows a positive relationship between the age of

---

3   Income generating activities are not scale-neutral and have differential utilities and effects for different groups of poor people. See chapter 12 of Hulme and Mosley (1996).

membership and the average size of household income. The Pearson's correlation analysis also shows a positive correlation between the loan size and income levels of the GB members (r=0.73). There are, however, some exceptions.

The average level of household income of the members at the end of the fourth year was somewhat lower than that in the third year. This may be due to some adverse factors, which influenced the rate of return for some particular member or group of members. This group of members, as mentioned, might belong to the group of *extreme poor*, who could not use the loan properly to increase productivity due to their pressing demand for consumption expenditures needed for their mere survival. A significant minority of investments fail leading to a decrease in income while many investments that increase income also soon reach a plateau, especially investments in operating a rickshaw, manually hulling rice mill, and adopting HYVs and inputs on a small farm. For the latter, credit schemes give borrowers an important *one step up* in income; however, such schemes rarely provide the entrepreneurial basis for poor borrowers to move on to the *escalator* of sustained growth of income (Hulme and Mosley 1996, 114). In general, it is reasonable to believe that with the age of membership the experience gained in utilising the loans increases considerably. It appears that the average income increases of first-time borrowers are not very impressive. For the members associated with the GB for two years or more, the increase is more-but still not sufficient to constitute major growth. However, the average household income of the 5th time borrower is 50 per cent higher than the 1st time borrower (Table 4.2).

Nevertheless, the importance of the income from loan-assisted enterprises in relation to total household income is significant. The majority of the borrowers reported that the incomes from loan-assisted enterprises accounted for 50 per cent of the total, and is by far the most important single source of household incomes. The other important sources of income were: incomes from agriculture (homestead gardening and yields from small plots of arable land), returns from household

Table 4.2   Number of Loans Taken, Average Size of Loans, and Household Income for GB Members, 1997-98

Number of Loans Taken	Number of Borrowers	Share of Borrowers	Average Size of Loan	Average Size of Household Income
	N = 300	Percent	Taka	Taka
First time	88	29.3	3,867	32,893
Second time	66	22.0	5,612	38,239
Third time	62	20.7	6,314	41,976
Fourth time	54	18.0	6,668	35,908
Fifth time & more	30	10.0	7,018	49,180
Total	300	100.0	5,576[a]	38,118[a]

Note: N is the size of the sample. [a] - parts do not add to total because of rounding
Source: Survey of 300 borrowers

livestock, wages from casual labouring and various types of rental income (petty cash and loans in kind). These results indicate an increasing dependency of the borrowers on the loan-assisted activities, but also reinforce the fact that such activities remain only a part, though significant, of the total livelihood pattern of the households.

It must, however, be mentioned that availability of the GB credit is only one amongst various factors that in general determine the average income of a household. Heterogeneity of the poor in terms of factors like: land owned; value of non-land fixed assets; number of working hands in the family; level of education of the members of the family; access to other kinds of resources, all exert significant influence on household income. Below is an analysis on the causal factors responsible for increase in incomes of the GB members.

Growth of Income: Causal Factors

Having observed that the microcredit operations of the GB enabled most of its members to enjoy higher income levels compared to non-members, it is, perhaps, pertinent now to look at the factors that have contributed to this increase in income.

Poor people face harsh reality when they become unemployed. Unemployment and underemployment in rural Bangladesh are critically high due to high landlessness (more than half of rural households are functionally landless); low absorptive capacity of agriculture; and high population growth (Hashemi 1997, 249). The poor deal with unemployment and underemployment, which is endemic in rural Bangladesh, by falling back on various mechanisms available at their disposal. They either borrow money from the moneylenders often at an exorbitant rates of interest, buy food from shopkeepers or dissave money. If they fail to deal with the situation in either of the ways they have to starve to balance the deficit.

Studies indicate that during the last 10 years the rural sector has experienced an even more declining trend in employment opportunities in an already aggravated situation of unemployment. The various groups of people, where the poor abound that is, day labourers, agricultural and non-agricultural workers, share croppers, fishermen and women heads of poor households were the hardest hit (Rahman and Rahman 1998, 11-3). One of the immediate impacts of the GB credit could be to increase the employment opportunities in the project areas. This would have a favourable impact on the existing wage rate to improve the often starving situation of these people. A higher level of employment with an increased wage rate can contribute to an increase in income and in addition, credit-induced additional investment and capital accumulation may also augment the asset income base of the members. Access to the GB credit at an institutionally determined interest rate is also likely to make substitution of private loans with high interest rate among the members. This accessibility will help reduce the debt burden and in the process sustain the increase in income of the rural poor households. The following analysis supported by empirical evidence, looks at how the different causal factors help to increase in incomes of the GB members.

Wage and Employment

In the resource-poor environment of the rural poor, the lack of availability of investible fund is considered as a major constraint to the expansion of output and employment. It follows, therefore, that providing credit to the poor is a solution to the problems of both unemployment and poverty since credit can be viewed as a means to overcome the constraint on their lack of access to other productive resources (other than labour).

The stated objective of the targeted credit programmes of the GB is to create opportunities of productive self-employment for the rural poor and thereby alleviate poverty. The analysis here attempts to assess how far this objective of creating productive self-employment has been successful. However, expansion of self-employment alone cannot be considered as a yardstick of success if it does not lead to an increase in total employment. Generation of credit-financed self-employment can increase total employment by unleashing forces on the demand side, which creates more employment or on the supply side, which makes it rational for workers to supply more labour.

The changes in employment may take place at the level of an individual worker and also at the level of households. These changes may take two forms: a change in the labour force participation, and a change in the hours of employment of a worker. Self-employment opportunities at the village level are also expected to influence the wage rate in the labour market, thereby influencing the labour supply behaviour of other households, not members of the GB programme.

Credit can also increase the demand for labour in self-employed activities by enhancing productivity through an increased investment in the existing activities or by creating a scope for new activities. Some of the self-employed workers may also resort to wage employment.

It is possible that an increase in self-employment may actually mean that the participants substitute self-employment for wage employment. The reasons for such substitution may be greater prestige attached to self-employment and access to cash money. Wage employment opportunities given up by the participants may be pursued by other wage-workers in the village. In most rural areas, wage-workers are fully employed in the peak season. In this situation, a shift of workers from wage labour market to self-employment can create an upward trend in wage rate.

Self-employment in rural areas especially in South Asian countries is considered to be more prestigious, compared to wage employment. Besides, self-employment has lower opportunity cost for women in terms of forgone household production because self-employment can conveniently be combined with household activities. In contrast, wage employment is mostly performed either in the employers' homestead or at market places. Because of these advantages of self-employment over wage employment, women's labour force participation is greatly enhanced if they find opportunities for being self-employed.

Table 4.3 shows the changes in the principal occupation of the GB borrowers as a result of their participation in the targeted credit programme of the GB.

New employment was generated mostly for female members, nearly half of whom reported having no occupation before joining the GB: at the time of the survey this proportion had been reduced to 17 per cent. Thus about one-third of the female members previously unemployed had become income earners.

Only 9 per cent of male members were unemployed before joining the GB. For them new employment was created mostly in livestock farming, and processing and manufacturing sectors. For those who were already employed, there was a change in occupational pattern from agricultural wage labour to petty trade and transport operations. The proportion of male members who reported agricultural wage labour as their principal occupation was nearly 19 per cent before joining the GB but only less than 2 per cent at the time of the survey, while the number of those who reported trading and shopkeeping, and livestock and poultry raising as their principal occupations increased from 34 to 48 and from less then 1 per cent to nearly 5 per cent, respectively (Table 4.3). The withdrawal of this significant proportion of the GB members from the agricultural labour market is expected to have an indirect positive effect on employment and earnings of the remaining agricultural wage labourers who did not join the GB.

The fact that the GB operations did increase the wage rate in and around the GB project areas is also evidenced from the Table 4.4. Wage rates in all seasons-normal, peak, and slack- increased substantially (varying from lowest 38 per cent

Table 4.3   Changes in Occupation of Borrowers after Joining GB, 1998

Principal Occupation	Before Joining GB			At Time of Survey		
	Male (N=144)	Female (N=156)	All (N=300)	Male (N=144)	Female (N=156)	All (N=300)
	(Percent of Borrowers)					
Cultivation	8.2	0.6	4.2	6.8	0.6	3.6
Wage labourer	18.6	1.8	9.9	1.8	0.1	0.9
Livestock & poultry raising	0.4	0.8	0.6	4.5	9.1	6.9
Processing & Manufacturing	15.2	38.8	27.5	13.5	55.4	35.3
Trading & Shopkeeping	34.2	6.2	19.6	48.3	13.5	30.2
Transport Operations	3.2	0.1	1.6	11.0	0.2	5.4
Construction & other services	11.2	2.3	6.6	14.1	4.1	8.9
Unemployed	9.0	49.4	30.0	0.0	17.0	8.8
Total	100.0	100.0	100.0	100.0	100.0	100.0

Note: N is the size of the sample
Source: Survey of 300 Borrowers

Table 4.4   Changes in Agricultural Wages due to Intervention of GB, 1998

| | Seasons/Period (Figures in Taka) | | | | | |
| | Peak | | Slack | | Normal | |
	With Meal	Without Meal	With Meal	Without Meal	With Meal	Without Meal
Before the intervention of Grameen Bank	22.00	30.00	18.00	25.00	19.00	27.00
At the time of survey	32.00	45.00	25.00	38.00	30.00	42.00
Percentage rise	0.45	0.50	0.38	0.52	0.58	0.55

Note: All values are expressed at 1998 constant prices
Source: Field Survey

to highest 58 per cent) at the advent of the GB. Admittedly, this rise in wage rates benefited not only the Bank members, but also the large number of non-members in the agricultural labour market. The Table depicts two measures of wage i.e., wage with meals and without meals. It is, perhaps, necessary to make it clear that in rural areas, especially in agriculture, there are two types of wages, as mentioned.

Direct evidence of the GB's impacts on the aggregate employment level in rural areas is not available. There is, however, ample evidence of new employment being generated through the operation of the GB-financed enterprises. There was a significant rise in the activity ratios (defined as the ratio of average number of workers in a family to the size of that family) of the mostly unemployed GB members. Studies indicate that the activity ratio of GB members, especially of female members is nearly double than those of comparable non-members (A. Rahman 1986, 17). The significant point is that the GB has contributed to the increase in female participation in the labour force, most of whom never participated in market-oriented income-generating activities. Although there remains the hard-nosed question over the nature of productivity of female workers, the initiative of the GB in creating new employment for women is indeed a step forward. The women's participation in the labour force has in turn reduced the dependency ratio, which is favourable for alleviation of rural poverty.

The most widely used measure of underemployment uses the time criterion, although this is difficult and costly to apply. Time budget studies based on rather painstaking accounting of the time spent by members of a household in a range of activities, corrected for intensity of work, show considerable underemployment in Bangladesh which is variously estimated to be about 25 to 40 per cent of the available labour time (Jazairy et al. 1992, 170). This study of underemployment is important because of the fact that poverty results not only from unemployment but also from underemployment; the underemployed labourer often receives wages well below the market rate.

It is rather difficult to quantify exactly the effect of the GB loans in terms of reducing underemployment without recourse to an expensive and time-consuming regular employment survey conducted throughout the year. This survey however asked the borrowers to report their average number of days of employment per month and average number of hours worked per day in the occupation for which the loan was taken, both before they joined the GB and in the year of survey. From this information, patchy and imprecise though, it is possible to estimate standard eight-hour days of employment in the GB-financed enterprises, which at least gives a qualitative indication of the change in underemployment as a result of the GB intervention.

Before joining the GB, an average worker in a member household was employed for approximately 8 standard day of work a month, while at the time of survey (not shown in the Table), such employment was estimated at 19 days. The GB loans thus generated additional employment in that activity for about 11 days a month. The additional employment generated was highest for manufacturing and transport services (21 days), and this did not vary much for other occupations (12 to 15 days), as well. It was found that the activity undertaken by female borrowers provided employment to other members of the household for 2 hours a day per household, or about 7.5 standard eight-hour days a month. This trend was more or less the same with the activities undertaken by male borrowers of the household.

It is important to note that, despite the GB is creating job opportunities for the rural poor, studies demonstrate that the performance of the GB in this front is not as impressive as that of BRAC (Rahman and Islam 1993, 60).

Employment impact, in terms of creation of wage employment for the rural poor, appears to be minimal. Eighty-five out of eighty-eight (97 per cent) first-time borrowers did not employ any wage labour and one hundred and eighty-seven out of two hundred and twelve (88 per cent) relatively *older* borrowers have also not used any one on a wage basis (not shown in the Table). There seems to be a very slight correlation between successive loans and incidence of wage-employment creation. Generation of employment, judged in terms of quantity by twenty-eight borrower households, who are each on average employing one full-time labour, is negligible in relation to the total sample size.

In order to achieve overall poverty reduction, employment outside the family is crucial, but the GB, in its policy of employment generation, does not consider wage employment as the happy road to success. The basic objective of the GB is to create self-employment opportunities for rural unemployed and underemployed human resources. Borrowers choose their own loan use and work in their own setting; and the possibility of conflict between their domestic duties and their income work is very slight (Todd 1996, 91).

Although less than 50 per cent of the GB borrowers (not shown in the Table) answered positively to the question of easy availability of new jobs, a significant number of these self-employed borrowers could not meet the basic needs of their families from the income of the GB-financed enterprises. The self-assessed position of the borrowers illustrated in chapter 5 confirms this marginal impact of the GB.

The impact of borrowing on employment is a natural consequence of the technology in which that borrowing is embodied. Across the sample as a whole, the technical change induced by borrowing was not significant, and neither as a consequence has been its influences on employment outside the family. Examination of the hiring patterns of different types of enterprises confirms the impression that rising levels of output financed by loans were initially accommodated by increased demands for family labour only, with significant hiring of non-family labour carried out only by larger enterprises with high return schemes. Seasonal peaks in output were met by the hiring of labour on a casual or on an exchange basis.

The section that follows highlights the trend of capital accumulation of the GB members, which will indicate the sustainability of the increased income, whatsoever, from the GB-financed enterprises.

Effect on Capital Accumulation

Because borrowers are poor, increases in consumption as a result of borrowing from a microcredit programme constitute an immediate welfare gain. The impact, thus, could be short-lived unless enhanced income from borrowing supports asset and capital accumulation. Capital accumulation helps sustained income-generating capabilities.

Moreover, as the loan repayment of the GB is on a weekly basis, critics argue that repayment by poor borrowers sometimes takes place not from the incomes of the GB-financed activities, but from other sources including sales of household assets. It is, therefore, necessary to examine whether borrowing in fact enhances net worth of the household (the value of current assets less the value of loans outstanding). This may apparently be judged by looking into the level of working capital the GB members use in their enterprises. The changes in working capital after joining the GB are illustrated in Table 4.5.

The nature of working capital differs in different business enterprises. Working capital mainly includes, bank loans, raw materials, seeds, fertilizers, insecticides, rubber, rent, wages, interest, and petty cash to run the day-to-day operation of the business enterprise.

Nearly 50 per cent of the borrowers reported investment in working capital before they joined the GB, but at the time of survey the corresponding figure was high at nearly 72 per cent for male borrowers and 67 per cent for female borrowers, indicating a majority of borrowers increased their working capital. The average amount of working capital per borrower increased nearly three times, from Taka 1217 to Taka 3,607, within about two years. About 65 per cent (not shown in the Table) of the households reported accumulation of non-agricultural capital and 45 per cent of the households reported some investment in crop agriculture after joining the GB. The increase has comparatively been faster for borrowers engaged in trading and shopkeeping, followed by processing and marketing, and others. For other activities, such as, livestock raising, investment in fixed assets is more important than working capital.

Table 4.5   Changes in Working Capital after Joining GB by Type of Borrower and Occupation, 1998

Type of Borrower	Number of Borrowers	Borrowers Reporting Working Capital		Amount of Working Capital per Borrower	
		Before Membership	At Time of Survey	Before Membership	At Time of Survey
		(percent)	(percent)	(Taka)	(Taka)
Sex					
Male	144	50.1	72.5	1,268	3,788
Female	156	46.2	66.9	1,170	3,468
Occupation					
Processing and Marketing	104	65.2	83.2	1,347	4,182
Trading and Shopkeeping	93	42.1	74.5	1,452	4,322
Other	103	36.3	51.5	875	2,380
Total	300	48.1	69.6	1,217	3,607

Source: Survey of 300 Borrowers

The level and growth of equity capital is another important indicator of the borrower's changing economic situation. Average investment from borrowers' own funds increased from Taka 1,207 for first time borrowers to Taka 5,128 for members who had borrowed four times and more. The share of equity in total investment increased from 25 per cent for the first time borrowers to nearly 48 per cent for members who had borrowed four times or more. This indicates that the more the length of membership with the GB, the more the growth of equity of the borrowers. This is evidenced in Table 4.6.

Livestock is an important asset base for the rural poor. More than 50 per cent (not shown in the Table) of borrowers did not own any cattle before joining the GB although some of them were engaged in raising the cattle of rich farmers on a 50-50 share basis. This figure of 50 per cent of borrowers who did not own any cattle was reduced to 33 per cent at the time of the survey. The average number of cattle owned increased by 59 per cent during this period.

It is to be noted that not all the GB borrowers have been equally successful in accumulation of assets. Polarization, between those who have made it out of the poverty group and those who have been left behind, was observed in the survey. Of course, the first-time borrowers are not a success-tested sample, repeat borrowers are. Whatever income is added to the repeat borrowers was spent for maintaining their livelihoods. This combined with the declining trend in incomes from GB-financed enterprises result in a marginal improvement in the overall increase in incomes of the repeat borrowers.

Table 4.6   Effect of GB on Growth of Equity Capital, 1998

Length of Membership	Average Amount of Current Loan	Average Accumulation of Capital After Joining Bank		Average Share of Equity in Accumulated Capital
		Total	Equity	
	(Taka)	(Taka)		(percent)
Less than one year	3,867	4,830	1,207	25
One to two years	5,612	6,318	2,452	38.8
Two to three years	6,314	7,194	3,152	43.8
Three to four years	6,668	7,157	2,818	39.4
Four years and more	7,018	10,728	5,128	47.8

Source: Survey of 300 Borrowers

While changes in total household asset values before and after joining the GB have not been very significant, however, there has been an increase in the value of working capital. This is particularly noticeable for the *old* borrowers, associated with the GB for more than two years. This tendency suggests that successive loans lead to a *build-up* of productive assets over time.

The social investment in education, housing, and sanitation increased positively with the length of membership of the GB. These social investments are not directly productive in the immediate short run, but in order to promote human capital for sustainable development in the long run, it is essential that they be invested in. Due to the decline in the rate of productivity of certain activities with the increase in loan size, a significant portion of borrowers were engaged in conspicuous consumption as opposed to being involved in social investment. Below is an analysis on productivity showing the rate of return of the GB-financed activities.

Productivity

The Productivity function shows the relationship between the amount of inputs used and the quantity of output produced. Income is a good proxy for productivity. Productivity is a crucial factor in determining the economic condition of the rural poor. Poverty cannot be alleviated unless there is a concomitant and secular rise in income, which again depends on the nature and trend of productivity of the microenterprises the borrowers are involved in. As productivity is crucial for an increase in income, the following section analyses the issue in more detail.

Table 4.1 provides comparative productivity trends of members belonging to credit programme of the GB and control respondents who do not belong to such an organization. The productivity of GB members is higher than those of comparable non-members in project and control villages. The positive effects of the GB finances are more obvious on the non-farm activities, which include livestock, poultry, fisheries, trading and shopkeeping.

Despite the productivity of the GB members is more than those of their counterparts, there is concern as to whether a level of productivity just above that of the non-members, who are living far below the *poverty level equilibrium trap*, can be justified as a reasonable achievement on the part of the GB members. The consumption level of most of the comparable non-members was far below the poverty line, and any further reduction in consumption might result in death, the possibility of which was close to unity. Moreover, the increase in productivity of the GB members in most cases was not sufficient to cross the poverty line. An attempt is made here to look into the existing level of productivity of the GB enterprises, especially those run by female borrowers.

In terms of potential expansion of the GB, this is a major issue because the demand for the GB loan will depend on whether the earnings of the borrowers in the activity pursued with the loan are higher compared to their earnings before the intervention of the GB.

Table 4.7 presents the distribution of workers employed in different sectors by gender.

The incidence of female worker employment is highest in processing and manufacturing sector. Within this sector, cottage industry absorbs most of the female borrowers. Investment in cottage industry generates much more additional employment than corresponding investment in other sectors. However, among the cottage industrial activities an inverse relationship is found between the labour productivity and the incidence of female employment. The proportion of female borrowers is very high in processing and manufacturing activities (Table 4.7). And within processing and manufacturing, the female borrowers are concentrated more on rice husking, mat making, cane and bamboo works and these are the activities which had a very low

Table 4.7   Distribution of Workers Employed in Different Sectors by Gender, 1998

Sectors	No. of Households	Average Number of Workers	Average Number of Male Workers	Average Number of Female Workers	Female Workers as a percent of all Workers
Processing and Manufacturing	104	2.14	1.06	1.08	50.5
Trading and Shopkeeping	93	1.74	1.42	0.32	18.3
Livestock, agriculture and other	103	1.66	1.18	0.48	28.9
ALL Sectors	300	1.85	1.21	0.63	33.10

Source: Field Survey

rate of return on labour. On the other hand, weaving, pottery and tailoring which gives positive rate of return have a small proportion of female borrowers.

What is actually the rate of return on investment in activities undertaken by the female and how does it compare with that for the male? Although it is difficult to estimate the incomes of a female member separately from the household in which she belongs particularly when she is self-employed. Due to fungibility of money, the resources of the household may be jointly pooled for the activity pursued by a female member and she may also help male members in other income earning activities of the household. However, to get some idea about the incomes earned by women, the study picked up those cases where only female members took loans from the GB and estimated the rate of return on labour and credit and compared it with those for households only with male members. The findings are reported in Table 4.8

Table 4.8   Return on Investment for all Activities by Gender, 1998

Indicators	Male Loanee N = 62	Female Loanee N = 48
Gross family income* (Tk per annum)	22,186	19,250
Size of loan (Tk)	5,102	4,105
Family labour (Hours worked per annum)	3,615	4,200
Net return to family (Tk per annum)	17,300	16,800
Net return to labour (Tk per hour)	4.78	4.00
Rate of return on credit		
a) Family labour imputed at market wage	37	-61
b) Family labour imputed at shadow wage		
of 80% of the market wage	96	25

* Includes income from trading, manufacturing and livestock activities.
Source: Field Survey

The net return (income) to the household of the female member is estimated at Taka 16,800 per annum. The labour productivity is estimated at Taka 4.00 per hour, about 19 per cent lower than that for the male member. If the cost of family labour is imputed at the agricultural wage rate (Taka 4.20 per hour), the rate of return on capital becomes negative, but if the opportunity cost of family labour is assumed at 80 per cent of the prevailing agricultural wage rate, the return on credit becomes positive (25 per cent). Appendix 4A estimates the rate of return to labour and credit.

One question that should be examined is whether the return from GB-financed activities is low and therefore inadequate for loan repayment at the current rate of interest. The returns to labour from many activities are high and only for some of the activities are returns lower than the market wage rate. Hossain (1984); and Rahman and Khandker (1994) also confirm that the returns to labour from many activities financed by the microcredit organizations in Bangladesh are sufficient enough for loan repayment. Some of the spare-time activities such as livestock raising may generate low returns, whereas most of the skill-intensive activities yield a higher return. Moreover, wage employment opportunities are not available to the rural poor women.

From the early days of the expansion of the MFIs, the sceptics have put forward the views that MFI-financed activities bring a low return and MFIs cannot therefore be instrumental in raising household income. A deep-rooted apprehension was that, given the low rate of return from most rural activities, investment opportunities would soon be exhausted and the scope for further expansion of MFIs would be limited. Such scepticism has been based on the assumption that the family workers especially women do not time to be involved in income generating activities and MFIs cannot increase family labour supply. Such assumptions are not, however, valid in reality and loans from MFIs have been found to increase women's labour force participation and employment. Many women, who did not previously have any involvement in directly productive employment, started such activities. Positive changes in labour force participation among women borrowing from GB has been revealed (Table 5.4) not only by this study but also by other studies (for example, Hossain 1988; and Khandker 1994; and Kabeer 1998). These studies have also demonstrated that the supply of labour among the female members of different MFIs does not show a negative response to the number of times they receive a loan.

Still another question and, perhaps a pertinent one, arise. Do activities which, have negative returns to labour help rural poor women to alleviate poverty? The answer is not straight- forward. In developing countries like Bangladesh, women perform three main responsibilities: production; reproduction; and social services. The opportunity costs of female workers are very low in the prevailing socioeconomic environment of Bangladesh. Therefore, women's economic behaviour does not follow a purely economic rationality, aiming for the maximization of individual profit or the pursuit of enterprise growth above all. Tinker (1995, 30-34) proposes that the yardstick of women's economic performance in microenterprises should be a human economic one because this takes into account women's multiple roles and their basic values. Such an approach to policy and programming would be more appropriate than the conventional liberal economic theories that give overriding importance to economic variables and tend to measure women on a men's scale.

Moreover, the rate of return has to be evaluated keeping in mind what alternative income earning opportunities these women had before joining the GB. In view of the prevailing socioeconomic conditions in rural Bangladesh, employment opportunities are often not available to women. Moreover, most of the rural female workers would not be available for work outside their homes except in post harvest operations. The relatively low productivity of women may be acceptable in these cases and whatever they can earn from home-based enterprises adds to the family income. If credit can generate self-employment for women, and if the employment generated a positive net return to the family labour, they would go for credit. In an environment of acute unemployment without any significant social security system, it is desirable though, but not necessary especially in the short run, for the rate of return on capital to be positive or productivity of labour to be higher than the agricultural wage rate.

This has an important implication for policy responses of the GB. The GB will fare well if it allocates resources, including credit, proportionately more in the activities which have higher rates of return, and improves technology which will help increase productivity in the activities where the rates of return are low.

As the expansion of the GB, both vertical and horizontal, depends on the incremental rate of return of the GB-financed activities, the following section highlights the role of technology in increasing the rate of return or productivity.

Technology can simply be defined as a method of operating on the environment for the operator's benefit. Such methods are usually seen in terms of sources of energy. Thus in farm and non-farm production, one has hand-power technology, animal-power technology, or mechanized technology. Technological progress means an improvement in any one or a combination of these technologies, and its effect is measured by *technical progress*, which means a measurable increase in the output per unit of some constraining input or combined bundles of inputs.

The highly influential analysis of Schultz (1964, cited in Quibria ed. 1993, 18) also supports the above view and states that households in traditional societies, including the poor, are *constrained-efficient*. This implies that the introduction of new technologies shift the marginal efficiency of capital schedule to the right. The interventions in the credit market may enable the poor to escape poverty in such a situation if there is a new technology, appropriate to the local conditions and needs of the poor.

The low productivity in rural microenterprises can be traced to a number of factors. The most important is that these enterprises use backward technology, and in fact, many of them are mainly dependent on manual skills. Although there are no comprehensive empirical studies to indicate the role of technology in poverty alleviation, micro studies of a fragmentary nature convincingly show that appropriate technology significantly assists to increase productivity.

The generation of rural non-farm employment should originate not only from the point of poverty alleviation, but also from its dynamic growth role (efficiency) point of view. In doing that emphasis should be given both on quantity and quality of product. Increasing productivity depends mainly on the application of appropriate technology, and improving the quality of product depends on product design. Both quantity and quality will need to be designed by keeping an eye to the prospective demand for those products. This, if realized, would help sustainability of its borrowers with relatively more incomes to alleviate poverty.

But the transfer of technical know-how sometimes may be a placebo, rather than a panacea for development of the most disadvantaged in the society. New technology has often replaced women's productive roles. Rice mills and large scale parboiling and drying equipment in Bangladesh have begun to replace traditional poor women's work. Women are displaced from certain activities in three principal ways: (1) by mechanization of sectors using female wage labour; (2) once these sectors are mechanized men take them over; and (3) by men taking over such activities following their commercialization. This raises the spectre of the marginalization of women at a time when there is evidence that their economic status is already at stake.

As noted in chapter 2, the rapid increase in mechanized rice milling has displaced an estimated 3.5 million to 5 million days of female wage-labour per year. The rice mills have displaced 29 per cent of the total husking labour and adequate availability of rice mills throughout the country will deprive the rural poorest of a total income of Taka 450 million annually by reducing the volume of employment. Another way the mills may have reduced the income of the poor is by depressing wages (Ahmed 1982, 120-24).

One outcome of the green revolution and its associated technology is that it has increased the amount of labour used in crop production very marginally, but has increased yields substantially. Therefore, the amount of income available through market exchange of commodities seems to rise. One consequence resulting from environmental degradation is that there has been a fall in income available from non-exchange sources, such as food obtained by gathering, fishing, collecting of thatching materials and fuel and the availability of free fodder and sustenance for livestock. This has particularly affected the ability of the rural poor women and children to supplement family income from such non-exchange sources. Studies (for example, Greeley eds. 1982), though not empirical and therefore not conclusive, indicate the 10 per cent of the grain which had been left in the field under traditional harvesting methods and which had been gleaned by the poorest for food was no longer available due to the introduction of green revolution. The mechanized harvesting technology, one of the many aspects of the green revolution, leads to minimum wastage of crops to be gleaned by the poor for their survival.

It is a matter of concern, and indeed a compelling one, that while women are being released from such tasks as water carrying, rice husking, wheat grinding, spinning, and feeding cattle, there were no serious productive alternatives being offered. Measures to transfer technology to these technologically-redundant women assume considerable importance as these would make poor women technologically more productive, reduce their dependence on nature, and more importantly, on family, preserve the environment, and would help the economy reap greater benefits from the technological change.

Having said all this, the impact of technology to increase incomes of the rural poor has been very marginal. For landless men and women, as well as marginal and small farmers, these technologies were either prohibitively expensive or a high risk because of the costs and delivery problems involved. Technologies that replaced labour with capital were of little relevance to the landless poor and marginal farmers. It was particularly inappropriate for landless labourers who in effect lost out twice with this technology: (1) they did not possess land, and therefore could not make use of new technologies; and (2) their jobs were displaced when large farmers adopted labour-saving technologies.

Considering the harsh implications of the poor-alienated technology policies, the GB needs to introduce productivity-enhancing, pro-poor technology for its unskilled members if it wants to increase their productivity. An appropriate technology policy will be the one that optimizes the mix between the intermediate and the indigenous technologies in such a way that would make technology growth- enhancing and poverty- alleviating (Appendix 4B).

A very fundamental limitation of the GB is that it not only leaves the choice of the activity to the members but it also does not provide extension services by way of technical advice, marketing support and so on. The GB though has fared relatively well in targeting the poor for supply of credit, it has done nothing significant to help them access to technology. With the enabling environment that the GB has created for its members through the group-based approach and the mandatory weekly meetings, it makes it all the more easier for the GB to deliver appropriate technology to its poor members.

Besides the lack of access to technology, the other important hindrances the poor members encounter are: the lack of proper design of technology; lack of awareness and information; lack of education and management skills; and institutional environment. These barriers make it difficult to realize development potential, and call for a variety of measures to promote technology adoption.

All this means that the GB provides opportunities for poor members to engage in income earning opportunities but the opportunities are not wide enough to have a significant impact in raising their incomes.

The following analysis on the impact of the GB in rural credit market will explore whether the GB members have been freed from the clutches of the informal moneylenders and are able to retain the incomes earned from the GB-financed enterprises.

Substitution of Non-institutional Loans with Institutional Loans

There are four broad categories of credit institutions in rural Bangladesh: the formal (nationalized and private) banks, oriented primarily to collateralized borrowers; government-targeted credit schemes, such as the BRDB RD-12; NGOs such as BRAC, Proshika; and informal lenders of various types. Within each of these categories considerable variety exists, especially amongst informal lenders; and some institutions are difficult to categorize. For example, the GB is a parastatal, and is somewhere between a formal bank and the more flexible and experimental *NGO* organizations (Hulme and Mosley 1996, 124). Although it is technically a bank rather than an NGO, its community-based approach and poverty alleviation objectives give it a quasi-NGO status.

Concerns are often raised about the overlapping and potential unhealthy competition amongst different credit institutions and NGOs. These organizations often work in the same locality, leaving aside some vast areas uncovered. In such a situation it is also possible that few people successfully maintain dual memberships of different organizations. Of course, the GB staff seemed to be quite strict about this, overtly because of practical rather than policy reasons.

However, in an atmosphere of, to use the term of Sanyal (1991), *antagonistic cooperation*[4], the presence of several credit programmes in a single area does raise questions about the impact of credit of a particular organization. Difficulties in estimating the size of IFM arising from reluctance of the lenders to discuss their credit operations for business, social, religious or legal reasons are also apparent.

Despite the operations of the financial institutions expanding over the years both in total amount of credit disbursed and in number of borrowers served, even this growth has not been sufficient enough to keep up with the growth in credit demand in the rural sector. The institutional sources, as evidenced from different studies, cannot even meet 20 per cent of the credit needs of the rural sector. It is, therefore, not surprising that the non-institutional sources or IFMs still play a very important role especially in rural sector of Bangladesh. Although there are no firm estimates, fragmentary evidence based on various microsurveys conducted over the last two decades, however, suggest that IFMs in Bangladesh may be providing as much as two-thirds of the total credit needs in rural Bangladesh (Chowdhury and Rahman 1989, 1). In a nationwide survey of 3,129 farmers who did not borrow from institutional sources, about 62 per cent of them obtained credit from informal sources and the rest sold properties to undertake projects they had hoped to finance through loans (Clapp and Mayne 1980, 102).

Table 4.9   Non-institutional Credit as a Source of Working Capital, 1998

Type of Borrower	Before Joining GB		During Year of Survey	
	Households Receiving Non-institutional Credit	Working Capital Financed with Non-institutional Credit	Households Receiving Non-institutional Credit	Working Capital Financed with Non-institutional Credit
	(percent)			
Sex				
Male	21.5	33.9	3.9	3.5
Female	19.8	31.2	3.5	3.3
Occupation				
Industry	22.7	17.2	5.4	5.1
Trading & Shopkeeping	24.8	32.2	4.8	4.1
Other	14.8	48.2	0.9	1.0
Total	20.6	32.5	3.7	3.4

Source: Survey of 300 Borrowers

---

4   This problem, particularly in relation to Government-NGO relations has been raised by Sanyal (1991, cited in Hulme and Mosley, 1996), p. 125

Given the limited role of the institutional lenders and the subsequent high demand level for credit, interest rates in the rural IFMs in Bangladesh have historically been high. In the case of professional moneylenders[5] or *loan* sharks the rates of interest charged are very high to compensate for the risk.

There are, however, studies on the contrary to indicate that the IFM in Bangladesh is not necessarily inefficient and exploitative under all circumstances and it is complementary to the formal financial sector[6]. A number of writers, especially belonging to the *Ohio School of Thought* maintain that IFM performs a useful function, socially as well as economically[7].

While the GB tends to stick by hard and fast rules in terms of repayment of loans, the moneylenders are more flexible, and the borrowers may opt to pay more to a moneylender in exchange for knowing that if difficulties make it hard to repay on time, the moneylender will typically extend the loan duration, often without extra interest charges.

In spite of all these blessings, the IFM cannot be a perfect substitute for formal financial system in Bangladesh. Although the formal financial system cannot meet the growing demand of the rural poor, no one will prefer to go back to the pre-banking system.

In order to enable the poor, especially women in the non-farm sector, to become independent of the rural financial and market intermediaries and help this group to retain the income now extracted by moneylenders, the GB has almost explicitly targeted these poor women, because they are excluded from normal banking process.

It was found during the survey of this study that nearly 21 per cent of GB members had received credit from the non-institutional sources before joining the GB (Table 4.9). This proportion was reduced to nearly 4 per cent as a result of intervention of the GB. Nearly 33 per cent of the working capital was financed from non-institutional sources before joining the GB; this was reduced to nearly 3 per cent for 1998, indicating the significant effect of the GB on the operation of the informal credit market[8]. Only 4 per cent of the GB members received very small amount of informal loans (average size of informal loan was Taka 96), whereas the average amount of loan from the GB was Taka 5,575. This relatively insignificant loan from nonGB borrowing perhaps could not contribute to any significant bias in the impact study.

---

5   Traditionally IFMs are dominated by professional moneylenders and landlords in developing countries. For a historical analysis of IFMs in Bangladesh see Chowhury and Rahman (1989).

6   See for details, Rahman (1994), pp. 635-40.

7   Von Pischke 1991, Ghate 1988, and Rahman 1992 cited in Martokoesoemo, (1994) p. 57.

8   The findings are comparable to the figures of the latest study on the issue. The corresponding figures in Hossain (1988) study for households receiving noninstitutional credit before joining the GB was 19 per cent, which was reduced to nearly 3 per cent as a result of the intervention of the GB.

Table 4.10 depicts a clear picture of the effect of the GB on the rural credit market. About 96 per cent of the GB members received an average of Taka 5,575 from institutional sources. The dependence of the Bank members for credit from non-institutional sources was low compared with similar groups of the project and control villages. Nearly 4 per cent of the GB members received loans from non-institutional sources compared with about 26 per cent with among comparable non-members of the project villages and more than 20 per cent of comparable non-members in the control villages. Most institutional credit outside of the GB was received by non-target group households; less than 6 per cent of the target group received such loans, compared with 30 per cent of the nontarget groups.

The membership with the GB allowed the rural poor easy and regular access to loans on better terms than those locally available in informal markets. However, the GB members admitted that taking such loans from IFMs was sometimes necessary to meet contingencies caused by illness in the family or the costs incurred by social obligations. There are additional forms of minor credit transactions commonly

Table 4.10   Amount of Loans Received from Various Sources by GB Members and Comparable Non-members in Project and Control Villages, 1998

Household Category	Number of Loans	Non-institutional Credit		Institutional Credit	
		Households Receiving Loans	Average Loan Received per Household	Households Receiving Loans	Average Loan Received per Household
		(percent)	(Taka)	(percent)	(Taka)
A. Grameen Bank Member	25	4.4	96	95.6	5,575
B. Non-participant Within target group in project villages	23	25.6	700	3.7	612
C. Grameen Bank Target group in Control villages	21	20.4	798	2.1	79
D. Non-target group	24	16.8	1,190	30.0	2,888
Total	93	16.7	686	34.8	2,413
Grameen Bank non member (B + C + D)	68	20.9	903	12.5	1,251

Source: Household survey in project and control villages

occurring among friends and relatives. These types of credit, which are sometimes interest-free, are often in kind (for example, rice), have negligible impact on the rural credit market due to their nature and size.

The factor of transaction costs in Bangladesh, especially in the context of the rural economy (which are traditionally low for those borrowing from informal lenders) is less significant than interest rates and loan sizes. In an environment of capital scarcity, and low creditworthiness, the type of services offered by the GB to the rural poor, especially women are far more attractive than those of informal lenders.

It may, however, be remarked that *despite taking the Bank to the people*, the GB imposes high costs for members in advancing loans to them. Each loan requires a considerable investment of time, effort and discipline by its borrowers. Participation in weekly meetings is a time-consuming activity, but this is the borrowers' only gateway to credit. Despite the transaction costs of the GB microcredit programmes are not small, and are sometimes greater than those incurred when going to a local landholder or trader for a loan. The GB members are prepared to bear these disciplinary and temporal costs in order to gain access to much larger amounts of capital on better terms than would otherwise be available to them.

What impact does the GB has on local informal credit markets? The question is a complex one and the survey data related to this issue is limited. However, until and unless proved otherwise, it would be safer to suggest that the supply of informal credit is low compared to the demand for capital. It can be said that the GB borrowers as well as borrowers from other MFIs, have partially, though not completely, been freed from the clutches of the informal moneylenders. Their monopoly in extracting higher rates of interest has been diminished to a certain extent.

However, it should be noted that while the GB and other MFIs/NGOs may be taking clients away from some moneylenders, programme coverage of these organizations is still sparse enough to ensure that there are plenty of other potential customers. Until now the GB and similar other targeted credit programmes have been able to cover only one-fourth of the rural poor, leaving aside three-fourths of the eligible rural poor who have a pressing demand for credit. It is also evident that 4 per cent of the GB borrowers and perhaps some members of other MFIs, as well, still borrow from informal lenders, and probably will continue to do so. This is because; the informal sector is still the main recourse when people quickly need credit in small amounts.

Despite the GB provides a *competitive* financial service for the poor, it is still not a substitute for the informal sector. In order to have a significant impact in the rural credit market, the lending policies of the GB be redesigned to be sensitive to household initial conditions. Designing a quality, flexible, and client-responsive financial services can provide a real choice to its member households. Only then the GB can seriously compete with the informal lenders.

However, moving on to the question of lessons for rural financial theory that can be learned from the institutional innovations of the GB, it can be said that the emphasis of the financial liberalization theory in interest rate reform in rural financial markets (RFMs), the performance of the GB is more impressive in terms of ensuring the access of the rural poor to the formal sources of finance. The elegant financial liberalization theory through changes in interest rates could not ensure the access of the rural poor to institutional sources of finance. The section that follows highlights the institutional innovations of the GB.

Financial Liberalization Theory and the GB

Financial Liberalization: Nice Theory

The theory of financial sector liberalization in the developing countries came to dominate financial policy discussion since the early 1970s due to two seminal contributions by McKinnon (1973) and Shaw (1973). The core of their hypothesis is that government intervention in the developing countries to control interest rates, put ceilings on lending rates, and ration credit to borrowers at below market clearing rate has repressed the development of the financial sector. Developing countries often pursued policies that kept interest rates artificially low, even negative in real terms, and in the process discouraged financial saving. This has hampered financial deepening, at times led to financial disintermediation.

Financial liberalization means the removal of government ceilings on interest rates and of other controls of financial institutions. It is primarily concerned with macroeconomic aggregates, that is, interest rates, savings and investment and conditions in formal financial institutions. Financial sector reform policies complement financial liberalization and include a broad range of measures aimed at improving the regulatory and supervisory environment in the financial sector and at the restructuring and development of financial sector institutions. Financial liberalization policies have been implemented in a wide range of developing countries since the 1970s, spanning Asia and Latin America and more recently in Sub-Saharan Africa.

It is widely believed that liberalizing financial markets would create an environment in which the financial intermediaries would offer better financial services to the poor. Liberalization of financial markets often influences current thinking on finance for the poor. Through the process of deregulation, financial liberalization should reduce entry barriers and stimulate the development of the financial sector, increase competition in banking and leading to a diversification in financial institutions (Baden 1996, 9). It is, therefore, believed that the poor will be able to have access to better financial services in an environment characterized by financial liberalization. Competition forces different financial institutions in producing attractive financial products and services and also in lowering transaction costs (Vogel and Adams 1997, 375-6). Financial sector liberalization is also intended to reduce financial resource misallocation and bring about financial development and hence accelerate and sustain economic growth.

Ugly Facts

This study highlights some shortcomings of the liberalization theory in terms of the main process by which presumably it could help the poor through greater market competition between the financial institutions. The study argues in particular for restraint in assuming that financial market liberalization is certain pro-poor strategies- in reality it appears to be more complex, and less certain. Undermining rural development with cheap credit (Adams et al. 1984) may be true at certain point in time, but also undermining the poor with overtly simplified ideas is likely to be true at this point in time.

Equating of the current microfinance industry with the old subsidized-rural development programs by the *Ohio School of Thought*, ignores several fundamental differences between the two. Numerous innovations (such as, group lending, small weekly repayments, and mobile banking) have significantly reduced the information asymmetries and transaction costs of providing financial services to the poor relative to the earlier experience. While many MFIs suffer from severe institutional deficiencies, the industry today includes a large number of well run MFIs where it is not unusual to find repayment rates of 98 per cent, far above the rate of traditional commercial banks, lending against material collateral. The fact is that the old subsidized rural development programs constituted one form of organization that existed at one point in time. One simply cannot extrapolate directly from them to existing MFIs.

In spite of predictions by financial liberalization theory, the poor are likely to remain underserved by the financial markets. There is growing evidence that even after liberalization, the commercial banks of different countries have been slow to innovate in lending and have found themselves with excess liquidity. Rather than thrusting into new markets to serve the poor, such banks have tended to be passive even after liberalization. Commercial banks in Bangladesh retreated from providing financial services to the poor after liberalization, being content to leave that part of the market to informal agents and NGOs (Yaqub 1998, 105). This means that contrary to the popular view liberalization tends to exclude rather than include the poor into their financial services.

Financial liberalization, according to its proponents, is supposed to bring about increased savings and investment through higher interest rates, as well as through a better allocation and productive use of resources. Basu (2002) provides a convincing theoretical analysis of why both financial liberalization and government intervention have been unable to achieve their intended goals of proper allocation of loans through market-determined interest rates. According to him, financial liberalization, instead of improving the financial environment, has brought financial crisis and reduced growth. Financial did not produce the intended results either in terms of faster economic growth or better distribution of wealth and resources.

Moreover, the gender-blind financial liberalization policies without taking into consideration of the different savings pattern of men and women have been of very little, if any, benefit to the rural poor women in terms of their access to savings services. There is a need for much greater attention to savings and investment behaviour of men and women. Study of the different savings patterns of men and women (for example, different marginal propensity to save, preferred type of savings, constraints on savings and so on) would provide insights into how financial liberalization policies might affect the value and form of savings by gender and how complementary policies could be designed to increase women's choices in terms of access to savings instruments.

The Grameen Experience

However, moving on to the question of lessons for RFM theory that can be learned from the institutional development of the GB, it can be said that given the present emphasis on interest rate reform in RFMs, the GB's performance is significant because the GB is the product of institutional innovation (that is, collateral- free group lending, mobile banking, and female- focused programs), and not of interest rate policy liberalization.

The situation of the GB supports the view that while the RFM model is a useful tool for the analysis of RFMs, it explains only one set of variables constraining the accessibility of credit for the poor. Interest rate reforms may be necessary to ensure institutional financial viability and to improve the allocation of scarce resources towards productive investment. However, there is no evidence that interest rates perform the World-Bank dictated role of efficient allocation of financial resources in rural communities which are largely non-monetized, or where people are faced with communication and infrastructural constraints, and where the density of financial institutions is very low.

Financial liberalization and other macro-sector reforms while necessary are grossly inadequate in providing the means by which the bottom 50 to 70 per cent of the economically active population can participate in economic growth and social development. Macro reforms in financial systems need to be complemented by measures that encourage the institutions, instruments, relationships and financing arrangements geared to providing sound, responsive financial services to the majority of enterprises that have not had access to those services.

Simple changes in interest rates associated with financial liberalization are insufficient to improve the access of the poor to formal credit at reasonable prices. As the experience of the GB demonstrates that building financial institutions which can increase access of the poor requires more than adjustments in interest rates (MacIsaac and Wahid 1993, 205). What matters most to the rural poor is access to money, not the cost of it or interest rate (Havers 1996, 148). In rural Bangladesh, the pressing need is not for the policies, which aim at liberalization of the financial markets. Rather, it needs financial innovations (for example, group-lending, demand responsive quality financial services) that can effectively reach the poor.

Microfinance is hardly a triumph of market reforms. The tendency to incorporate microfinance into the market paradigm misses a major contribution of group-based microfinance, namely, that it is a proven example of selfish motives channeled into cooperative behaviour. Such behaviour helped to ameliorate some information problems, making collateral-free credit possible. The poor were previously thought unbankable, the GB and other microfinance innovations proved this wrong.

The Need for Innovations

Satisfactory though the performance of the GB and some other MFIs in reaching the poor and alleviating poverty of some of them, it could have been even more impressive if the MFIs had introduced the much desired, client-responsive product innovation, such as, introducing deposit products with less restriction in access and lending products that allow for more flexible terms and conditions.   These products innovations are considered to be more desirable by the extreme poor whose general livelihood conditions are immersed with uncertainty and vulnerability. The client-responsive, flexible financial services help smooth consumption and reduce vulnerability. The GB, through its Phase II has introduced some client-friendly changes to its products, although the recent changes in terms of introducing a full range of client-responsive services both financial and non-financial, is as yet only one step toward a goal lying several miles away.

There is a need for an on-going programme of *product innovation* to seek to improve the quality of services being made available to clients. This is the challenge for the future. The eventual impact of microfinance on poverty alleviation and the sustainability of MFIs will ultimately depend on organizations' systems and products. The more appropriate and the higher the quality of services is on offer, the better impact on poverty alleviation and financial sustainability.

No one, of course, argues seriously that microfinance programmes alone will be the answer to all the problems of poverty. The best evidence to date suggests that making a real dent in poverty situation will require increasing overall levels of economic growth and employment generation. But the promise remains that MFIs that go for regular innovation in client-responsive financial and non-financial products may be able to alleviate (not remove) poverty of their clients significantly.

Final Thoughts on Institutional Innovation

Given the major financial innovations made by the GB and many other successful MFIs, the strong lesson of microfinance must surely be that *institutional innovation*- rather than *laissez faire liberalization*- is the way to produce new services useful to the poor. Institutional innovation is, however, not perfect, but compared to other approaches to providing financial services to the poor, institutional innovation appears to be doing very well. The GB inclines to the views of Braverman and Guasch (1986, 1256) for more study of institutions and institutional environments as key elements in understanding financial markets and their role in the development process. There is a role for donor agencies here in supporting institutional change favouring poor women borrowers, through staff training programmes and innovative changes in management structures and practices. The GB may serve as an example of the importance of institutional development in increasing the accessibility of financial services for the poor, especially the rural poor women.

Summary and Conclusions

Identification of programme's benefits requires a participant-level impact analysis that measures effects on individual and household welfare, such as per capita income, accumulation of capital, increase in productivity, substitution of informal loans, and so on. Given the complexity of different biases, the task of programme impact evaluation becomes difficult. First, programmes set their objectives at the start, and hence are not randomly placed. Thus, without controlling for programme placement endogeneity, it is difficult to determine a programme's effects. Second, participation in a programme is self-selective, so comparing outcomes between participants and non-participants does not indicate any significant impact.

It is likely that the borrowing is determined by household characteristics, including the characteristics of the other members of the credit programme in a group or village. Programme impacts differ between individual and household, as there are some unmeasured differences in the ability of individuals or households that cannot be controlled. Similarly, there might be some village specific characteristics, as microcredit programmes, in general, do not randomly place programme without regard to some characteristic, for example, poverty status. Programmes may be placed in a village where people, in general, support the women's role in supporting the family. Similarly, there are other impacts such as social barrier by being member of a MFI, opportunity cost of time spent for group based activity. Thus the unobserved household and village specific characteristic affect the programme status of the household.

The best way to handle such endogeneity is to compare between programme and control households outcome in terms of socio-economic indicator (see Khandaker 1998). This study, however, resolved these issues to a greater extent as the study-administered questionnaires are of quasi-experimental nature. Households were chosen at random from both programme and control villages, from both target and non-target groups.

The incomes of the GB members were higher than the comparable non-members both in the project and control villages. The increases in income were, however, observed among non-poor or not-so-poor members. The extreme poor did not experience any significant increase in incomes.

A positive correlation was observed between the loan size and the income levels of the GB members. There were exceptions, though. The GB credit is only one amongst various factors that determine the average income of a household. The increases in income, in many cases marginal though, were due to the self-employment opportunities initiated by the GB credit. However, expansion of self-employment alone cannot be considered as a yardstick of success if it does not lead to an increase in total employment.

The GB operations helped increase wage rates in and around the GB project areas. There was also a significant rise in the activity ratios of the GB women members. There was also the growth of equity of the GB members, but all members did not experience identical growth.

The productivity of the GB members was higher than their counterparts in project and control villages. But there is a concern as to whether a level of productivity just above those of the non-members, who are living far below the *poverty level equilibrium trap*, can be justified as a reasonable achievement on the part of the GB members. Moreover, the increase in productivity of the GB members in most cases was not sufficient to cross the poverty line. The productivity of the female members in most of the enterprises had negative returns to labour.

Do activities with negative returns to labour help rural poor women to alleviate poverty? The answer is not straight-forward. Given that women in Bangladesh perform three main responsibilities: production; reproduction; and social services, women's economic behaviour does not follow a pure economic rationality. The yardstick of women's economic performance in microeneterprises should be a human economic one because this takes into account women's multiple roles and their basic values (Tinker 1995).

Moreover, the rate of return has to be evaluated keeping in mind what alternative income earning opportunities these women had before joining the GB. In view of the prevailing socioeconomic conditions in rural Bangladesh, employment opportunities are often not available to women. If credit can generate self-employment for women, and if the employment generated a positive net return to the family labour, they should go for credit. In an environment of acute unemployment without any significant social security system, it is desirable though, but not necessary especially in the short run, for the rate of return on labour to be higher than the prevailing agricultural wage rate.

The most important factor limiting the higher productivity is the lack of productivity-enhancing technology. A very fundamental limitation of the GB is that it not only leaves the choice of the activity to the clients but it also does not provide extension services by way of technical advice, marketing support and so on. Through the provision of credit, the GB provides opportunities for poor clients to engage in income earning opportunities but the opportunities are not wide enough to have a significant impact on their standard of living.

In terms of impact of the GB on local informal credit markets, it can be said that the GB borrowers as well as borrowers from other MFIs have partially been freed from the clutches of the informal moneylenders. Their monopoly in extracting higher rates of interest has been diminished to a certain extent. Despite the GB provides a *competitive* financial service for the poor, it is still not a substitute for the informal sector. Designing a quality, flexible, and client-responsive financial services can provide a real choice to its member households. Only then the GB can seriously compete with the informal lenders.

Never the less, the institutional innovation of the GB has enabled the rural poor, especially the rural poor women, for the first time in Bangladesh to access the formal sources of finance. The GB may serve as an example of the importance of institutional development in ensuring the access of the rural poor women to the institutional sources of finance.

Appendix 4A   Estimation of Family Income

The gross family income from the trading activities for a week has been estimated as follows:

$$Y_B = SL + (STK_E - PRC - STK_B - C_O)$$

where,
Y_B =   Gross family income from the activity for the week of survey
SL =   Amount of sales valued at sales prices during the week
STK_E = Stock of the tradeable commodities at the end of the week valued as sale prices
STK_B = Stock of the tradeable commodities at the beginning of the week valued at purchase prices
PRC = Purchases of the commodities during the week valued as purchase prices
C_O = Other cash costs incurred for operating the trade during the week. This includes travelling expenses, transport charges, wage bill to workers, rent for shops and other bills or taxes paid.

The information on SL and PRC was recorded for each day for all seven days preceding the period of survey.

For manufacturing activities the gross family income is calculated as follows:
$$Ym =   (SLQ + STQ_E - STQ_B) - (STR_B + PRCR - STR_E) - C_O$$

where,
Y_M = The gross family income from the manufacturing activity
SLQ = Value of sales of output during the week
STQ_E = Stock of the output at the end of the week
STQ_B = Stock of the output at the beginning of the week
STR_B = Stock of raw materials at the beginning of the week
$PRCR$ = Value of purchases of raw materials during the week.
STR_E = Stock of raw materials at the end of the week
C_O = Other cash costs incurred for operating the trade during the week. This includes travelling expenses, transport charges, wage bill to workers, rent for shops and other bills or taxes paid.

As seasonal variations in income are expected, the information on all these items was collected for three weeks at different points of time during August to December 1998, and the value per annum has been estimated from the weekly averages. The amount of investment in the trading activities has been estimated by the weekly averages of the sum total of the value of stock, cash costs incurred and the value of purchases during the week. For manufacturing activities, however, the raw materials are often purchased in bulk (not very frequently) so it is difficult to estimate working capital from three weeks' data. Also some of the loans may be used to acquire fixed assets such as *dhenki*, handloom, *ghani* and various tools and equipment. This study used the amount of loan taken as the amount of investment in the case of manufacturing activities.

Three alternative measures of the return from investment have been estimated: (i) Net return to family, I, (ii) Net return per unit of labour employed, R_L, or the productivity of labour and (iii) Rate of return on capital, R_K.

(i) $I = Y - (1+r) K$
(ii $)R_L = I/L$
(iii) $R_K = (Y - _w.L - K)/K$

where,
Y = Annual gross family income from the activity
L = Family labour hours worked on the activity per annum.
K = The amount of credit taken for the activity (amount of working capital used for trading activities, where KA actual loans used and KT loans taken.
r = Annual rate of interest on the loan per annum
w = The wage rate for agricultural labour per hour

The rate of interest is taken to be 22 per cent per annum which includes the five per cent compulsory deduction of loan for Group Fund.

Return from Investment in Trading Activities, 1998

Activities	No. of Obs	Gross Income (Tk per annum)	Working Capital Employed (Tk)(KA)	Working Hours (per annum)	Loan (Tk) (KT)	Net Income (Tk/ annum)	Return on Labour (Tk/hr)	Return on capital (%)
Paddy trading	7	17640	4100	2910	4010	12638	4.34	32
Seasonal crop trading	11	18873	4210	2760	4000	13737	4.98	72
Livestock & forestry products	7	11500	1760	1990	4400	9353	4.70	78

Cottage Industrial products	10	17390	2110	3950	4370	14816	3.75	-62
Peddling	6	17800	2005	4090	4570	15354	3.75	-68
Shopkeeping	12	19740	1972	3816	4276	17335	4.54	88
All Activities	53	17531	2719	3292	4251	14214	4.39	30

For Comparison: Agricultural wage rate Taka 4.20 per hour.
Annual rate of interest on loan is 22 per cent.
Source: Three weekly input-output surveys for the activities.

Return from Credit in Industrial Activities

Industrial Activities	No. of Obsv	Gross Income (Tk/ annum)	Loan (Tk)	Family Labour (hr/ annum)	Net Return to Family (Tk/annum)	Return on Labour (Tk/hr)	Return on credit (%)
Cane & bamboo works	7	15,050	3,500	3,700	10,780	2.91	-114
Pottery	11	22,300	4,100	3,815	17,298	4.53	53
Rice husking	5	14,000	3,600	3,760	9,608	2.55	-148
Oil pressing	7	17,000	2,901	3,950	13,461	3.41	-85
Mat making	8	16,500	3,600	4,100	12,108	2.95	-120
Weaving	6	23,100	4,200	4,200	17,976	4.28	30
Dairy & misc. industries	8	23,400	3,910	4,105	18,630	4.54	58
All Industries	52	19,182	3,715	3,945	14,649	3.70	-35.9

Note: Tk. means Taka
Source: Field Survey

The net return to family would be the most appropriate measure of the return if labour employed in the activity had no opportunity cost, that is, the labour would have remained idle if the investment on self-employment had not been made with GB credit. At the other end (Y -wL) is the most appropriate measure of the income if all the labour could be alternatively employed in agriculture or other similarly paid activities. These are two extreme situations and the reality may be in between. The study estimated the net return per labour hour employed, so that one can compare it with the agricultural wage rate and one's notion of the opportunity cost of labour to make a judgement about the desirability of the investment. The net profit (Net Income-Cost of Family Labour - Cost of Credit) has been expressed as a per cent of investment (or amount of credit taken) to get the rate of return from credit. This would have been the most appropriate indicator for the viability of investment with GB credit when the proprietor runs the activity mostly with hired labour. If the rate of return is higher than the cost of investment it is profitable to make that investment.

The GB members however, run the activities mostly with family labour which face inadequate and uncertain employment opportunities in the market. Hence the rate of return on capital, R_K, may not be an appropriate guide for investment decision. Also, since the amount of investment is small, R_K would be very much sensitive to the assumption of the wage rate and to error of measurement of such variable as labour hour employed on which accurate information is difficult to collect.

Source: Field Survey, 1998

Appendix 4B   Technology for the Poor

Appropriate Technology

The debate around whether the rural poor have been able to benefit from the new technologies that were developed, adopted and disseminated in the second half of the twentieth century has added more to heat than to light. At one end of the continuum is the idea that although new technologies did initially favor larger farmers, over time more of the benefits have been captured by poorer groups. Distribution biases that emerged did not reflect problems with the technology *per se*, but rather with local institutional structures that led to social biases in access to the technology and to the related credit, information and technical support services that would have helped poor farmers take advantage of these new technologies. At the other end, is the idea that the rural poor have been excluded from the benefits of this modernization.

However, it can safely be said that advanced, high capital-intensive technology has failed to benefit the poor in a significant way. This is what has happened in Bangladesh and other developing countries. An appropriate technology policy will be the one that optimizes the mix between the intermediate and the indigenous technologies in such a way that would make technology growth- enhancing and poverty- alleviating.

Efforts to achieve reforms have come under headings such as *appropriate technology, integrated pest management, low-input technology*, and more recently, *sustainability* (Ruttan 1990, 400-401). The fact that the introduction of technology does not necessarily increase the desired productivity for all adopters raises the question of *appropriateness* of technology. The idea of *appropriate* implies the existence of limits. When something is inappropriate, it means it is too large or too small, too advanced or too simple, too slow or too fast, too expensive or too cheap. The concept is a relative one and takes its measure from the thing it serves. Appropriate to what? When speaking of technology, the consensus of most is that it refers to high productivity. The higher the productivity, the more appropriate is the technology.

Not only do appropriate technologies need to be locally developed, but also proper organizational management that caters to the needs and wishes of the local poor. To solve the problem of Third World poverty means building the capacity of poor women and men to choose and use technology. The rural poor themselves should adapt it, develop it, and improve it; and manage its sustainability over time. Without addressing these factors, no technology can be successfully applied to their livelihoods. And it means subjecting any new technology choice to the *three As'* analysis. From the point of view of poor people, is a technology option: Affordable to people living on less than $ 1 a day? Accessible to poor people in developing countries? Appropriate, meaning is it adapted to their social, economic and cultural needs (Practical Action 2006, 1). Technical assistance programmes of the past have deliberately ignored the poor and it is perhaps justified to agree with what Robert Chambers (1983) called *a tragic gap between those who perceive the needs of rural societies and those who create appropriate technologies.*

In an answer to the question of appropriate technology, Leopold Kohr (1980, 190-191) observes that for developing countries the appropriate technology is an infinitely less costly *intermediate* technology. Considering their reduced maintenance requirements, very often the intermediate technology is enough to provide equally high and, indeed, higher living standards than can be achieved in developed countries with the most advanced technology. Moreover, as Kohr argues, though intermediate technology is *mechanically* less efficient, it is infinitely more efficient in *human* terms, since in this age of crippling unemployment, it can achieve the highest standard of living through ensuring maximum employment for the rural poor.

The intermediate technologies are soft technologies and there are dozens of different kinds of soft technology. Each one is used to do what it does best; none are intended as a panacea. These technologies are renewable: they run on sun, wind, water, farm and forestry wastes, and conceivably a few other renewable flows-not on depletable fuels. They are cheaper, relatively simple and understandable from the users' point of view, but can still be technically very sophisticated. Putting it differently, the reduced efficiency of intermediate technology provides the same amount of goods, but at a higher cost in labor, than can be achieved under conditions of labor-saving advanced technology. It is unemployment-the prohibitive cost of which no society can afford to pay in the long run. The following section analyses the technology for the poor in farm and nonfarm sector.

Technology in the Farm Sector

Improved seeds, irrigation, fertilizers, pesticides have received important theoretical and practical consideration. Farmer's tools and technology, however, have been relatively neglected. There is enormous scope for development in them.

Most of the rural farmers are very poor and it is unlikely that they will adopt changes in methods of production that require outlays of cash. Studies indicate that the mechanized equipment is eighteen times more expensive than the traditional ox-powered equipment. This differential concerns only the initial capital outlay, and does not take into account the further differences in running costs (Macpherson and Jackson 1975, 102), not to speak of the expertise needed to operate it. Even though the tractorized equipment is more efficient in handling large acreage, and can substantially raise employment in the rural sector (Rao 1972, 393), the reality of the farming situation is that such a cost differential puts the mechanized equipment out of reach of the great majority of the poor farmers. It is therefore important to develop a tool technology that is accessible to poor farmers.

To avoid failure, innovation should start at the current level of technical competence of the rural people. In most villages there are people skilled in the use of the axe, the ladder, the plough and the hoe. In many villages there are carpenters who make chairs, tables, ladders, ploughs, doors and houses using these implements, while in some there are blacksmiths who forge axes, knives, hoes and other small tools. This provides a reservoir of basic skills that can be tapped into for the benefit of all.

The implements of advanced technology are mostly of metal. This requires labor skilled in welding when repairs are needed. Welding is very often beyond the technical capacity of the poor farmers, nor is the cash readily available for such repairs.

It is therefore necessary to develop a rural technology where both construction and repair can be undertaken by the rural poor farmers. This can be done in many cases by substituting wood for metal. This enables the poor farmers, with the help of a simple and inexpensive tool-kit and their everyday skills, to construct and keep in working order a whole variety of agricultural equipment. This type of technology provides a valuable lesson in self-reliance because implements are no longer seen as shop-bought and alien, but as self-created and capable of modification and redesign to meet special needs. This type of technology facilitates production and exchange within the rural economy, and thereby provides an important means for the growth of rural output as an alternative to trade between rural agriculture and urban industry. By providing income for those with spare labor-time, rural technology contributes to rural development.

Detailed specification of appropriate tool kits necessary for rural poor farmers goes beyond the remit of the study, however, a discussion on *cultivator* and plough, as representative tools of the rural poor, will be attempted here. Weeding being a time-consuming but essential task is one of the notorious bottlenecks in peasant agriculture, and the lack of adequate weeding can account for yield losses. Weeding between rows is traditionally carried out by hoe and is highly labor-intensive. It is technically quite feasible to do the weeding by an animal-powered implement called a *cultivator*. This machine is pulled along between the rows of plants with its adjustable blades cutting the weed roots. Hand-weeding can then cope with the few remaining weeds between plants.

It is possible to make a rural technology plough, but the field experience suggests it does not do as good a job as the intermediate technology iron plough which is well tested and widely in demand in rural areas of developing countries. An alternative, and perhaps a more feasible one, is the use of small hand-tractors for ploughing.

It is also possible for the rural poor to adopt traditional low-cost techniques for irrigation. These techniques include swing basket, dugwell and unsophisticated cross dams. But these techniques can not be recommended for farmers, as the returns are very low. Appropriate rural technology does not necessarily exclude intermediate technology when the latter is technically superior and the cost difference is slight.

Bamboo tube wells, which are traditional techniques, and low-cost hand tube wells, which are intermediate technique may be the best method for poor farmers' irrigation needs. These microirrigation techniques of hand pump and bamboo tube well can help many rural poor people for many years.

It will, however, be fruitless to plead for a ban or curb for a further extension of rice mills, which may bring substantial post-harvest problems including milling and storing. It is, however, advisable to take steps to alleviate the imbalances in the employment and income situation of the poor due to rice mills. A potentially rewarding approach for the poor engaged in paddy processing business lies in switching over from dhenki husking to custom husking. This switch over may increase their turnover by three to four times. The paddy processing business thus may offer profitable alternative employment for the poor displaced by rice mills.

It is thus observed that an appropriate technology for rural poor farmers comprises of a variety of technologies. It also takes into account the cash constraints of poor farmers, while at the same time reducing the labor input per unit of output and lightening much of the physical arduousness of agricultural work.

Technology in the Nonfarm Sector

The issue around generating rural nonfarm employment stems primarily from a concern with poverty amelioration and human resource mobilization rather than seeing the sector as having a dynamic and growth contributing role to play.

The cases of China and Taiwan have been cited in some studies as success stories of using rural industrialization as a key element in rural development strategies. Rural non-farm sectors are perceived to provide dynamic backward and forward linkages with agriculture. The rural nonfarm sector absorbs 34.5 per cent of the labour force in rural areas of Bangladesh (Asaduzzaman and Westergaard eds. 1993, 141).

Once the importance of rural nonfarm employment is established in quantitative terms, the next question that needs to be addressed is whether these activities are productive enough to ensure a decent income and a standard of living for the rural poor or are they more of a symptom of distress adaptation to growing poverty and landlessness.

The general consensus that emerges from different empirical studies is that the rural non-farm sector especially the manufacturing sector is characterized by a dualistic structure in terms of productivity and returns (Rahman 1995, 32). At one end of this structure is a small but growing segment which is comprised of activities having high capital intensity, a certain degree of technological sophistication, and high factor productivity and returns. At the other end of the spectrum are activities, which are often seasonal, mostly run with unpaid family labour using rather primitive technology, if any, and catering mostly to the local market and responding more to the supply side of the labour market than to the market demand for output.

While petty trades and other odd jobs in the informal sector fall mostly in the residual group, activities such as tailoring, masonry, sweet making, house repairing, and transportation in which skill requirement and capital intensity per worker are relatively high have been characterized by higher levels of returns and growth.

Any observed low rate of return in activities of this sector is largely attributable to problems with technology. The problem of low rate of return is accentuated when many of these activities are faced with serious problems of product displacement. The displacing products are either new or improved products or same products produced by more productive technologies within or outside the rural sector. The upgrade of traditional technology and the introduction of new ones have to go beyond providing subsistence income only and become a dynamic element in the growth process.

When poor women are provided with credit to set-up *dhenki* of their own, they compete with mechanized rice processors. When marketable surpluses are available, food losses to farmers during post harvest operations (due to problems of collection, transportation, storage, and subsequent processing) are in fact substantial, and the problems can be alleviated by the use of improved technology like *pedal threshers* which are labor-intensive and have proved to be economically viable.

Hand-operated grinding machines for wheat, corn, and spices; and rice hullers that could replace the traditional *dheki* for husking rice would save women from the long, laborious hours of work which only result in low returns. Since livestock raising is also a popular category of women's projects, women need veterinary services that could reduce the risks of expanding the size of the livestock.

In terms of comparative advantage of alternative oil processing technologies, although there is an increase in labor productivity and decrease in processing cost as someone moves along the technology scale, the displacement of labor in the *expeller*, the most modern technology in oil processing, compared to *ghani* (bullock-driven oil extractor) is significant. An integrated approach, utilizing the by-product, would offset the disadvantages to a certain extent. Instead of utilizing the by-product for cattle feed, oil cake may be exported to European countries in exchange for dairy products, which would compensate more than the loss incurred due to non-use of *expeller* (Bangladesh Task Force Report 1991).

In case of hand loom sector, instead of using the traditional weaving machinery, the introduction of intermediate technology on textile production would have a more significant impact in terms of productivity for the poor weavers. In certain cases, a small improvement in the existing technologies (dhenki, coir products, blacksmithy and so on) may produce significant improvements in productivity without adversely affecting employment opportunities.

In Bangladesh only 30 per cent of the total population has access to grid electricity. The scenario is worse in rural areas. Due to the shortage of electric power, development of agriculture and rural industrial sectors are hampered. Since more than 70 per cent of Bangladeshi people live in rural areas, there is an increasing unmet demand for electricity in the rural farm and nonfarm sectors.

Although the GB often maintains a reluctant relationship with its clients in terms of increasing the skills of its members, it is good to mention that the Grameen Shakti, a member of Grameen family of companies, which is a pioneer renewable energy technology organization, is devoted to promote and popularize solar home systems with other renewable energy resources to the off grid rural people of Bangladesh. The vision of the Grameen Shakti, which came into being in 1996, is to bring well-being for the rural people using renewable energy resources. The mission of the organization is: promoting solar home systems; providing maintenance services; alleviating poverty; protecting environment; research and development of renewable energy based technologies; and utilization of renewable energy for the benefit of the rural poor. The Grameen Shakti has installed 30,560 solar home systems with the installed power capacity of 1.5 MW with more than 180,000 beneficiaries up to October 2004 using its 105 unit offices throughout Bangladesh. The organization has a plan to install 100,000 solar home systems by 2007 (Grameen Shakti 2004).

Concluding Remarks

Access to microfinance and technological services, though very necessary, these are not sufficient to lift the poor out of poverty. The other important hindrances are: the lack of proper design of technology; lack of marketing facilities; lack of awareness and information; lack of education and management skills; and institutional environment. These barriers make it difficult to realize development potential, and call for a variety of measures to promote technology adoption. The technology development program should be directly related to poor people and evolve with the changes in their lives. It needs to take into account their resources, education, skills, family composition, and their environment. Initial technology must be low cost, and with no undue reliance on external expertise, capital know-how and equipment. Most importantly, technology needs to be based on the active participation of the rural poor themselves. They may be involved from the definition of problems to the selection, application and evaluation of possible solutions. When this process occurs the technology can be internally sustainable as each stage of development becomes more sophisticated. The conditions of the poor must be reflected in the development of technology, and the poor must be brought into efficient process by removing institutional barriers to their movement from a lower to a higher level of technology.

It is to the MFIs' interest to introduce technological innovation for their poor clients. With the enabling environment that the MFIs have created for their clients through the mandatory weekly meetings, it makes it all the more easier for the MFIs to deliver appropriate technology to their poor clients. Given that 95 per cent of MFIs' members are women, it remains to be seen whether the MFIs will be able to contribute to the alleviation of rural female poverty significantly or whether they have targeted the poor women for the hidden reasons that poor women are accessible (being at home during working hours); more likely to repay on time; and more pliable, and patient than men.

It is obvious that poor women clients are in need of more appropriate technology in order to draw them out of their disadvantaged position. Nonetheless, the introduction of technology and the transfer of technical know-how sometimes may be a placebo rather than a panacea for the development of most of the disadvantaged in the society. Technology assistance program must act slowly but steadily, and pay close attention to how the poor women entrepreneurs perceive the possible deficiencies of their enterprises. If the assistance fails to adopt such a slow and incremental approach, poor women entrepreneurs will be unable to adapt to new technologies and the investments will be lost.

Given the above scenario, this study suggests that the MFIs which are perhaps still a beginner in terms of innovation of technology policies suited for the poor in both farm and nonfarm sectors, may go through a three tier technology policy. In the immediate short run the technology policy has to be one of supporting and protecting existing traditional technologies for purposes of sustaining the significant level of employment that exists in these activities. In the medium term, the thrust has to be on upgrading technology in these activities in a way so as to raise productivity without adversely affecting the employment situation. In the long run, the choice of technology for the rural poor has to be made in line with the needs and ability of the rural poor to absorb the improved technologies.

Even once such an appropriate technology is introduced; there is a need for an on-going program of technology development- to seek to improve the quality of services being made available to the rural poor. Designing technological services is rarely a fixed process. Clients' needs and preferences may change with the changes in economic and regulatory environments. The eventual impact of MFIs on poverty will ultimately depend on organizations' systems and products. The more appropriate and the higher the quality of services is on offer, the better would be the impact on poverty alleviation for their clients.

Source: Various sources including:
M. Asaduzzaman and K. Westergaard eds. (1993), pp. 1-27
I. Ahmed. (1983), pp. 48-63
J. U. Ahmed. (1982) pp. 105-27
J. James, and H. Khan. (1997), pp. 153-65
T. Islam, and M. A. Taslim. (1996), pp. 734-70

Chapter 5

Poverty Alleviation Impact of Grameen Microcredit

Introduction

Chapter 4 considered the issues in approach and methodology of the empirical study on the GB. A critical evaluation of the GB's impact in raising the economic situation of its members was also made there. The analysis looked into the economic impact of the GB microcredit programme upon the members in terms of income, employment, capital accumulation, productivity and substitution of informal loans by the GB credit. The gains in terms of economic benefits, though marginal in many cases, were not identical for all GB members. The gains were positive for the moderately poor members. The extreme poor members did not experience any significant increase in their incomes. Based on the extent of the economic benefits the GB members enjoy, this chapter finally attempts to assess the GB impact in alleviating poverty of its members.

The GB was founded to alleviate poverty and it strives to achieve its goal of poverty alleviation. The basic premise behind the setting up of the institution is that if credit is extended to the poor at reasonable terms and conditions, it can generate self-employment and thereby improve their economic condition. Credit is thus seen as a means to the ultimate end of alleviation of rural poverty. The aim of this chapter is to assess the extent to which this objective has been achieved.

An individual's decision to participate in a credit programme can be based on the joint production and consumption behaviour of a household that is constrained in the formal credit market, lacks sufficient savings to finance an income-earning activity, or cannot rely on informal credit because of its high cost. It may be more efficient for such a household to borrow from a group-based credit programme which charges less than informal lenders, in order to make efficient use of available resources, mainly family labour, with an elastic supply of labour. The poor participate in the credit programmes in the expectation that credit will increase their income and sustain self-employment.

The following analysis looks into the success of the GB's efforts to alleviate poverty. This being the ultimate test, the success of which will mainly, though not exclusively, determine the success of the GB. Based on the findings of the GB's credit programme on income, employment, productivity, and credit market together, the analysis will explore the extent and nature of poverty alleviation for different groups of the poor.

Alleviation of Poverty

Given the changes in incomes of the GB members, an attempt is made here to assess the impact of the GB to alleviate poverty amongst its rural poor members. The extent of inequality in the distribution of income for the different groups of households and the proportion of poor households within the total households are shown in Table 5.1.

The Gini-concentration ratio is comparatively lower among the GB members than among the target groups in control villages. The difference between the GB members and the comparable non-members of project villages is not statistically significant. The proportion of the population living in moderate poverty was 79 per cent for comparable non-members in project villages, 74 per cent for the comparable non-members in control villages, but 64 per cent for GB members.

Table 5.1   Proportion of Poor Population Among Participants and Comparable Non-participants

		Target Group Non-participants		All Households	
Variable	Grameen Bank Members	Project Villages	Control Villages	Project Villages	Control Villages
Gini concentration ratio of income	0.263	0.269	0.289	0.287	0.286
	Percent				
Proportion of moderately poor population	64.1	78.6	74.2	62.8	71.6
Proportion of extremely poor population	46.1	63.8	60.4	53.4	55.2

Source: Income distribution data obtained through the household survey in project and control villages.

On the other hand, those living in extreme poverty were estimated at 46 per cent for members of the GB, compared with about 62 per cent for non-members in project and control villages. This indicates that the GB has been able to alleviate poverty of a proportion of its members.

In rural Bangladesh, lack of access to food is synonymous with poverty. A household having no access to food needed for a healthy life is treated as a poor household. Achieving household food security remains a critical objective of poverty alleviation and rural development. Food security, at the household level, is defined as access by all people at all times to the food needed for a healthy life (Zeller 1999, 28). Improvement in the standard of living of the GB members is also reflected through a comparison of the level of expenditures on food and nonfood basic needs for different groups of households (Table 5.2). The per capita expenditure on food for the GB members was 6 per cent higher than for non-members of the same groups in project villages, and 15 per cent higher than the comparable target-group in control villages[1] Similarly, the expenditure on clothing for the GB members was 13 per cent higher than nonparticipants in project villages and 29 per cent higher than the comparable non-members in control villages. As shown in Table 5.2, household expenditure in housing by GB members was 32 per cent higher than that of the target groups in project villages and 310 per cent higher than the comparable non-members in control villages. Although no significant statistical differences in food expenditure were observed among the GB members, comparable non-members in project and control villages (Table 5.2), differences in non-food expenditure among those groups were statistically significant (P<0.000). The differences were mainly for higher housing expenditure of GB members, which indicate their improved standard of living compared to their counterparts.

Although the GB could fare well in achieving food security through consumption credit, it has nonetheless helped improve the living standards of its members through its emphasis on credit programmes.

Tables 5.1 and 5.2 reflect a comparatively better situation of the GB members than their counterparts in the project and control villages. However, a closer look at the self-perception of the GB members (Table 5.3) depicts a rather trivial picture of the role of microcredit in poverty alleviation. As noted earlier, the GB members on the average appeared to be benefiting notably from credit. The members were experiencing increases in income, equity capital, employment, productivity, and access to institutional credits.

Due to differences amongst the poor in terms of economic and social endowments, however, all members of the poor did not experience identical improvements in terms of alleviation of poverty.

---

1 This increase in expenditure in foods stuff, though marginal, indicates the improved standard of living of GB members. This view is confirmed by Hulme and Mosley (1996, 138) when they observe that if income changes were having a significant impact on the standard of living it might be expected that essential expenditure on foods stuff would fall.

Table 5.2   Expenditure on Basic Needs by GB Members and Comparable Control Groups in Project and Control Villages, 1998

Variable	Members	Non-participants in project villages	Target Group in Control Villages	Difference of project over control groups	
				Non-participants in project villages	Target Group in Control Villages
		(Taka/person)		(per cent)	
Expenditure on food	2,980	2,805	2,583	6	15
Expenditure on cereals	2,040	1,935	1,771	5	15
Expenditure on non cereal food	940	870	812	8	16
Expenditure on clothing	210	185	163	13	29
		(Taka/household)		(per cent)	
Expenditure on education	300	221	198	36	52
Expenditure on health	350	287	258	22	36
Expenditure on housing	1,190	898	290	32	310
	(per cent)				
Households incurring expenditures for education	45.5	32.6	30.0	40	52
Households incurring expenditures for housing	61.2	52.1	48.1	17	27

Source: Household survey in project and control (Insert Table 5.2 – Portrait)

Table 5.3 shows that 23 per cent of all members had *reasonably improved* their positions, while 50 per cent of members had experienced a *marginal improvement* only. Nearly 17 per cent of members experienced *no change*, and 10 per cent of members experienced *further deterioration* in their positions. This means that nearly 77 per cent of the members did not experience any significant improvement in their

Table 5.3   Borrowers' Perception of Change in their Economic Position

Economic Condition	Male Borrowers (N=144)	Female Borrowers (N=156)	All Borrowers (N=300)
Improved	22.5	23.6	23.1
Improved (marginally)	50.0	50.1	50.0
Unchanged	17.6	16.2	16.9
Deteriorated	9.3	9.8	9.6
No response	0.6	0.3	0.4
Total	100.0	100.0	100.0

Note: N is the size of sample
Source: Grameen Househousehold Survey

positions as a result of their membership with the GB. Contrary to general findingsof many studies, the present findings are not the first to depict such a comparatively gloomy picture[2].

This trend in poverty alleviation is comparable with the studies that indicate that a decade of one's membership with the GB has done little more than keep one's head above water (Sobhan 1997, 132-4). In Bangladesh there is significant differentiation within the ranks of the poor. Roughly about half of the poor constitute what is referred to as the *extreme poor*, who are forced to subsist on a daily calorie intake of less than 1740 and a per capita income that is less than three-fifths than that of the poverty line (Rahman 1995). While the poverty situation seems to have improved a little over the last seven years, a little less than a quarter of the rural population still seems to be within the ranks of the *extreme* poor (Hashemi 1997, 253). The GB has failed miserably to target this group effectively, resulting in most of them remaining outside the microcredit net.

It is clear that most of the GB members, especially the *extreme poor*, could not alleviate poverty. In some instances, rather than improving their situations, they had experienced a further deterioration. These members, experiencing further deterioration, probably had some inherent weaknesses beside the low level of productivity and income in the GB-financed microenterprises. These members were either trapped in previous debts with the informal lenders and as such could not use the loan money for productive purposes, or had faced any natural calamity or illness or some unexpected incidents like the theft or death of the livestock purchased with the loan money. These factors, in single, or in combination, have resulted in further deterioration of their position. This tendency, drawn essentially, but not conclusively, from the empirical findings, suggests important conclusion about the limitations of credit as a poverty alleviation strategy in Bangladesh.

---

2   Todd found that 17 families out of 40 were still under poverty line even after a decade of membership with the GB, Todd (1996), p. 220. For limitations of credit in alleviating poverty see Rahman (1997), pp. 271-88.

Finally, to evaluate the GB impact on social welfare indicators, the study looked at 75 female GB members randomly selected from three projects, one each from three different zones. Forty five comparable female nonmembers from both project and control villages were also randomly selected to compare their performance with those of the GB female members.

The survey settled on four variables in evaluating the social welfare impacts of the GB women members. They were: the activity ratio; the percentage expenditure on children's education; the percentage expenditure on family nutrition; and the percentage expenditure on family health care services. In general, the performance of the GB female members (Table 5.4) in terms of all the above variables was satisfactory.

Table 5.4   Welfare Indicators of GB Female Borrowers

Welfare Indicators	GB Members	Target Group non members in project villages	Target Group non members in control villages
Activity Ratio	0.50	0.35	0.31
Expenditure on education for children	0.18	0.08	0.06
Expenditure on family nutrition	0.14	0.09	0.09
Expenditure on health services	0.11	0.07	0.09

Source: Field Survey of 75 female borrowers

The investment pattern of female members was more efficient in terms of human capital formation compared to comparable non-members. Their increasing expenditure towards their children's education and family health care clearly demonstrates that they are more concerned regarding the human capital formation of their family members. These types of investments have significant social returns and intergenerational payoffs. In terms of human capital formation, the GB female members were more cautious not only from comparable non-members, but more importantly, from their male counterparts.

The Khandker (1998) study based on data from a multipurpose household survey of 1,798 households in Bangladesh also commends the performance of the GB female members on efficiency grounds. The study added that besides the impressive indicator of loan repayment, the GB women members are more efficient in terms of accumulation of net worth or working capital.

The above study also confirms that in terms of human development efforts, female members had a large impact on the well being of both male and female children, compared with their male counterparts. At the mean 1 per cent increase in the GB credit provided to women increased the probability of school enrolment by 1.9 per cent for girls and 2.4 per cent for boys. In contrast, for the same increase in male credit increased boy's school enrolment by 2.8 per cent, with no impact on girl's schooling. The female members had a large impact on the nutritional well being of both male and female children.

In terms of productivity, the performance of the female members was, however, not as satisfactory as those of their male counterparts (discussed in chapter 4 around *distribution of workers in different sectors*). But, it would perhaps be justified before commenting on the overall productivity of female members to look into the prevailing socioeconomic condition and the place of rural poor women in that environment. One has to evaluate the productivity (rate of return) in GB-initiated women microenterprises, keeping in view what alternative income-earning opportunities these poor women have had before joining the GB.

In rural areas of developing countries, men are increasingly drawn into a world emphasizing individual pursuit of wealth and happiness, whereas women are often left behind with their household works to manage and rearing their children and struggle to provide for them within a human economy frame of reference. Women's economic behaviour does not follow a purely economic rationality, aiming for the maximization of individual profit or the pursuit of enterprise growth above all. The yardstick of women's economic performance in microenterprises should be a human economic one because this takes into account women's multiple roles (Tinker 1995, 25).

If credit can generate self-employment in home-based enterprises, and if the employment generates a positive net return to the family labour, it is imperative in terms of human economics that the women would go for such credit. However, the productivity of rural poor, illiterate women cannot be expected in any way to be identical with those of the modern educated women in Bangladesh or other developed, developing, and economically-transforming countries. The productivity of rural poor women should be judged by keeping in mind their elastic supply of labour and their traditional three roles of production, reproduction, and social services. These women would be seen as productive as long as they make any contribution to the family income.

It is widely believed that as long as women, who unlike their male counterparts suffer the double burden of poverty and discrimination, are not provided with demand-responsive, effective financial and nonfinancial services, mere participation of the rural poor women in the development process does not and probably cannot help them climb out of poverty. The broad conditions of endemic poverty and deliberate gender discrimination have been the main stimulus for the provision of quality financial and skill-enhancing nonfinancial services to generate productive employment for the growing rural poor women.

Limitations of Microcredit in Alleviation of Rural Poverty

The microcredit's ability to help reduce the vulnerability of the poor to downward mobility pressures, to develop their microenterprises, and to increase their net wealth is well documented. This simplified analysis overlooks the dynamic nature of poverty and the fact that today's vulnerable, not-so-poor may be tomorrow's very poor if they do not have access to client-responsive financial services (not credit alone) to help them mange the risks and crises that beset their households.

Most of the MFIs provide short-term financial services and are still in the process of developing more appropriate operating financial schemes for longer-term types of finance for their clients' enterprises necessary for significant poverty alleviation (Almeyda 1996, 120). Short-term financial services help smooth consumption, it does not alleviate poverty (Morduch 1998, 1).

The efforts of the GB though succeeded in alleviating household poverty to some extent, its contribution to alleviate overall poverty is very marginal. Two points must be made here in terms of the GB impact in poverty alleviation. The first one to note is that, contrary to much recent writings, microenterprise and small enterprise development should not be equated with poverty-reduction. At times the two will coincide but this needs empirical validation and should not be assumed, as is commonly the case. There are very real dangers involved in uncritically adopting microcredit strategies as a rule and cheap panacea for poverty (Wood and Sharif 1997eds. 29).

The second point, partially related to the first, is that most of the poor households cannot be viewed simply as microentrepreneurs, self-employed poor. The vast majority of households are, to use the term of Chambers (1995, 23), are *foxes* not *hedgehogs*. The poor are generally seeking to diversify income sources-no single income source is expected to provide an *escalator of sustained growth of income*. Hulme and Mosley (1996) observe,

> depending on season, prices, health and other contingencies, they pursue a mix of activities that may include growing their own food, labouring for others, running small trading, hunting and gathering, and accessing loans from friends and relatives and sometimes even from money lenders. In terms of occupational pattern, they are managers of complex multiple enterprises and not just the manager of a single enterprise, normally financed by the Bank.

Also the assumption that credit alone can automatically translate into successful microenterprises is fatal. This is the familiar debate of *minimalist* credit strategies versus the *integrated* approach to microenterprise promotion. Microcredit though a very necessary but not a sufficient condition for microenterprise promotion. Other inputs, for example, business and production training, establishing of market linkages for inputs and outputs, sub-sectoral analysis and policy reform are required.

As the GB has entered a phase of expansion, it faces new challenges. The major concern about microcredit is whether the poorest households have benefited from microcredit. Since poverty alleviation has been the major objective of microcredit, concerns related to their ability to reach the poorest households need to be examined.

The rhetoric surrounding microcredit remains extraordinary. For years programmes blithely asserted that they were serving the *poorest of the poor*. Part of this is because of the efforts to promote microcredit as a *panacea* or *cure all* for poverty. Any MFI seriously claiming it reaches the *poorest of the poor* is either not monitoring its clientele properly or simply being economical with the truth unless the institution is offering revolutionary quality financial services that attract the poorest and destitute. Wright (2000, 56) remarks that certainly none of the larger MCIs including the GB operating in Bangladesh are serving the poorest of the poor through their mainstream credit and savings activities.

Relying on microfinance interventions in isolation *is like a carpenter using only a hammer to build the platform upon which the poor will stand. Other tools are necessary* (ibid. 2000, 36). Robinson (2001, 20) observes that providing credit by MFIs to the extremely poor is like trying to build a house by using a saw to hammer the nails and a screwdriver to cut the boards.

Credit by itself, to quote Matin et al. (2001, 1), *is not a magic sky-hook that reaches down to pluck the poor out of poverty*. The justification for treating credit as a potentially powerful anti-poverty instrument is that first, it is properly administered with client-responsive financial services and, second, that the skills of the rural poor are enhanced. These caveats create the need for the word *potentially*.

The ADB (1997) report remarks that in the longer perspective, microenterprise promotion can never be a substitute for a variety of social sector programmes such as, primary health care, environmental sanitation, education, nutrition, family planning and child care. Continued investment in basic infrastructure, an overall favourable economy, and structural changes like land reform also remain a necessarily high priority.

While there is no denying that such programmes can be run more cost-efficiently and that they can be better targeted to the poor, the replacement of such programmes with microcredit programmes may be double disaster for the rural poor.

While recognizing and accepting this, we should not lose sight of the fact that because of the scarcity of development resources, the poor cannot rely on government programmes, and are therefore forced to taking care of themselves with whatever inputs are made available to them.

Whereas the availability of microcredit enhances income among the poor and with continuous membership with those MFIs, some of them have moved out of poverty, there is still, as noted, a group of *extreme poor* households who have not been reached by the microcredit programmes. The increase in income of microcredit members is directly proportional to their starting level of income- the poorer they were to start with, the less the impact of the loan. This study observes that less than half of target households in progamme villages participated in microcredit programmes even where the programmes had been available for more than three years. The poorest of the poor (extreme poor) did not join microcredit programmes.

This exclusion of the poorest households is in line with the concerns about the heterogeneity amongst the poor. Those living below the *poverty line* are located at various distances from it. It may be comparatively easier to lift those who are closer to the line. The self-perception of members (Table 5.3) reinforces the fact that the GB targets those who are above the poverty line (*non-poor*) and or closer to the line (*moderate poor*) at the neglect of those who are far below the poverty line (*extreme poor*).

There is, of course, a special group among the *extreme poor* identified as suspect. They are the work-averse beggars, disabled, vagabond, street singers and performers etc. These people are so destitute that they sometimes think themselves not credit-worthy. They do not think they can repay the loan and *self-select* themselves out of credit programme membership. In order to maintain its excellent record of repayment, very often the GB also excludes this group of people from their credit programmes. This group is mainly unable or unwilling to perform hard physical labour and their exclusion is easily justified. In order to perform hard physical labour, one needs more calorie intake, sometimes up to 7,000 calories, as against the normal calorie intake of 2,122. There is another group of poor households who constitute a type of *floating population*. They may easily shift their residence and move to other areas. This type of household is considered a bad credit risk and is excluded from the microcredit programme.

The self-selected groups for peer monitoring, the principle which the GB adheres to, have also not been inclusive of the poorest people. People select those with whom they want to form a group on the basis of their own knowledge of the likelihood that these people will make timely payment of loan instalments. Even the low-asset and land-holding ceiling which the GB has used to target loans away from better-off people has not necessarily meant that the poorest are included in the GB credit programme.

There has been no adequate understanding of the reasons behind the exclusion of the extreme poor. The most important reason is the poor loan repayment prospects by the extreme poor households. Perfect recovery of loans, the measuring rod of the overblown claims of success of the GB, may be an obstacle if loans are given to these groups of households.

However, studies on the default of agricultural credit reinforce the fact that the large scale defaults are within the non-poor farm households. Even among NGO clients, *the not-so-poor* do not always demonstrate their superiority to the *poorest of the poor* in terms of good repayment and stable group behaviour[3].

Poverty alone is not responsible for the inability to repay. There are a number of characteristics of the poor, which differentiate their ability to repay. It is, therefore,

---

3   It can be well argued that the entire extreme poor cannot be accused of loan default. The large NGOs (that is, ASA), which show 99 per cent loan recovery, have a substantial portion of extreme poor (the percentage is, perhaps, more than the GB) as their members. See Rutherford (1995).

imperative to analyse these factors to understand why the poorest households are not credit-worthy.

A large percentage of the poorest households, who self-select themselves out of the credit programmes may have stayed away because of their own reservations and fear, which may be termed *demand side consideration*. The exclusion of the poorest households can be explained in terms of the interaction of *demand* and *supply* factors[4]. Poor households' demand for microcredit will be generated from their ability and willingness to make a profitable investment of the fund. The pertinent question that boils down to whether for the poorest households such ability and willingness is lower than for the less poor and why this is so. The answer to the question lies mainly, though not exclusively, on the operational basis of microenterprises and the factors associated with poverty. The answer then will shed light on how the same factors work as constraints to the expansion of microenterprises and account for low profitability of those enterprises among the poorest households.

By definition microenterprises are family enterprises, which means that the family labourers are primarily utilized in these enterprises. Of course, it is a rather limited view to consider the utilization of family labour input as the only objective of microenterprises without considering the complementarities of input use in microenterprises. A proper view, therefore, is to take into account all the major types of inputs and to identify what actually is a binding constraint for microenterprise development.

Agricultural land is not directly related to microenterprise development. However, the homestead area and the house itself are important in determining the demand for loans for microenterprises. For example, the rickshaw puller needs a safe place to keep his rickshaw at night. Paddy processing requires a place for drying the paddy.

An important determinant of the extent of poverty of households is the size, skill, and gender composition of family labour force. It will be seen that these factors have an important role in determining the profitability of microenterprises.

Skill and physical ability enable workers to pursue activities of high return. For example, a person with the physical ability to ply a rickshaw can generate a high rate of return. With such a high return the loans from the microcredit institutions can easily be repaid. Households with such skilled labour do not usually constitute the *extreme poor* and they are attractive as clients of microcredit institutions as against households with no skilled family labour force and a larger dependency burden.

A similar argument holds for the gender composition of a family labour force. The worst position is likely to þe occupied by families with only one adult woman. The households headed by women face so many problems. However, enterprising

---

4   The division between exclusion by the clients themselves and exclusion by the MFI is arbitrary since it is the systems of the MFI which will determine whether clients self-exclude or not. An MFI's ability to attract the poorest depends mainly on the services it offers, and whether the services have been designed to be appropriate for the poorest. See for details Rahman (1997), pp. 271-88.

women who run their own business without help from any male family members are also substantial in number.

Microcredit does not require equity capital on the part of the borrower member. Though one's own capital is not necessary to start a business, it may determine the returns to labour by raising the capital/ labour ratio and also by affecting the choice between fixed capital and running capital, which, in turn, determines the type of activity pursued. Recent studies on limitations of microcredit demonstrate that it (microcredit) may often be more effective in terms of poverty reduction to support existing user-owned enterprises[5]. Those who do not possess their own capital are likely to use a smaller proportion of the borrowed fund as fixed capital. This constraint arises when the repayment schedule is strictly set at one year. With such terms of repayment, the borrowers having no savings to guard them against failure of such repayments, hesitate to come within the microcredit net of these programmes.

The literature put forward by microcredit institutions assume that borrowers invest in business that will produce a steady stream of income out of which the loan will be quickly repaid. The proportion of borrowers that do invest in such income-generating activities is not known: estimates vary and are hotly contested. But it is clear that many spend their loans in a wide variety of ways that do not produce a stream of income (Rutherford 1997a, 368). Credit is a form of debt and for those *extreme poor* households who are subsisting far below the *poverty line*, taking loans constitutes considerable risk. For activities such as petty trading, and rickshaw driving, returns may be regular and yield income which is sufficient to meet the weekly repayments. For other activities, such as livestock, returns may be more irregular. Some borrowers at various times may have to service their loans from non-assisted enterprise sources. For those without regular incomes especially the *extreme poor* households, even the small amounts required can be a burden (Montgomery et al. 1996, 153-4). This is the main, although not the only, reason for self-exclusion.

The poorest households are more likely to invest in activities, which require little fixed capital. This limits their choice to certain processing activities or peddling which generate a low return to labour. Moreover, after a certain level of working capital/labour ratio is attained in these activities, the marginal productivity of capital declines sharply. Thus the poorest households, who do not have any saving to supplement the borrowed fund, will be discouraged from entering into the microcredit programmes.

A substitute for one's own fixed capital to fund a microenterprise can be provided from a supplementary wage earning occupation by a second working member of a family. These earnings can be used to repay a part of the loan and thereby the fixed capital acquired using the borrowed fund can be saved. This linkage demonstrates how a family's human resources may work as a substitute for physical or financial capital.

---

5   For limitations of microcredit see Johnson and Rogaly (1997), pp. 10-12, as well as Lipton (1988).

In analysing the impact of *poverty lending*, an approach used by the GB in reducing poverty, Malhotra (1992, 19) observes that lending of this type limits investments to the most traditional and least profitable or productive activities. While the small size of activities financed sometimes leads to income increases, it does not generate new employment. The insignificant rise in income, if any, and lack of employment opportunity, do not attract the extreme poor to participate in microcredit programmes. Appendix 5A summarizes the distinguishing features of poverty lending and financial systems approaches to lending in MFIs.

Terming microcredit as *microdebt*, Hulme (2000, 26) observes that not all microdebt produces favourable results, especially for poor people working in low-return activities in saturated markets that are poorly developed. Because of lack of skills and knowledge, a proportion of borrowers encounter great difficulties in repaying loans. While MFIs suggest that such problems are overcome through social support in some painless way this is often not the case-the increasing number of dropouts of MFIs contradicts the contention of the MFIs.

As donors and practitioners place increasing emphasis on microfinance as opposed to microcredit, the poor are likely to join the microfinance programmes in order to save. Over time the poor may also enjoy the benefits of scale that microfinance institutions' more affluent clients allow-in terms of interest on savings, a broader range of financial services and possibly even lower cost loans (Rutherford 1995).

It is also not clear that the poorest are best assisted through financial programmes. The poorest 10 to 15 per cent of people may require initial help to get over food, health, or labour market thresholds before they can respond to policy changes that successfully reach less poor people. This appears to suggest that the extreme poor are more likely to use public works programmes than credit-based interventions (Khandker 1998, 142).

As a result of all these constraints, a significant portion of the *extreme poor* households self-exclude themselves from entering into the microcredit programmes and even if they enter at all, the programme impact rarely becomes positive for them.

Usury, lending at interest or excessive interest and practiced in various parts of the world, is prohibited in Islam. Bangladesh is predominantly an Islamic country, but despite the huge demand for financial services including credit among the rural poor, these people are reluctant to join the interest-bearing microfinancial services of the NGOs/MFIs. Over 2,500 Islamic NGOs, employing about 25,000, are operating in Bangladesh. The fundamental principle of the Islamic NGOs is that they are interest-free and most of them run on profit-sharing basis.

The GB, as noted earlier, has done many things right, including its programme on *Beggar members*. Given its high standard of professionalism, the GB could succeed in implementing some projects based on Islamic principles. The GB may well discover that the outreach or expansion of the GB would be significantly higher than what it has experienced during the last couple of years.

On the supply side, the fear that the poorest households may not be able to generate sufficiently high returns from investment in microenterprises may discourage the GB and other MFIs to provide loans to the groups of extreme poor. The MFIs consider serving the extreme poor is too inefficient, and too unprofitable.

Even if the demand side plays a crucial role, it may be difficult, if not impossible, to remove the constraints which account for low profitability of microenterprises for the poorest households. Knowledge of these factors may help the GB to adopt proper policies so that the credit offered by the GB suits the needs of the poorest. A closer look at the operational principles of the GB reveals that immediate attention to the following issues are desirable to reach the poorest of the poor and at the same time maintain its sustainability.

The floor size of loans of the GB is set at around BDT 5000. Many poor households complain that the loan sizes are small; at the same time there are very poor households who are not courageous enough to borrow as large an amount as BDT 5000. For this group of people, a loan larger than the capacity to invest will lead to consumption use of the rest of the money, which will then be difficult to repay. There should be no minimum floor regarding the size of the loan, especially for the extreme poor. Borrowers' initial situations should determine this.

The effective rate of interest of the GB ranges from 28 to 32 per cent[6]. Despite the fact that access to credit may be more important than rates of interest, a low rate of interest is obviously preferred by the borrowers. It may enable many of the poorest clients to enter into the credit market. Of course, the problem of reducing the rate of interest is that it cannot be done only for the poorest. A uniform reduction of the rate of interest will diminish the prospect of financial sustainability of the GB.

However, for an organization, like the GB, the largest rural financial institution in Bangladesh, a lowering of the rate of interest may not necessarily reduce its earnings. Interest elasticity of demand for credit may be such that a reduction in the rate of interest will expand the total volume of credit, and raise the number of borrowers per branch. The loss due to a decrease in interest rates will be compensated through increased gains in total interest earnings.

Choice of projects and their actual implementation is usually left to the borrowers. This autonomy may be relevant for experienced investors, but for new borrowers from the poorest group, besides lower rate of return in productivity, this may also lead to a leakage of funds and inefficient use. Closer supervision by the GB's field officials may help them to guard against misuse of funds. However, such supervision may be expensive for the GB. The way out of this is to adopt different policies for the new, hesitant and *extreme poor* borrowers in contrast to the older, more experienced, and *moderate poor* borrowers.

Fail-safe business plans, often claimed by the GB, are not generally available. There is no free lunch: returns in business plans can, as a rule, only be bought in return for the acceptance of risks; high or low. In such a situation credit for *extreme poor* borrowers' means that there are multiple responsibilities thrust upon them. By simply loosening a liquidity constraint it can enable those borrowers to simply

---

6   Rahman from the BIDS, however, argues that the rate of interest can range from 16 to 50 per cent. For details see Wood and Sharif eds. (1997), p. 282.

enlarge the scope of operations, so that vulnerability is not increased; which may be called the *protectional* role of credit. However, if their income is successfully increased through a series of loan operations, this may itself influence their attitude to risk, so that the risk-aversion constraint rotates clockwise. In this event borrowers, emboldened by the success of previous loans, may choose to borrow again for the purpose of *capital-deepening*. Such a move will increase their expected income, but at the same time it will also increase their vulnerability. Credit operations, which have this effect, may be called *promotional*.

Even if loans are made available to the *extreme poor*, there is still debate over the design of appropriate financial services for the poorest. Studies have demonstrated that providing credit for microenterprises is unlikely to help this group to increase their incomes. Some design features of savings and credit schemes are able to meet the needs of the *extreme poor*. Access to reliable, monetized savings facilities can help the poor smooth consumption over periods of cyclical or unexpected crisis, thus greatly improving their economic security. It is only when the extreme poor have some economic security that access to credit can help them move out of poverty by improving the productivity of their enterprises or creating new sources of livelihood (Johnson and Rogaly 1997, 12).

The above analysis suggests modifications in a number of fronts of the basic features of the lending operations by the GB. Most of the policies, such as small, flexible loan sizes to suit the poor, longer repayment periods, close supervision, and savings mobilization, are likely to increase the cost of credit operation, making it more difficult, although not impossible, to achieve the goal of financial sustainability. Mobilization of savings, of course, will ensure the financial viability of both the GB and the borrowers. Financial sustainability is desirable, but at the same time the GB should also consider whether the attainment of such sustainability involves too large a cost in terms of the sacrifice of excluding the poorest. The objective of poverty alleviation and service to the poorest should be treated as a criterion of success of the rural financial institutions, especially for an institution like the GB, which was founded mainly to alleviate poverty.

In an apparent trade-off between sustainability and outreach, some MFIs are relatively successful. Those that seem to have come closest to self-sufficiency have generally confined themselves only with credit without an emphasis on non-financial services. This *credit-alone* approach though necessary for financial sustainability, is not helpful for poverty reduction, particularly for the extreme poor (Berger 1995, 211).

While microfinance can help alleviate poverty to some extent, significant poverty alleviation is dependent on economic and social changes well beyond the reach of financial intermediation. Thus, financial services may be a necessary but not sufficient condition for poverty alleviation. Important interventions at the microlevel such as microfinance need to be matched with supportive macroeconomic policies to create an enabling environment for the poverty alleviation process (Wood and Sharif eds. 1997, 374-5). The MFIs, without any link to the overall macroeconomic policies of a country, are no panacea for poverty alleviation. While these organizations have some comparative advantages over the public sectors, it would be an illusion to imagine that the patchwork of services that the MFIs provide could substitute for the state provision of basic education, primary health care, welfare services and essential infrastructure (Turner and Hulme 1997, 218).

While the GB and other credit-oriented MFIs' staff may be screening out some of the poorest, it is the MFIs' policies that seem to play a particularly important role in the exclusion of the poorest. There seems to be an opportunity to examine still more flexible financial services (for example, entirely voluntary, open access savings accounts, without the compulsory weekly deposit requirements) to attract the poorest. Although the GB has recently introduced the voluntary open access savings accounts, it has yet to go a long way to meet the ever growing needs of the flexible financial services of the poorest households. Such a service would, however, demand a total commitment of the GB.

As the microfinance revolution continues, there is a growing awareness that improved client-friendly savings facilities can provide not only an important financial service to the poor, but also that such facilities will actually provide more capital funds for the MFI than the compulsory, locked-in savings systems that have been so prevalent. More importantly, there is a wide-spread belief that voluntary and accessible savings facilities may result in the inclusion of the poorest 10-15 per cent of the population, who are averse to risk (and thus to taking credit), and are therefore not being served by most MFIs (Wright 2000, 146).

Taking into considerations the factors of both demand and supply responsible for exclusion of the poorest from the credit operations, it is presumably the supply side factors i.e., the GB itself exclude the extreme poor in order to ensure an impressive rate of loan recovery. Except for a very few groups of the *extreme poor*, most of the poorest households have a pressing demand for microfinance services.

It should also be noted with concerns that the GB's targeting appears to have shifted in recent years against the poorest. With the introduction of technology-intensive projects through the *Grameen Network and Grameen-created Companies* (Appendix 5B) this problem has become more acute. Most of the members who have recently joined the GB appear to be better endowed from the old, first-time members. This will lead the GB further away from the concerns of the *extreme poor*.

The call of the Microcredit Summit (1997) as well as the intense desire of the MFIs to achieve sustainability, there has been a sudden increase in the disbursement of loans. In view of the limited scope for horizontal expansion, the GB has started rapid credit deepening and an increase in the incidence and severity of mistargeting. Introduction of a seasonal loan by the GB in 1992 is considered one of the factors of its increased mistargeting.

As Gresham's law[7] reminds us, if the poor and non-poor are combined within a single programme, the non-poor will always drive out the poor. For the poverty alleviation programme to be effective, the delivery system must be designed and

---

7   Gresham's law generally refers to the tendency of people to hoard the more valuable of two types of specie (currency), letting the inferior type circulate more freely. Here, it refers

operated exclusively for the poor. That requires not only a strict definition of who the poor are-but also a committed adherence to that definition.

All this amounts to saying that the secular trend of the GB to exclude the extreme poor and the inability of some of the extreme poor to turn their livelihood enterprises to microenterprises, as well, are responsible for the limited impact on the alleviation of rural poverty.

This lends support to the argument that credit for the poorest is not as practical as programme rhetoric suggests[8]. The common assumption that MFIs work with the poorest of the poor needs to be dropped, unless they (MFIs) can provide clear evidence that this is the case. The grandly named CGAP (through disseminating microfinance best practice) has spent its first three years as the Consultative Group to Assist the not-so-Poor if one examines its portfolio (Hulme 2000, 27)

The microcredit programme of the GB in reaching the poorest of the poor has been far less impressive than that of the BRAC. The experience of the Income Generation for Vulnerable Group Development (IGVGD) programme of the BRAC indicates that the project has been successful in targeting the most destitute rural women, who generally are either excluded from NGO programmes or who self-select themselves out because they are too destitute to be considered credit-worthy[9].

The limited impact of the GB in alleviating poverty has been confirmed by the Grameen itself when its former Deputy Managing Director, Khaled Shams remarks that micro-scale interventions may move borrowers from just below to just above poverty line; families will have three meals a day where once they had one; and children may go to school where before they did not (Holcombe 1995, 75). The Grameen microfinance services thus have, at best, ensured this regular meals for some of its clients, at worst, these have left most of the clients' situation unchanged and in some cases, even deteriorated.

The implicit but widespread assumption regarding nongovernmental financial institutions in Bangladesh has been that they are indeed placed in special poverty-stricken areas. A study on three leading NGOs in Bangladesh, by Sharma and Zeller (1999, 2123) shows those branches tend to be located in relatively well-developed areas than in remoter, less developed regions. The GB also tends to open new branches in developed areas. By doing so, the GB excludes the vast majority of the poor both moderate and extreme, which leads to the overall limited impact on rural poverty alleviation.

---

to the tendency of one group (non-poor) to *crowd out* another's (poor) ability to gain benefits from a programme.

8   Most of the NGOs describe in their literature the goal of helping the *poorest of the poor*, but in practice, put little effort to ascertain whether the benefits of their work accrue to the poorest or merely the poor. For a convincing discussion on the issue see Clark (1990), p. 54, as well as Hulme and Mosley (1996), Vol. 2, p. 154.

9   Professor Hashemi was the former Director of the Project for Rural Poverty Alleviation of the GB. For a detailed analysis of the failure of the GB to reach the extreme poor see Hashemi (1997), pp. 248-57.

If one judges the performance of the GB in terms of its efforts for ensuring access to the large numbers of rural poor women, hitherto been excluded from institutional finances, the performance of the GB is good. However, if the GB microcredit programme is instead seen as a form of employment programme that attempts to realize the goal of increased employment opportunities and incomes, the performance of the GB is not encouraging.

It is true that poor people want microfinance services. Even when they have to pay the full cost of those services, they use them, and come back to use them again and again. But, as to the power of microfinance to alleviate poverty, the evidence is still ambiguous. Microfinance is being over advertised, far beyond a level that present evidence supports.

The impact of the GB microlending to the recipient household's income tends to increase at a decreasing rate as the recipients' volume of loans increased. This relationship can be explained in terms of the greater preference of the poor for consumption loans, their greater vulnerability to asset sales forced by adverse income shocks and their limited range of investment opportunities. In such a situation, where average loan impacts diminish with repeated loans, attempts to alleviate poverty through the GB microcredit is bound to hit rapidly diminishing returns.

Apart from low level of productivity, poor households are vulnerable to economic stresses caused by a variety of factors: (1) structural dimensions of the rural economy (investment and return); (2) familial or life-cycle effects; and (3) sudden crises such as death or illness in the family or natural calamities. The many factors influencing economic well being and the inherent vulnerability of poor people suggest that providing client-responsive credit, and open-access voluntary savings and insurance services are likely to be more successful in coping with such vulnerabilities. Poor people suffer not only from persistently low incomes but also from the precarious nature of their existence. It is of no matter that they have experienced a reasonable increase in incomes from credit-induced enterprises.

The GB's contribution in reducing vulnerability of its clients is limited. There are institutions that provide relatively low transaction cost savings services that permit vulnerable households to *store cash,* which earns interest. These savings can be readily accessed in times of crisis. Although of late the GB has introduced an *open access current account scheme* which can be used even by non-members, and wherein the depositors earn a competitive market interest rate and are allowed to withdraw money irrespective of whether they have an outstanding loan or not. The fact remains, however, that in contrast to the sophistication that has developed in the lending activities of the GB, the range of saving services does not seem to be as well-developed.

The GB's impact on alleviating poverty through changes in the consumption pattern of the rural poor is favourable for the majority of individual clients and households. However, its impact on village-level poverty reduction is somewhat smaller. The Khandker (1998, 149) study confirms that overall only one per cent of rural households can free themselves from poverty each year through microcredit.

Are the poverty alleviation impacts even if only marginal, sustainable? If poverty reduction is achieved mainly through changes in consumption rather than changes in income and productivity, poverty reduction impacts are difficult to sustain. Participants in the GB microcredit programmes, particularly the women, tend to have low levels of skills and knowledge. They are limited therefore to borrowing for self-employment in non-farm projects that have low growth potential. Unless activities with high growth potential are supported by microcredit programmes, the possibility of long-run poverty reduction on a sustained basis through microcredit programmes is remote. Despite the operations of the GB and other MFIs in Bangladesh which have expanded over the years both in total volume of financial services provided and in number of clients served, the institutional sources cannot even meet one-fifth of the credit needs of the rural sector, let alone the needs for voluntary savings mobilization. It is, therefore, not surprising that the non-institutional sources of finance still play a role in the rural sector of Bangladesh. However, given the limited role of the non-institutional sources in providing credit for investment on a sustained basis and their high interest rates, these sources of finance cannot be a perfect substitute for a formal financial system in Bangladesh.

The GB, despite being a formal financial institution, has incorporated some of the principles of the non-institutional sources of finance in its credit policies. Its microlending services had a positive impact both directly and, in some cases indirectly, by inducing informal financial institutions such as moneylenders, to lower the element of monopoly profit in their interest rate and widen their product-mix. In an environment of scarcity of capital and low credit-worthiness, the type of services offered by the GB to the poor, especially women are far more attractive than those of non-institutional sources of finance.

Nonetheless, this has by no means stopped the GB clients from taking loans from the non-institutional sources. Such loans are often necessary for members to maintain the regularity of weekly loan repayments of the GB and to meet contingencies caused by illness or the costs incurred by social obligations. The incomes earned by the GB members may again be extracted by the non-institutional sources of finance.

In seeking an answer to the question of the impact of the GB in the RFM, it can reasonably be argued that the rural non-institutional sources which still finance more than two-thirds of the rural sector, do not consider themselves as being in competition with the programme of the GB. In order to have a significant impact in the rural credit market, the GB needs to redesign its lending policies to incorporate flexibility both in the amount of loan disbursed and the repayment schedule on the basis of household resource endowment. Designing a differentiated and diverse lending policy sensitive to the individual absorptive capacity of different clients can provide a real choice to its member households. This may go side by side with its present group-based lending. This will enable the GB to compete more successfully with the informal lenders. Despite the GB provides a competitive financial service for the poor, it is still not a substitute for the informal credit market in rural Bangladesh.

In order to attract the extreme poor into the microcredit net, the rate of return of the GB-financed enterprises needs to be increased. To increase the rate of return in those activities in rural Bangladesh, where the impact of microcredit on productivity is generally low compared to other rapidly growing economies for example, Indonesia, Malaysia, and Bolivia the introduction of appropriate technology is often the only way out (Hulme and Mosley 1996, 89-91).

The limited impact of its *minimalist* credit programme in alleviating poverty leads one to question the inflated claims of the GB on its success as a model of poverty alleviation. The broad conclusion that is emerging seems to suggest that the credit-alone approach without emphasis on voluntary savings mobilization and growth-enhancing technology and training on the use of the technology will not alleviate rural poverty significantly. In response to the research question related to the poverty alleviation impact of the GB microfinance programmes, it can safely be said that the impact has been modest.

In an environment of *macrofailure* and *economic stagnation*, it is, of course, a positive step forward toward the alleviation of poverty in rural Bangladesh. But the achievements made so far through its slow, often frustrating step-by-step processes are not substantial and the GB definitely cannot be labeled as perfect. The rate and level of progress made so far is not enough to claim that the GB model is the one to be uncritically replicated. There is room for improvements in its effort to alleviate poverty, especially poverty of the *extreme poor*. The GB, in order to be viable and in the process replicable, must demonstrate sufficient progress and success in alleviating poverty in a significant and meaningful way.

Given the limited impact of the GB in alleviating poverty, this study presumes that such impact, even if marginal, should not be dismissed altogether as unimportant. One has to compare the benefits; keeping in view what alternative income-earning opportunities the poor, particularly poor women have had before joining the GB. Targeted credit programme of the GB for the poor though not a panacea for poverty alleviation, is a key step forward to opening the door and enabling them to harness their own underutilized capacity.

Sustainability of Poverty Alleviation Impact

How effective the GB microcredit programmes are in reducing poverty in a sustained way is an important policy question that merits careful programme evaluation. An answer to this question will indicate whether the poverty alleviation impact is sustainable over time.

A sustainable poverty reduction can occur through a secular increase in income due to an increase in productivity. This increase in productivity may result from an increase in efficiency, which again may result from different efficiency-enhancing efforts of the lending institution: development of proper technology; training; product design; and marketing channels. There also needs to be a reasonable impact in the rural credit market to meet different financial needs of the rural poor so that the poor need not go to the informal lenders, and proper steps are taken to protect the poor from vulnerabilities.

This study has shown that the GB is performing relatively well and perhaps better than other specialized financial institutions operating in oligopolistic competition in Bangladesh. The GB is a unique financial institution that has succeeded in providing credit, without collateral, to the poor, particularly poor women, with very low default rates. The GB is, however, more than a bank, since its objectives include alleviating the poverty of the rural poor. The important aspect of the GB is its outreach to women who constitute about 95 per cent of its membership.

In considering the sustainability of the poverty alleviation impact of the GB microfinance programmes, the answer to which is not straightforward, it can safely be said that in terms of consumption smoothing its performance is good but in terms of significant poverty alleviation, the performance is not encouraging. Nonetheless, the GB microfinance programmes appear to be more effective than other formal finance and targeted poverty alleviation programmes.

This study however, does not in any way support the microcredit *evangelists'* unrealistic prescription of a worldwide blanket replication of the GB model in alleviating rural poverty. There is not a GB blueprint that can be handed out universally and replicated. An approach or method cannot be replicated in a fixed, prescriptionary way. Replication demands a lot of experimentation and adaptation. With proper modifications, where necessary, the GB approach has a fair chance of success in densely settled poverty-stricken areas in rural Asia. In Africa and Latin America, however, an appropriate delivery mechanism specific to each case has to be worked out through trial and error.

Can the Impact on the Extreme Poor be Enhanced?

The limitations of the GB in alleviating poverty of the poor, especially the extreme poor, have been well documented. The question, which the study faces now, is whether the GB can increase its poverty impact, and if it can, what are the costs of doing so? As a prelude to an overall discussion of policy options to increase the impact on the extreme poor, the following arguments may be taken into consideration:

1. In principle, the GB can easily control the components of impact. It can avoid what Cornia and Stewart (1993, 459) call E-mistakes (intervention reaching the non-target population) by simply refusing to lend to all borrowers except those who declare assets or income below the poverty line and the GB, in most cases, does this. Despite this, the percentage of non-poor borrowers into the GB credit net is increasing over time. Fixing a small loan size, particularly for the first time borrowers, appears to be a more effective way of excluding

the non-poor than refusing loans to them.
2. An alternative strategy consists of trying to increase the extent of impact, which on the evidence of the present study can be achieved by:

   a) measures to improve the efficiency of savings mobilization, especially voluntary savings;
   b) measures which reduce the (transaction and transport) costs of doing business by opening mobile banking centres where low income people are concentrated;
   c) political changes which allow for greater freedom of interest- rate policy and pursuit of overdue borrowers;
   d) measures which remove demand constraints to which the borrowers are subject;
   e) measures which increase the labour- intensity of credit- supported activities and thus motivate borrowers to hire more people from the pool of landless workers per unit of output;
   f) measures which create opportunities for women to enter into new fields, to acquire new skills, and to introduce new technologies in their enterprises;
   g) measures to provide financial and non-financial services;
   h) intensive loan collection;
   i) measures to build confidence amongst the hesitant borrowers;
   j) measures to integrate microfinance programmes with the local level planning.

Measures of type (d), and (j) of course lie partly, and measures of type(c) wholly, outside the control of the GB.

A second alternative strategy consists of taking the limitation of the impact as given, but deliberately seeking to build up business amongst the extreme poor. If this strategy is successful both in increasing customer numbers and in screening out the bad borrowers it may over time lead to both higher overall impact and greater poverty impact, than that achieved by those lenders who seek to play safe by confining their lending, after a time, to borrowers above the poverty line.

Besides the above options, as 95 per cent of the GB's clients are women, the development of women enterprises actually contributes to the maintenance and even enhancement of clients' viability. Women face additional and different problems from men. The *environmental constraints* in their totality constitute the most obstructing stumbling block to the development of women enterprises. Even when women's access to the GB's microfinance is achieved, women's inclusion apparently seems to be partly for the institutional viability of the GB itself, not the viability of women clients. Women are good credit risks, and this helps easy and regular instalment payment-which is key to the GB's claim of nearly hundred per cent loan recovery rate. In order to make the poverty alleviation programme a success, programme design of the GB should take into account that most of the rural poor women have dual responsibilities and assist them in dealing with their multiple roles.

It is obvious that poor women clients are in need of more appropriate technology in order to draw them out of their disadvantaged position. Nonetheless, the introduction of technology and the transfer of technical know-how sometimes may be a placebo rather than a panacea for the development of most of the disadvantaged in the society. Technology assistance programme must act slowly but steadily, and pay close attention to how the poor women entrepreneurs perceive the possible deficiencies of their enterprises. If the assistance fails to adopt such a slow and incremental approach, poor women entrepreneurs will be unable to adapt to new technologies and the investments will be lost.

Empirical studies (Berger 1995, 208; Almeyda 1996, 111-2) confirm that credit projects with training components have a higher probability of success, particularly as far as women microentrepreneurs are concerned. After credit, training is the most frequently included component in the GB's microenterprise projects although it remains a relatively nebulous activity. Like the diffusion of appropriate technology, pro-poor training is also an integral part in the process of making the unskilled women more skilled. Nonetheless, such training components, if not properly designed, may place undue burdens on these poor women given their responsibilities toward both domestic and market work, and the formidable time constraints they face in regard to participation in training courses. Given these concerns, training must be selectively used and carefully designed if it is to serve the function of improving women's productivity.

The training needs of poor women who initiate their own economic activities in the informal sector can be grouped under mainly two categories: training for very poor women in their livelihood projects; and training for women with microenterprises. The scope of training programmes for the women in the first category, by necessity, has to be broader than programmes designed for women with microenterprises. The experience of many agencies suggests that women with survival or livelihood projects minimally require training in technical production skills as well as counselling in family-life education. Training for women microentrepreneurs points mainly toward entrepreneurship development such as business training including training on product design and planning, interpersonal skills, product control, marketing, record-keeping, and accounting. Skills training, though essential for survival and livelihood projects, is of more relevance to those women involved in microenterprises.

Most of the women entrepreneurs moving into microenterprises with larger operations are in older age groups who are no longer occupied by child-care responsibilities. Young married women are consciously limiting their enterprises to relatively smaller home-based operations that permit reconciliation of the family and the enterprise roles. This finding calls for growth-oriented, pro-poor technologies for the women in the older age groups, and relatively indigenous home-based technologies including the apprenticeship training in the garment industry for women in the younger age groups. The training on garments, which is a booming industry in Bangladesh, has a very bright prospect for wage-employment with a relatively better wage rate.

Realistic Policy Options

In the light of the above, this study concentrates here on instruments available to the designers and managers to make the GB more poverty alleviating and financially self-sustaining.

The obvious option is to increase the extent of impact by introducing design features, amongst those identified in (a), (e), (f), (g), (h), (i), and (j) above. These features will help the GB to achieve the twin goals of poverty alleviation and sustainability.

The most effective way of targeting credit to the poor is not to apply an explicit means test, but rather to offer very small loans, as these would be taken up by the poor, would inflict less risk on them and save the GB the huge administrative costs of targeting. But as very small loans cost more to process per Taka of portfolio than large loans, a combination of incentives for the GB staff may be offered. Incentives to staff have been offered for several years by the GB. What is new here is the suggestion that the incentive should be harnessed so as to motivate the staff to work explicitly for higher poverty impact.

If the GB is to find it financially attractive to offer small loans and hence reach the poor the step forward for it is to charge for those loans at cost, replacing standard charges for credit with a tapered tariff in which the higher the interest rate the smaller the loan. Will this choke off demand for such loans? Considering the interest rate of the informal sector, and the non-availability of credit in the formal sector, the answer is, probably not.

By opening new branches (or simply supplying mobile banking services) in regions currently not serviced by any institutional lender, it is possible for the GB to increase its outreach and in the process reduce the costs of transport, information transmission and social intermediation to poor people, and thereby raise the expected rate of return on (impact of) its projects.

Moreover, the GB and the other MFIs need to develop a much higher level of cooperation and coordination among themselves and, more importantly, among the local government institutions. None of the MFIs including the GB has the whole solution nor the resources for sustained impact. Bringing together the variety of services that the poor need, and linking the work at the base with broader policy advocacy, will demand a high level of coordination among different organizations, including the government organizations.

Managing growth is a balancing act. The GB apparently strives for balance between outreach and sustainability-that is, balance between its social mission of poverty alleviation and its commercial strategy of sustainability. In considering the trade-off between poverty alleviation and sustainability, it is emphasized that as the GB is the product of some desperate economic situations prevailing in the country immediately after its liberation, it is more of a poverty alleviation organization than just a traditional commercial financial institution. The main objective of poverty alleviation is the *end*, to which the GB should try to reach with its *means* of a sustainable financial structure-through the provision of quality, client-responsive, and flexible financial and non-financial services for its clients.

Grameen Phase II

This book was written in 2006 on the basis of research findings on the GB. It is very good to note that in 2002, the GB introduced the Grameen Phase II, incorporating some client-responsive changes in its product design. The introduction of Grameen Phase II indicates that the Classic Grameen model with its *Credit-alone approach* was not sustainable.

As different approaches in microfinance evolve, we are learning more and more about their possibilities and limitations. However, learning will only translate into improved programmes when the interveners are self-critical, when they face the limitations of various types of interventions, and make a commitment to clearly articulated goals. As ingenuous as it may sound, we cannot solve problems unless we face them. Interventions will only improve if the interveners look critically at projects and learn from experience how to do better.

This observation helps to explain as to why microcredit has worked so well in Bangladesh and many other developing countries, while other institutional arrangements like co-operatives have not. Microfinance is not based on static ideas or theories; rather it represents an evolving and dynamic system that can respond to the changing and varied needs of the poor. Microcredit is a learning-by-doing process, ready to incorporate new innovations and learn from experience.

Background of GB Phase II

The GB started as a project to deliver credit to poor rural Bangladeshis in 1976. Led by its founding Managing Director, Muhammad Yunus, it steadily developed what it now calls its *classic* microcredit system. But the *classic* Grameen's method with its credit-alone approach grew piecemeal, as lessons of clients' dissatisfaction were learnt and new ideas emerged. In 2000 work began on the design of Grameen II, or, more formally, the *Grameen Generalised System* (GGS). Grameen II consolidates many of the lessons learnt in regard to clients' dissatisfaction, and also made some fundamental changes. In the Grameen Classical System, the uniform treatment of clients and the persistent efforts to ensure that borrowers repay their loans, in many cases, meant being tough on clients in times of need.

What are the Changes?

The GGS, with a new *easy* loan product that allows rescheduling with ease is designed instead to create *tension free* microlending by giving staff ways to accommodate clients in temporary crises. The other important changes made in Grameen II are:

Public deposit services; extended member deposit services; improved loan contracts
These client-responsive changes alongside the introduction of *Scholarship, and Higher Education Loan* for GB clients' children are a step forward in meeting the varied needs of the rural poor women.

The GB has introduced an *open access current account scheme* which can be used even by non-members, and wherein the depositors earn a competitive market interest rate and are allowed to withdraw money irrespective of whether they have an outstanding loan or not. The Grameen Pension Scheme (GPS), earning 12 per cent compound interest and ultimately getting back 187 per cent of the clients' deposits is very popular among the GB clients. Given a low rate of inflation, the return is generous and the clients will be able to build up tidy sums through the power of compound interest rate (Aghion and Morduch 2005, 153-4). Despite GPS turns out to be popular with clients in its own right, ten years is a long time, and the GPS has not yet been operating long enough to know how clients will manage to meet their obligations in stressful times.

Grameen II has fostered a sharp growth in membership, after a relatively stagnant growth during the late 1990s. Grameen II has taken an ambitious target for new branches, and for client numbers per branch and per worker which helped membership grow from 2.36 million in mid 2002 to 5.2 million in September 2005, indicating nearly a 200 per cent increase in membership in less than three years.

In terms of financial performance, the GB in 2003 had experienced a six-fold increase in net profits over 2002-from 60 to 358 million taka (US$ 6 million). The improvement in the GB's financial performance is real, and is related to the greater intake of Grameen II's wider range of more user-friendly loan products and to its decision to attract deposits in much greater volume, which has allowed it to expand its loan portfolio and serve many new members. The year 2003 was the first full year of Grameen II, so this increase in profits look like a good return on the decision of the GB to launch Grameen II (Hossain 2005).

The two field surveys in 2004 and 2005 of the author of this study reveal that though the GB has not tried to present Grameen II as a consolidated *one-stop* answer to their members' financial needs, the performance of the Grameen II is so far so good. The Grameen II answers many of the criticisms made against the credit-alone approach under the Grameen classical system. While the need for continued product development, based on the changing needs and preferences of the clients, remains, the introduction of Grameen II is really a good start, probably with good future.

The main changes in Grameen II are to the range of products. The environment in which the products are offered, however, has remained the same-meetings that are attended by all of the five-person groups in the village, and served by a visiting fieldworker. The preponderance on women members remains a striking feature (Rutherford 2005, 1).

Why Now Not Before?

In recent years, there has been considerable self-examination by the GB along with criticism from analysts about product rigidity. The horizontal expansion of the GB with its credit-alone policy virtually came to a halt during the late 1990s. A severe flood in 1998 affected many Grameen members and revealed the internal weaknesses in the Grameen classic system. The main weakness was rigidity in the loan scheme: members had no choice but to follow a uniform schedule of borrowing and repaying. Once a borrower fell off this track, she found it very difficult to get back on. Floods and other factors exposed this vulnerability in classic Grameen. On-time loan repayment declined sharply, and many members failed to attend meetings. The Grameen II, with its key weapon of flexibility in financial products was designed to overcome these problems.

The push to embrace changes is a welcome one, because it recognizes the clients' demand for flexibility in financial services. By August 2002, the GB had fully switched over to GGS. It is too early to comment on the impact of the recent changes made in the Grameen II. Furhter empirical study at village level will help assess the extent to which Grameen II has become a reality in the field. It will indicate to what degree, under what conditions, and through which mechanisms these changes are being implemented and how the members are reacting with those changes. If the changes are well-received by the clients and the programme is successfully implemented by the Grameen, then the other big MFIs in Bangladesh like the BRAC and the ASA, both followers of the Grameen model, could also go for such changes. Although because of the lack of banking status, these MFIs cannot accept public deposits, none the less, they can introduce other changes. Otherwise they risk losing their members in a purely competitive microfinance market in Bangladesh.

The introduction of Grameen II is definitely a step forward in meeting the increasing client demand for flexible financial services, but it could have been even better if the GB had introduced some structural changes that allowed for more options than just the group lending method. The GB in Bangladesh has enjoyed a worldwide reputation as leader in the microcredit movement. It is now being hoped that it can successfully move into the next phase of supplying demand-driven financial services.

Be that is it may, while there are no magical strategies to reduce poverty with microfinance alone, a set of measures, each with its own dosage and timing without distracting the greater emphasis on provision of demand-induced microfinancial services may be undertaken. Such a set would include several of the following in one form or other, with greater or lesser intensity, and to be applied either immediately or in the future: encouraging the participation of the poor in planning and implementation of poverty alleviation projects; provision of access to productive assets and public infrastructure to the poor; elimination of the bias against females in the access to resources through policy inducement; removal of policy bias against rural development; and finally, instituting a set of fair and effective laws and regulations governing resource use.

Summary and Conclusions

In this chapter the potential and limitations of microcredit in poverty alleviation have been analysed wherein it has been revealed that supply-driven microcredit alone does not and perhaps cannot alleviate poverty significantly. Demand-responsive financial and non-financial services can help the poor to help themselves overcome their problems. The findings of this study indicate that nearly 77 per cent of the clients did not experience any significant improvement in their positions as a result of their membership with the GB. This alarmingly limited impact in poverty alleviation is due to, among other things, the lack of demand-responsive, flexible financial services including voluntary savings.

In order to make microfinance more client-responsive, the following changes in credit and savings products may be considered. Credit shouldn't be limited only to business investment. A more flexible mandate which encourages enterprise use but does not exclude other uses needs to be pursued. Assessment of creditworthiness needs to take account of different household income sources including credit-supported enterprise. The ceiling of loan amounts needs to be linked to specific requirements as well as creditworthiness. The scope for bringing down effective interest rates should be explored by reducing transaction costs, pushes for high growth, high repayments and portfolio turnover. And finally, repayment of loans should preferably be based on cash flows of different livelihoods. Dairying is a common loan use, instalments can be adapted to the milking cycle. In case of savings, withdrawal of interest and a proportion of savings too may be allowed after one year. Such a package of financial services would provide the GB members with a range of convenient and useful services.

Providing flexible financial services only may improve the welfare of the very poor women but not necessarily lift them out of poverty because of their lack of required skills and efficiency that raise incomes by expanding their production frontier. Enhancing skills of clients has been an utterly neglected, if not completely forgotten, part of the GB. The GB could go even further in unlocking the creative and productive potential of the rural poor through a properly designed and sensibly implemented women-friendly, skill-enhancing programme.

The limitations of microcredit should be as deeply understood as its successes are widely recognized. After nearly twenty years of experimentation and research and development, microfinance is poised to sour. Embracing pragmatism over principle and practice over theory, the GB as well as other MFIs should focus on the real job in hand: developing institutions that can create and provide the broad range of microfinancial services and skill-enhancing non-financial services that will support poor people in their efforts to improve their poverty situation. Developing such flexible financial services is, however, a complex task and one that takes time-not the donors' prescribed time of 3 to 5 years. Microfinance is not a quick fix but the kind of slow, often frustrating step-by-step process that is usually the hallmark of real change.

Even after such a microfinance system is implemented, there is a need for an on-going programme of *product development* to improve the quality of services being made available to clients. This is the challenge for the future. The eventual impact of microfinance on poverty alleviation will ultimately depend on organizations' systems and products. The more appropriate and the higher the quality of services on offer, the better will be impact on poverty alleviation.

The real taste of microfinance depends mainly on two big *ifs*. *If* microfinance is meant to include only microcredit, it usually tastes sour. *If*, on the other hand, microfinance services include broad range of client-responsive, quality financial and non-financial services, it does really taste sweet. The time has come to re-think the purpose and potential of microfinance, going far beyond microcredit for enterprise development so as to encompass the provision of flexible financial services to poor people, regardless of whether they own enterprises or not.

Despite its limited impact on poverty alleviation, the Grameen movement has demonstrated the importance of thinking creatively about institutional innovations, and is forcing economists and other social scientists to rethink the traditional wisdom about the nature of poverty and its alleviation. In the end, this may prove to be the most important legacy of the movement. Moreover, the introduction of Grameen II might help the GB to achieve the apparently contradictory goals of significant poverty alleviation for its poor clients and financial sustainability of its own. This is a goal desired by many but achieved by very few.

Appendix 5A Distinguishing Characteristics of the Poverty Lending and Financial Systems Approaches

Characteristics	Poverty Lending	Financial Systems
Objectives	Advance well-being, self-worth, empowerment, attempts to address multiple constraints through provision of multiple services.	Develop viable sustainable financial institutions to serve financial needs of poor MSEs.
Target Group	The *Poorest of the poor*, the most marginalised operators of the *survival economy*, those at risk of malnutrition.	The specialised financial institution that serves poor entrepreneurs.
Methodology	Loan ceilings, client graduation.	Financial discipline. Streamline procedures and systems at institutional level.
Services	Credit and non-financial assistance.	Financial mediation between savers and borrowers.
Costs	Typically high costs per borrower.	Can be streamlined to a minimum.

Interest Rates	Grappling with issue of full cost-recovery. Moving from charging subsidised to commercial rates.	Advocates full cost-recovery through interest rates to sustain services to the poor.
Subsidies	Social benefits justify subsidy elements.	Subsidies will stunt the possibility to provide sustainable services. Can be justified at start-up and rapid expansion phases.
Sustainability	Community organisation sustainability viewed as critical. Financial sustainability not viewed as germane to programme success. Is now an increasing concern.	Is the fundamental objective of the financial institution, without which services and benefits would not continue to clients.

Source: M. Malhotra. (1992), p. 8.

Appendix 5B   Grameen Network and Grameen-Created Companies

Grameen Network

Grameen Bank does not own any share of the following in the Grameen network. Nor has it given any loan or received any loan from any of these companies. They are independent companies, registered under Companies Act of Bangladesh, with obligation to pay all taxes and duties, like any other company in the country.

1. Grameen Phone Ltd.
2. Grameen Telecom
3. Grameen Communications
4. Grameen Cybernet Ltd.
5. Grameen Software Ltd.
6. Grameen IT Park
7. Grameen Information Highways Ltd.
8. Grameen Star Education Ltd.
9. Grameen Bitek Ltd.
10. Grameen Uddog (Enterprise)
11. Grameen Shamogree (Products)
12. Grameen Knitwear Ltd.
13. Gonoshasthaya Grameen Textile Mills Ltd.
14. Grameen Shikka (Education)
15. Grameen Capital Management Ltd.
16. Grameen Byabosa Bikash (Business Promotion)
17. Grameen Trust

Grameen-Created Companies

The following companies in the Grameen network were created by Grameen Bank, as separate legal entities, to spin off some projects within Grameen Bank funded by donors. Donor funds were transferred by Grameen Bank to these companies.

1. Grameen Fund
2. Grameen Krishi (Agricultural) Foundation
3. Grameen Motsho (Fisheries) Foundation
4. Grameen Shakti
5. Grameen Kalyan (Wellfare)

Source: M. Yunus "Grameen Bank At A Glance", 2004

Bibliography

Abdullah, A. and Shahabuddin, Q. (1997), 'Critical Issues in Agriculture: Policy Reforms and Unfinished Agenda' in M.G. Quibria (ed.), *The Bangladesh Economy in Transition* (New Delhi: Oxford), pp. 28-75.

Abugre, C. (1993), 'When credit is not due-financial services by NGOs in Africa', *Small Enterprise Development*, 4:4, 24-33.

Aghion, B., de Armendariz. and Morduch, J. (1998), *Microfinance beyond Group Lending*, Working Paper, (London: University College).

---------- . (2005), *The Economics of Microfinance* (Cambridge: MIT Press, MA).

Ahmad, Q.K. (1986), *Promotion of Employment and Income through Rural Non-crop Activities in Bangladesh*, Research Report # 45 (Dhaka: BIDS).

Ahmed, A.U. et al. (1991), 'Poverty in Bangladesh: Measurement, Decomposition and International Comparison', *The Journal of Development Studies*, 27: 4, 48-63.

Ahmed, I. (1983), 'Technology and rural women in the Third World', *International Labour Review*, July-August, 493-505.

Ahmed, J.U. (1982), 'The Impact of New Paddy Post-Harvest Technology on the Rural Poor in Bangladesh', in Greeley (ed.), *Rural Technology, Rural Institutions and the Rural Poorest*, Centre on Integrated Rural Development for Asia and the Pacific (Comilla : CIRDAP), pp. 105-27.

Ahmed, Z. and Kabiruzzaman, M. (1984), 'Landlessness in Bangladesh: Realities and Constraints', in Ahmed et al., *Landlessness in Bangladesh*, (Dhaka : BRAC), 35-46.

Alamgir, M. (1978), *Bangladesh: A Case of Below Poverty Level Equilibrium Trap*, (Dhaka : BIDS).

Almeyda, G. (1996), *Money Matters: Reaching Women Microentrepreneurs with Financial Services*, (New York: Inter-American Development Bank).

Ameen, F. (1996), *The Economics of the Grameen Bank*, PhD Dissertation, Virginia State University.

Amin, R. et al. (1994), 'Poor Women's Participation in Income-Generating Projects and their Fertility Regulation in Bangladesh, *World Development*, 22: 4, 555-65.

Annis, S. (1987), 'Can Small-scale Development be Large-scale Policy?', *World Development* (Supplement) 15.

APDC (Asia and the Pacific Development Cooperation). (1992), *Banking with the Poor*. (Brisbane: APDC)

Ariff, M. and Khalid, A.M. (2000), *Liberalization, Growth, and the Asian Financial Crisis: Lessons for Developing and Transitional Economies in Asia*. (UK and USA : Edward Elga Publishing).

Asaduzzaman, M. and Westergaard, K. (1993), 'A Summary View of Growth and

Development in Rural Bangladesh', in M. Asaduzzaman, and K. Westergaard eds. *Growth and Development in Rural Bangladesh: A Critical Review*, (Dhaka: University Press Ltd.), 1-27.

Asaduzzaman, M. and Westergaard, K. eds. (1993), *Growth and Development in Rural Bangladesh: A Critical Review*, (Dhaka: University Press Ltd).

Asian Development Bank (ADB). (1993), *The Gender and Poverty Nexus: Issues and Policies*, Economics Staff Paper # 51, (Manila: ADB).

---------- . (1997), *Microenterprise Development: Not by Credit Alone,* (Hongkong: Oxford University Press).

Bamberger, M. and Cheema, S. (1990), *Case Studies of Project Sustainability: Implications for Policy and Operations from Asian Experience*, EDI Seminar Series, (Wahington, DC: World Bank).

Bangladesh Bureau of Statistics (1986), *The National Household Expenditure Survey 1981-82 for Rural Areas,*(Dhaka: Bangladesh Bureau of Statistics).

---------- . (1991-92), *The Household Expenditure Survey of Bangladesh, 1988-90,* (Dhaka: Bangladesh Bureau of Statistics).

Bardhan, P. (1993), 'Women and rural poverty: Some Asian Cases', in M.G. Quibria ed., *Rural Poverty in Asia: Priority Issues and Policy Options*, (Hongkong : Oxford University Press). pp. 316-29.

Basu, S. (2002), Financial Liberalization and Intervention: a New Analysis of Credit Rationing, <http://www.politicalreviewnet. com/polrev/reviews>, accessed 11 august 2004.

Beltran, S. (1997), *The Grameen Bank: Panacea or Placebo? A Critical Examination of the Bank's Successes and Failures*, A thesis for the Bachelor' Degree, (Arizona: Arizona State University).

Berger, M. (1995), 'Key Issues on Women's Access to and Use of Credit in the Micro-and Small-Scale Enterprise Sector', in L. Dignard and J. Havet eds., *Women in Micro-and Small-Scale Enterprise Development*, (London: Westview Press, IT Publications), pp. 189-215.

Bornstein, D. (1997), *The Price of a Dream: The Story of the Grameen Bank and the Idea that is Helping the Poor to Change their Lives*, (Chicago: University of Chicago Press).

Brand, M. *New Product Development for Microfinance: Evaluation and Preparation, and Design, Testing, and Launch*, (updated 15 Jun 1998) <http://www.mip.org/ pubs/MBP/Newprod.html>

Braverman, A. and Guasch, J.L. (1986), 'Rural Credit Markets and Institutions in Developing Countries: Lessons of Policy Analysis from Practice and Modern Theory', *World Development*, 14:10, 1253-67.

Chambers, R. (1983), *Rural Development: Putting the Last First*, (Harlow: Longman).

---------- . (1995), *Poverty and Livelihoods: Whose Reality Counts?*, IDS Discussion Paper # 347, (Brighton: Institute of Development Studies).

Chaudhuri, S. and Gupta, M.R. (1996), 'Delayed formal credit, bribing and the informal credit market in agriculture: A theoretical analysis', *Journal of*

Development Economics, 51, 433-49.

Chowdhury, F.A. and Rahman, A. (1989), *Urban Informal Financial Markets in Bangladesh*, Research Report # 103, (Dhaka: BIDS).

Choudhury, S.A. and Phare, L.C. (1993), 'Paraproject or Megaproject as Instrument of Durable Change: Answers from Financial Viability Analysis of the Grameen Bank', in A. N. M. Wahid ed., *The Grameen Bank: Poverty Relief in Bangladesh*, (USA: Westview Press), pp. 281-96.

Christensen, G. (1993), 'The Limits to Informal Financial Intermediation', *World Development*, 21:5, 721-32.

Churchill, C. *Managing Growth: The Organizational Architecture of Microfinance Institutions*, <http://www.mip.org/pubs/ MBP/ MG. organ.htm> , accessed 20 July 1997.

Clark, J. (1990), *Democratizing Development: The Role of Voluntary Organizations,* (USA: Kumarian Press).

Clapp and Mayne Inc. and Proggani Consultants Ltd. (1980), *Rural Finance Experimental Project: Baseline and Sociological Survey 1,* (Dhaka.: Clapp and Mayne Inc. and Proggani Consultants Ltd.)

Cornia, G.A., and Steward, F. (1993), 'Two Errors of Targeting', *Journal of International Development*, 5:5, 459-96.

Credit Development Forum (CDF), (2004), *Annual Report 2004*, (Dhaka: Credit Development Forum).

Dahlquist, D.A. (1994), *Replication of the Grameen Bank*, A thesis for the degree of Master of Arts in Economics, University of Wisconsin.

The Daily Sangbad. (1996), August 12, Dhaka.

The Daily Star. (1997), June 23, 1997.

---------- . (1998), August 27, 1998.

---------- . (2001), April 20, 2001.

---------- . (2006), "Bangladesh ranks 141st in economic freedom index," January 6, 2006.

Ditcher, T.W. (1996), 'Questioning the Future of NGOs with Microfinance', *Journal of International Development*, 8:2, 259-69.

Dowla, A.U. (1998), *Micro Leasing: The Grameen Bank Experience*, (Dhaka: BIDS).

Dreze, J. and Sen, A. (1991), *Hunger and Public Action*, (Oxford: Clarendon Press).

Easterly, W. et al. (1993), 'Good Policy or Good Luck?', *Journal of Monetary Economics*, 32, 459-83.

EDA Rural Systems. *The Maturing of Indian Micro-finance*,< http://www. edarural. com /impact.htm >, accesessed on 29 July 2005.

Food and Agricultural Organisation (FAO). *Microcredit: effects on rural poverty and the environment,* <http://www.fao.org/ docrep/x4400e/x4400e06.htm> , accessed on 30 October 2000.

Fuglesang, A. and Chandler, D. (1994), *Participation as Process: What We Can Learn from Grameen Bank*, Bangladesh, (Dhaka: University Press Ltd).

Gaile, G.L. and Foster, J. (1996), *Review of Methodological Approaches to the Study the Impact of Microenterprise Credit Programms*, (Washington DC: Management Systems International).

Germidis, D. et al. (1991), *Financial Systems and Development: What Role for the Formal and Informal Financial Sectors?* (Paris: OECD Publication).

Getubig, I.P. et al. (1993), *Overcoming Poverty through Credit: The Asian Experience in Replicating the Grameen Bank Approach*, (Kualalumpur: APDC).

---------- . (1997), *Creating the Vision: Microfinancing the Poor in Asia -Pacific-Issues, Constraints and Capacity-building*, (Kuala Lumpur: APDC).

Ghai, D. (1984), *An Evaluation of the Impact of Grameen Bank Project*, (Dhaka: Grameen Bank).

Ghate, P. et al. (1994), *Informal Finance: Some Findings from Asia*, (Hong Kong: Oxford University Press).

Ghate, P. (2000), 'Linking Formal Finance with Micro and Informal Finance', *The Bangladesh Development Studies*, 26: 2-3, 201-15.

Gibbons, D.S. (1992), *The Grameen Reader: Training Materials for the International replication of the Grameen Bank Financial System for Reduction of Rural Poverty*, (Dhaka: Grameen Bank).

Goetz, A.M. and Gupta, R.S. (1996), *Who Takes the Credit? Gender, Power and Control over Loan Use in Rural Credit Programme in Bangladesh,* (Brighton: Institute of Development Studies).

Government of Bangladesh. (1992), Report of the Task Forces on *Bangladesh Development Strategies for the 1990s*, (Dhaka: The University Press Ltd.).

---------- . (1997), *Bangladesh Arthanaitik Shamixma*, (Dhaka: Government of Bangladesh).

---------- . (1997), *Statistical Yearbook of Bangladesh*, (Dhaka: Government of Bangladesh).

Grameen Bank. (1994), *Grameen Dialogue* nos. 19 and 20.

---------- . (1996), *Grameen Dialogue* nos. 26 and 27.

---------- . (1997), *Grameen Dialogue* no. 31.

---------- . (1999), *Grameen Dialogue* no. 37.

---------- . (2001), *Grameen Dialogue* no. 45.

---------- . *Grameen Bank at a Glance*, <http//www.grameen-info.org/ bank/ GBGlance.html>, accessed on 28 November 2005.

---------- . *Annual Reports* of various years.

Greeley, M. ed., (1982), *Rural Technology, Rural Institutions and the Rural Poorest*, (Comilla: CIRDAP), pp. 105-27.

Griffin, K. and Khan, A.R. (1978), 'Poverty in the Third World: Ugly Facts and Fancy Models', *World Development*, 6:3, 295-304.

Haque, T. (1989), *Women and the Rural Informal Credit Market in Bangladesh*, (Dhaka: BIDS).

Hashemi, S.M. (1994), *Desperate Responses to Men's and Women's Health Problems: Evidence from Rural Bangladesh*, (Dhaka: Development Research Centre).

---------- . (1997), 'Those Left Behind: A Note on Targeting the Hardcore Poor',

G. D. Wood and I. Sharif eds., *Who Needs Credit? Poverty and Finance in Bangladesh*, (London: Zed Books), pp. 249-61.

----------, Schuler, S.R. and Riley, A.P. (1996), 'Rural Credit Programs and Women's Empowerment in Bangladesh', *World Development*, 24:4, 635-54.

Havers, M. (1996), 'Financial Sustainability in Savings and Credit Programmes', *Development in Practice*, 6:2, 144-50.

Hems, B. (2003), Microcredit for enterprise development vs microfinance as an industry, <htpp://www.microfinancegateway.
       org/content/article/detail/13566>, accessed on 1 July 2004.

Hoff, K. and Stiglitz, J.E. (1997), 'Moneylenders and Bankers: Price-Increasing Subsidies in a Monopolistically Competitive Market', *Journal of Development Economics*, 52, 429-62.

Holcombe, S. (1995), *Managing to Empower: The Grameen Bank's Experience of Poverty Alleviation*, (London: Zed Books).

Hossain, A. and Rashid, S. (1997), 'Financial Sector Reform', in M.G. Quibria ed., *The Bangladesh Economy in Transition*, (Manila: ADB), 221-74.

Hossain, I. (2005), "Financial Performance," *MicroSave Briefing Notes on Grameen II*, 4, 1-2.

Hossain, M. (1988), *Credit for the Alleviation of Rural Poverty: the Grameen Bank in Bangladesh*, International Food Policy Research Institute in collaboration with the BIDS, Research Report # 65, (Washington, DC: International Food Policy Research Institute).

---------- . (1992), 'Socio-Economic Characteristics of the Poor', in H.Z. Rahman and M. Hossain eds. *Rethinking Rural Poverty*, (Dhaka: BIDS).

---------- et al. (1994), 'Bangladesh', in M.G. Quibria ed. *Rural Poverty in Developing Asia, Volume 1: Bangladesh, India and Sri Lanka*, (Manila: ADB), pp. 69-187.

Hulme, D. (1990), 'Can the Grameen Bank be Replicated? Recent experiments in Malaysia, Malawi and Sri Lanka', *Development Policy Review*, 8, 287-300.

---------- . (1997), *Impact Assessment Methodologies for Microfinance: A Review*, Paper prepared for the Virtual Meeting of the CGAP Working Group on Impact Assessment Methodologies, April 17-19, 1997.

---------- . (2000), 'Is Microdebt Good for Poor People? A Note on the Dark Side of Microfinance, *Small Enterprise Development*, 11:1, 26-8.

---------- and Mosley, P. (1996), *Finance Against Poverty*, Vol. 1, (London: Routledge).

---------- . (1996), *Finance Against Poverty*, Vol. 2, (London: Routledge).

Humphrey, C.E. (1990), *Privatization in Bangladesh: Economic Transition in a Poor Country*, (Colorado: Westview Press).

International Labour Organisation (ILO). (1986), *Report iv: The Promotion of Small and Medium-Scale Enterprises*, (Geneva: ILO).

Islam, R. (2001), *Poverty Alleviation, Employment, and the Labor Market: Lessons from the Asian Experience*, Paper presented at the "Asia and Pacific Forum on Poverty," held at the Asian Development Bank, Manila, 5-9 February, 2001.

Islam, T. and Taslim, M.A. (1996), 'Demographic Pressure, Technological Innovation and Welfare', *The Journal of Development Studies*, 32: 5, 734-70.

Ito, S. (1999), *The Grameen Bank: Rhetoric and Reality*, a PhD thesis, Institute of Development Studies, (UK: University of Sussex).

Jackelen, H.R. and Ryne, E. (1991), 'Towards a More Market-Oriented Approach to Credit and Savings for the Poor', *Small Enterprise Development*, 2:4, 4-20.

Jain, P.S. (1996), 'Managing Credit for the Rural Poor: Lessons from Grameen Bank', *World Development, 24,* 79-89.

James, J. and Khan, H. (1997), 'Technology Choice and Income Distribution', *World Development*, 25: 2, 153-65.

Jazairy, I. et al. (1992), *The State of World Rural Poverty: An Inquiry into its Causes and Consequences*, (New York: New York University Press for the IFAD).

Jong, M.D. and Kleiterp, N. (1991), 'Credit for Small Businesses and Microenterprises in Developing Countries', *Small Enterprise Development*, 2:4, 21-39.

Johnson, S. (1998), 'Programme Impact Assessment in Microfinance', *IDS Bulletin*. 29:4, 21-30.

Johnson, S. and Rogaly, B. (1997), *Microfinance and Poverty Reduction*, (London: Oxfam and ACTIONAID).

Kabeer, N. (1998), 'Money Can't Buy Me Love', *Re-evaluating Gender, Credit and Empowerment in Rural Bangladesh*, Discussion Paper # 363, (Sussex: IDS).

Karim, M.R. and Osada, M. (1998), 'Dropping Out: An Emerging Factor in the Success of Microcredit-based Poverty Alleviation Programmes', *The Developing Economies*, 36:3, 257:88.

Khan, A.R. (1990), 'Poverty in Bangladesh: A Consequence of and a Constraint on Growth', *The Bangladesh Development Studies*, 18:3, 19-34.

Khalily, B. et al. (2002), *Impact of Formal Credit on Agricultural Production in Bangladesh,* (Dhaka: University of Dhaka).

---------- and Meyer, R. (1993), 'The Political Economy of Rural Loan Repayment: Evidence from Bangladesh', *Savings and Development*, 1:17, 23-35.

Khandker, S.R. (1996), 'Grameen Bank: Impact, Costs and Program Sustainability', *Asian Development Review*, 14:1, 97-130.

---------- . (1998), *Fighting Poverty with Microcredit: Experience in Bangladesh*. (Washington, DC: World Bank).

---------- et al. (1995), *Grameen Bank: Performance and Sustainability*, World Bank Discussion Paper # 306. (Washington, DC: World Bank).

---------- and Chowdhury, O.H. (1996), *Targeted Credit Programs and Rural Poverty in Bangladesh*, World Bank Discussion Paper # 336. (Washington, DC: World Bank).

Kohr, L. (1980), 'Appropriate Technology' in S. Kumar et al., *The Schumacher Lectures*, (London: Blond and Briggs Ltd.), pp. 182-92.

Koppen, B. V. and Mahmud, S. (1996), *Women and Water Pump in Bangladesh: The Impact of Participation in Irrigation Groups on Women's Status*. (London: Intermediate Technology Publications).

Krishna, A. et al. (1997), *Reasons for Hope: Instructive Experiences in Rural*

Development. (West Hartford: Kumarian Press).

Leidholm, C. and Mead, D. (1987), *Small-Scale Industries in Developing Countries: Empirical Evidence and Policy Implications*, MSU International Development Paper # 9, Michigan State University.

Lewis, W.A. (1992), 'Economic Development with Unlimited Supplies of Labour', in D. Lal ed., *Development Economics*, Vol. 1, (UK: Elgar) pp. 117-69.

Lipton, M. (1988), *The Poor and the Poorest: Some Interim Findings*, World Bank Discussion Paper # 25, (Washington, DC: World Bank).

MacIsaac, N. and Wahid, A.N.M. (1993), 'The Grameen Bank: Its Institutional Lessons for Rural Financing', in A.N.M. Wahid ed., *The Grameen Bank: Poverty Relief in Bangladesh.* (Colorado: Westview Press) pp. 191-208.

Macpherson, G. and Jackson, D. (1975), 'Village Technology for Rural Development: Agricultural Innovation in Tanzania', *International Labour Review*, Feb, 97-118.

Mahmud, W. *Bangladesh Faces the Challenge of Globalization*, <http://yaleglobal. yale.edu /article>, accessed on 28 July 2005.

Mahmud, W. and Ahluwalia, I.J. (2004), 'State of the Bangladesh economy: Pluses and minuses', *Journal of Economic and Political Weekly* (September 04, 2004 issue), 14-8.

Malhotra, M. (1992), *Poverty Lending and Microenterprise Development: A Clarification of the Issues*, Gemini Working Paper # 30. (Maryland: Bethesda)

Martokoesoemo, S.B. (1994), *Beyond the Frontiers of Indonesian Banking and Finance: Financial Intermediation to Mobilize the Potential of Small Entrepreneurs,*. (Jakarta: Central Bank of Indonesia).

Mascarenhas, R.C. (1993), 'Explaining Success in South Asian Rural Development: the Importance of Routine', *Public Administration and Development* 13, 475-87.

Matin, I. (1998a), *Rapid Credit Deepening and a Few Concerns: A Study of Grameen Bank in Madhupur*, (Dhaka: mimeo)

---------- . (1998b), 'Mis-targeting by the Grameen Bank: A Possible Explanation', *IDS Bulletin.* 29:4, 51-65.

---------- et al. (2001), '*Financial Services for the Poor and Poorest: Deepening Understanding to Improve Provision*, Paper # 9. (Manchester: Institute of Development Policy Management).

McKinnon, R.I. (1973), *Money and Capital for Economic Development.* (Washington, DC: The Brookings Institution).

Meyer, R.L. (2002), 'The Demand for Flexible Microfinance Products: Lessons from Bangladesh', *Journal of International Development* 14, 351-368.

Meyer, R.L., Khalily, A.B.and Hushak, L.J. (1988), *Bank Branches and Rural Deposits: Evidence from Bangladesh*, Occasional Paper # 1462. (Ohio State University: Economy and Sociology Department).

Microcredit Summit. (1997), *Declaration and Plan of Action*, Microcredit Summit, February 2-4.

Microcredit Summit. (1998), *Draft Declaration*, Result Education Fund. (Washington, DC).

Mody, P. (2000), *Gender Empowerment and Microfinance*, Working Paper, (Evans School).

Montgomery, R. et al. (1996), 'Credit for the Poor in Bangladesh', in D. Hulme and P. Mosley eds., *Finance Against Poverty*, vol. 2, (London: Routledge) pp. 94-176.

Morduch, J. (1998), *Does Microfinance Really Help the Poor? New Evidence from Flagship Programs in Bangladesh*, (Princeton University: MacArthur Foundation Project on inequality working paper).

---------- . (1999), 'The Microfinance Promise', *Journal of Economic Literature* 37:12, 1569-1614.

Mosley, P. (1997), *The Use of Control Groups in Impact Assessment for Microfinance*, Mimeo, (Washington DC: CGAP).

Mosley, P. and Hulme, D. (1998), 'Microenterprise Finance: Is there a Conflict between Growth and Poverty Alleviation?', *World Development* 26:5, 783-90.

Nabi, K.A. (1995), *Grameen Bank Model and its Replication in the USA*, (University of Illinois: Research Monograph).

Osmani, S.R. (1989), 'Limits to the Alleviation of Poverty through Non-farm Credit', *The Bangladesh Development Studies* 17:4, 1-18.

---------- . (2001), 'Growth Strategies and Poverty Reduction', Paper delivered at *the Asia and Pacific Forum on Poverty: Reforming Policies and Institutions for Poverty Reduction,* held at the Asian Development Bank, Manila, 5-9 February 2001.

PKSF (Palli Karma Sahayak Foundation). 'Coverage of microfinance program in Bangladesh' <http://www.unescap.org/ pdd/calendar/ povDecade/RT%20>, accessed 5 November 2005.

Pitt, M.M. and Khandker, S.R. (1996), *Household and Intra-household Impact of the Grameen Bank and Similar Targeted Credit Programs in Bangladesh*, World Bank Discussion Papers #320. (Washington, DC: World Bank).

Quasem, M.A. (1991), 'Limits to The Alleviation of Poverty Through Non-Farm Credit: a Comment', *The Bangladesh Development Studies* 19: 3, 129-33.

Quibria, M.G. ed. (1993), *Rural Poverty in Asia: Priority Issues and Policy Options*. (Hongkong: Oxford University Press).

---------- . (1997), *Bangladesh Economy in Transition*. (New Delhi: Oxford University Press).

Rahman, A. (1999), *Women and Microcredit in Rural Bangladesh: An Anthropological Study of Grameen Bank Lending*. (Boulder, Colorado: Westview Press).

Rahman, A. (1986), *Consciousness-Raising Efforts of Grameen Bank*. (Dhaka: BIDS).

---------- . (1992), 'The Informal Financial Sector in Bangladesh: An Appraisal of its Role in Development', *Development and Change* 23, 147-68.

---------- . (1994), "The Informal Financial Sector in Bangladesh: A Reply," *Development and Change*, 25, 641-3.

---------- . and Haque, T. (1988), *Poverty and Inequality in Bangladesh in the Eighties: An Analysis of some Recent Evidence,* Research Report # 91. (Dhaka:

BIDS).

---------- . and Islam, M.M.(1993), "The General Performance of the Grameen Bank," in A.N.M. Wahid ed., *The Grameen Bank: Poverty Relief in Bangladesh*, (USA: Boulder Co., Westview), pp. 49-67.

Rahman, H.Z. (1990), 'Not Quite, Not Enough: Institutional Approaches at Rural Development in Bangladesh', *The Journal of Social Studies*, 47, 10-17.

---------- . (1995), *Analysis of Poverty-Trends Project-Rural Poverty Up-date.* (Dhaka: BIDS).

---------- . and Hossain. M. eds. (1995), *Re-thinking Rural Poverty: A case Study for Bangladesh*. (Dhaka: BIDS).

Rahman, M.S. and Rahman, A. (1998), 'Poverty in Bangladesh-A Monitoring Exercise with Qualitative Tools', in A. Rahman eds., *South Asia Poverty Monitor: The Bangladesh Chapter*. (Dhaka: BIDS), pp. iv-1-iv-33.

Rahman, R.I. (1986), *The Wage Employment Market for Rural Women in Bangladesh*, BIDS Research Monograph # 6. (Dhaka: BIDS).

---------- . (1997), 'Poverty, Profitability of Microenterprises and the Role of Credit', in G.D. Wood and I. Sharif eds., *Who Needs Credit? Poverty and Finance in Bangladesh*. (London: Zed Books), pp. 271-88.

---------- . and Khandker, S.R. (1994), 'Role of Targeted Credit Programmes in Promoting Employment and Productivity of the Poor in Bangladesh', *Special Issue of the Bangladesh Development Studies on Women, Work and Changes*. (Dhaka: BIDS).

Rahman, S.M. '*Commercialization of Microfinance in Bangladesh Perspective*' <http://www.gdrc.org/icm/country/bangla-> , accessed on 1 January 2001.

Rakowski, C.A. (1994), 'Convergence and Divergence in the Informal Sector Debate: A Focus on Latin America, 1984-92', *World Development* 22:4, 501-16.

Rana, P.B. (1986), *Improving Domestic Resource Mobilization through Financial Development: Bangladesh*. (Manila : ADB).

---------- . (1997). 'Reforms in Bangladesh', M.G. Quibria ed., *The Bangladesh Economy in Transition*. (Oxford University Press for ADB) pp. 7-26.

Rao, C.H.H. (1972), 'Farm Mechanisation in a Labour-abundant Economy', *The Journal of Economic and Political Weekly* 7: 20, 393-400.

Ravallion, M. and Chen, S. (1996), *What Can New Survey Data Tell Us about the Recent Changes in Living Standards In Developing and Transitional Economies*, Policy Research Working Paper 1694. (Washington, DC: World Bank).

---------- . and Sen, B. (1996), 'When Method Matters: Monitoring Poverty in Bangladesh', *Economic Development and Cultural Change* 44: 4, 761-92.

Renteria, L. (1996), *Cost Efficiency and Replication of Grameen Bank: An Action Research for Mexico*, A PhD dissertation, University of New Orleans.

Rhyne, E. and Otero, M. (1991), *A Financial Systems Approach to Microenterprises*, Gemini Working Paper # 18. (Maryland: Bethesda).

Robinson, M.S. (1994), 'Savings Mobilization and Microenterprise Finance," in M. Otero and E. Rhyne eds., *The New World of Microenterprise Finance*, (West Hartford, Connecticut: Kumarian Press) pp. 27-54.

---------- . (1997), *Introducing Savings in Microcredit Institutions: When and How?* CGAP Focus Note # 8.

---------- . (1998), 'Microfinance: The Paradigm Shift from Credit Delivery to Sustainable Financial Intermediation," in M. S. Kimenyi et al., *Strategic Issues in micro-finance: Contemporary Perspectives on Developing Societies*, (UK: Ashgate Publishing Ltd.), pp. 55-85.

---------- . (2001), *The Microfinance Revolution: Sustainable Finance for the Poor.* (Washington, DC: World Bank).

Rock, R., and M. Otero eds. (1997), *From Margin to Mainstream: the Regulation and Supervision of Microfinance. (*Washington, DC: ACCION International).

Rogaly, B. (1996), 'Micro-Finance Evangelism, Destitute Women, and The Hard Selling of a New Anti-Poverty Formula', *Development in Practice* 6: 2, 100-112.

Rosenberg, R. (1998), *Independent Review of UNCDF Microfinance Activities*, Report. (United Nations Capital Development Fund (UNCDF)).

Rostow, W.W. (1960), *The Stages of Economic Growth: An Anti-Communist Manifesto*, (Cambridge: Cambridge University Press).

Roy, D.K. (1994), *Rural Poverty and Public Policy in Bangladesh: A Review of Some Issues*, Research Report # 136. (Dhaka: BIDS).

Rutherford, S. (1995), *Self-help Savings and Loan Groups*, Unpublished Report. (New Delhi: ODA Urban Poverty Office).

---------- . (1997a), *A Critical Typology of Financial Services for the Poor*, Action Aid Working Paper #1. (London).

---------- . (1997b), 'Informal Financial Services in Dhaka's Slums', in G.D. Wood and I. Sharif eds., *Who Needs Credit* ? (London: Zed Books Ltd.), pp. 351-70.

---------- . (1998), 'The Savings of the Poor: Improving Financial Services in Bangladesh', *Journal of International Development* 10:1, 1-15.

---------- . (1999), *The Poor and Their Money: An essay about financial services for poor people* (UK: Institute for Development Policy and Management, University of Manchester).

---------- . (2005), *What is Grameen II? Is it Up and Running In the Field Yet?* MicroSave Briefing Notes on Grameen II # 1.

Ruttan, V.W. (1990), 'Sustainability Is Not Enough', in C. K. Eicher eds., *Agricultural Development in the Third World*. (USA: John Hopkins University Press), pp. 400-403.

Schultz, T.W. (1964), *Transforming Traditional Agriculture*. (New Haven: Yale University Press).

Scobie, H.M. et al. (1993), *Informal Financial Markets in Developing Countries,*. (Oxford: Blackwell Publishers).

Sen, A.K. (1981), *Poverty and Famines: An Essay on Entitlements and Deprivation.* (Oxford: Clarendon Press).

Sen, B. (1988), *A Study on Moneylenders in Rural Informal Financial Markets*, Working Paper # 11. (Dhaka: BIDS).

---------- . (1997), *Evaluation of Rural Poverty Alleviation Programmes*. (Dhaka:

BIDS).

---------- . (1998), 'Crisis of Poverty Alleviation', in A. Rahman and B. Sen eds., *South Asia Poverty Monitor: The Bangladesh Chapter*. (Dhaka: BIDS,), pp. ix-1-ix-20.

Sharma, M. and Zeller, M. (1999), 'Placement and Outreach of Group-based Credit Organizations: The Cases of ASA, BRAC, and Proshika in Bangladesh', *World Development* 27:12, 2123-36.

Shaw, E.S. (1973), *Financial Deepening in Economic Development*. (New York: Oxford University Press).

Singh, I. (1990), *The Great Ascent: The Rural Poor in South Asia*. (Washington DC: World Bank).

Sobhan, R. (1992), *Planning and Public Action for Asian Women* (Dhaka: University Press Ltd).

---------- . (1997), The Political Economy of Microcredit', in G.D. Wood and I. Sharif eds., *Who Needs Credit? Poverty and Finance in Bangladesh*. (London: Zed Books), pp. 131-44.

Steinert, A. (1996), *Bangladesh: The Grameen Bank Health Programme* (Geneva: ILO).

Stiglitz, J.E. (1990), 'Peer Monitoring and Credit Markets', *The World Bank Economic Review* 4:3, 35-6.

Task Force on Poverty Alleviation. (1991), 'A Report prepared for the Adviser, In-charge of the Ministry of Planning, (Dhaka: Government of Bangladesh).

Taslim, M.A. (1988), 'Tenancy and Interlocking Markets: Issues and some Evidence', *World Development* 16:6, 655-64.

Third World Network. (1989), 'Half of the Humanity could be Absolutely Poor', *Feature* 533, 1-17.

The Times. April 28, 1997, London.

Tinker, I. (1995), 'The Human Economy of Microentrepreneurs', in L. Dignard and J. Havet eds., *Women in Micro-and Small-Scale Enterprise Development*. (USA: Westview Press), pp. 25-39.

Todd, H. (1996), *Women at the Center-Grameen Bank Borrowers after One Decade*, (USA: Westview Press).

Turnham, D. et al. (1990), *The Informal Sector Revisited*. (Paris: OECD).

United Nations. (1999), *World Survey on the Role of Women in Development: Globalization, Gender, and Work*, Report of the Secretary-General. (New York: United Nations).

---------- . (1999a), *World Economic and Social Survey*, (New York: United Nations).

United Nations Development Programme (UNDP). (1997), *Microstart: A Guide for Planning, Starting and Managing a Microfinance Programme*. (New York: UNDP).

---------- . (2004), *Human Development Report 2004*. (New York: Oxford University Press).

Varian, H.R. (1990), 'Monitoring Agents with Other Agents', *Journal of Institutional and Theoretical Economics* 146, 153-74.

White, S.C. (1992), *Arguing with the Crocodile: Gender and Class in Bangladesh.* (London: Zed Books).

Wikipedia. 'Demographics of Bangladesh', <http://en.wikipedia.org/wiki/ Bangladesh , accessed on 30 September 2005.

Woller, G. (2002), 'From Market Failure to Marketing Failure: Market Orientation As The Key to Deep Outreach In Microfinance', *Journal of International Development* 14, 305-24.

Women's World Banking. (1995), *The Missing Links*: *Financial Systems that Work for the Majority.* (Washington DC: Global Policy Forum).

Wood, G.D. and Sharif, I. eds. (1997), *Who Needs Credit? Poverty and Finance in Bangladesh.* (Dhaka: University Press Ltd.).

World Bank. (1990), *Bangladesh: Strategies for Enhancing the Role of Women in Economic Development.* (Washington, DC: World Bank).

---------- . (1994), *Enhancing Women's Participation in Economic Development*, A World Bank Policy Paper, World Bank, Washington, DC.

---------- . (1995), *Bangladesh: From Stabilization to Growth*, A World Bank Country Study. (Washington DC: World Bank).

---------- . (1996), *Poverty Reduction and the World Bank: Progress and Challenges in the1990s.* (Washington DC: World Bank).

---------- . 1999), *Bangladesh: From Counting the Poor to Making the Poor Count*, A World Bank Country Study (Washington DC: World Bank).

---------- . (2005a), *World Development Indicators.* (Washington DC: World Bank).

---------- . (2005b), 'Helping to Prevent Arsenic Poisoning'<http ://www.worldbank. org.bd/ we bsitexternal/ countries? southasiaext/ Bangladesh>, accessed on 6 July 2005.

Wright, G.A.N. (2000), *Microfinance Systems: Designing Quality Financial Services for the Poor.* (Dhaka: University Press Ltd.).

Yaron, J. (1992), *Successful Rural Finance Institutions*, World Bank Discussion Paper # 150. (Washington DC: World Bank).

Yaqub, S. (1998), Financial Sector Liberalization: Should the Poor Applaud?, *IDS Bulletin* 29:4, 102-110.

---------- . and McDonald, B. and Piperk, G. (1997), *Rural Finance Issues, Design and Best Practices.* (Washington DC: World Bank).

Yunus, M. (1992), *Grameen Bank: Experiences and Reflections* (Dhaka: Grameen Bank).

---------- . and Jolis, A. (1998), *Banker to the Poor.* (Dhaka: University Press Ltd.).

Yusuf, S. and Kumar, P. (1996), *Developing the Non-farm Sector in Bangladesh: Lessons from other Asian Countries*, World Bank Discussion Paper # 340. (Washington DC: World Bank).

Zeller, M. (1999), 'The Role of Rural Financial Services for Alleviation of Food Insecurity and Poverty', *Agriculture and Rural Development* 6:2, 28-32.

---------- . and Meyer, R.L. eds. (2002), *The Triangle of Microfinance*: *Financial Sustainability, Outreach, and Impact.* (Washington DC: International Food Policy Research Institute).

Index